WHY SCIENCE MATTERS

Robert W. Proctor and E. J. Capaldi

Understanding the
Methods of
Psychological Research

WHY SCIENCE MATTERS

Blackwell
Publishing

© 2006 by Robert W. Proctor and E. J. Capaldi

BLACKWELL PUBLISHING
350 Main Street, Malden, MA 02148-5020, USA
9600 Garsington Road, Oxford OX4 2DQ, UK
550 Swanston Street, Carlton, Victoria 3053, Australia

The right of Robert W. Proctor and E. J. Capaldi to be identified as the
Authors of this Work has been asserted in accordance with the UK
Copyright, Designs, and Patents Act 1988.

First published 2006 by Blackwell Publishing Ltd

1   2006

Library of Congress Cataloging-in-Publication Data

Proctor, Robert W.
    Why science matters : understanding the methods of psychological research /
Robert W. Proctor and E.J. Capaldi.
        p. cm.
    Includes bibliographical references and index.
    ISBN-13: 978-1-4051-3357-9 (hardcover : alk. paper)
    ISBN-10: 1-4051-3357-0 (hardcover : alk. paper)
    ISBN-13: 978-1-4051-3049-3 (pbk. : alk. paper)
    ISBN-10: 1-4051-3049-0 (pbk. : alk. paper)   1. Psychology—Research—
Methodology.   2. Psychology, Experimental—Research—Methodology.   I. Capaldi,
E. John.   II. Title.

    BF76.5.P68   2005
    150'.72—dc22

                                                                    2005014826

A catalogue record for this title is available from the British Library.

Set in 10/12.5pt Palatino
by Graphicraft Limited, Hong Kong
Printed and bound in India
by Replika Press, Pvt Ltd, Kundli

The publisher's policy is to use permanent paper from mills that operate a
sustainable forestry policy, and which has been manufactured from pulp
processed using acid-free and elementary chlorine-free practices.
Furthermore, the publisher ensures that the text paper and cover board
used have met acceptable environmental accreditation standards.

For further information on
Blackwell Publishing, visit our website:
www.blackwellpublishing.com

CONTENTS

Contents

Contents

PREFACE FOR INSTRUCTORS

It is the feeling of the authors that this text is an important supplement to current methodology textbooks. One of our major intentions is to provide students with a more complete and up-to-date understanding of important aspects of methodology that are generally not covered to any great extent in methodology texts. We think that students would become better consumers and producers of psychological research if they were better acquainted with these important topics. This supplementary textbook is meant to complement methodology textbooks by covering a variety of additional important topics useful for providing students with a more adequate basis for understanding and practicing scientific psychology. Such a text is needed because the understanding and practice of science, both in general and in psychology, is not static but is constantly being modified and expanded in new directions. Currently, it seems that our conceptions of science in general and psychological science in particular are developing in two antithetical directions. On the one hand, they are in the process of being modified in new and useful directions, and on the other, they are being challenged and undermined.

The text is primarily about methodology and training students to be more sophisticated methodologists. But methodology does not stand alone. All methodologies have to be evaluated both relative to other methodologies and to the wider context in which they are embedded. Our conception of the worth of a particular methodology is influenced by our more general conception of science, and it is neither wise nor appropriate to separate methodological considerations from more general scientific ones.

There are three scientifically important aspects of this text that we consider to be unique. One is to provide students with a view of science that is contemporary and up to date, which reflects the best current thinking about how science should be practiced and methodologies evaluated. A second unique aspect is to explicate how hypotheses and theories are to be evaluated. The view we describe differs from that provided in most methods textbooks, which tend to follow Popper's emphasis on falsification of a hypothesis taken in isolation and neglect the implications of the problems in doing so implied by the Duhem–Quine thesis. Our emphasis here is that hypotheses and theories must necessarily be evaluated in the context of other hypotheses and theories, and never alone. The third unique emphasis is in suggesting that the proper approach to devising and evaluating hypotheses and theories is given by abduction, and not by induction or deduction alone. We consider abduction to be the most important form of reasoning that is commonly used by scientists, despite the fact it has gone largely unrecognized.

Chapters 1, 2, and 3 describe the changing conceptions of science from ancient times to the present. The modern conception of science, naturalism, introduced in Chapter 3, is expanded and developed in some detail in Chapters 4, 5, and 6. The ideas developed in the first six chapters are applied to analyzing and evaluating certain contemporary methodological issues in psychology in Chapters 7–10. Some of the methodological proposals described in those chapters are in opposition to the way that psychology as a science is normally practiced. The purpose of this book, then, is to acquaint students with methodological issues, both ancient and modern, so as to make them better consumers and producers of psychological science.

We would like to express our appreciation to Christine Cardone, Executive Editor, Psychology for the extensive help she has given us throughout all phases of this project, Kim Vu for providing comments on a draft of the book, and Julie Smith, our secretary, for her assistance in preparation of the manuscript and a variety of related matters. We also thank Don Dulaney, Emeritus Professor of Psychology, University of Illinois, for the various forms of intellectual help he has given us.

PREFACE FOR STUDENTS

Methodology is among the more fundamental topics in science in general and psychology in particular. Consider two facts that indicate the importance attached to methodology by academic psychologists. First, almost all departments require most undergraduate psychology majors to take research methods and statistics courses. Second, the significance attached to particular empirical findings is seriously determined on the basis of the methodology that gave rise to those findings. For example, most experimentalists would not place too much emphasis on uncontrolled observational findings until they were verified in the laboratory.

The changing conceptions of science alluded to above are giving rise to new methodologies and to new means of evaluating them. These new methodologies may vary from statistical and measurement techniques to broad proposals that have the potential to fundamentally alter the methodological, empirical, and theoretical landscape. These broader methodological procedures, and some of the less broad ones, are often proposed within a general context that includes a variety of assumptions whose purpose it is to justify the new methodology. These newly introduced justificatory assumptions may vary from being more or less reasonable to being of dubious validity. Often the assumptions employed to justify the new methods may be characterized as being based on one's ontology, or worldview. Inescapably, then, proper evaluation of a particular methodology necessarily requires in turn evaluation of the more general context in which the method is embedded. Many of the assumptions that are employed to justify a particular methodology can be characterized as propositions that fall within the boundaries of philosophy of science. That this is the case is clearly apparent in many of the methodological articles that frequently appear in the *American Psychologist*, the flagship journal of the American

Psychological Association that is sent to all of its members, and other journals. Thus, to properly understand a particular methodology, it is necessary to have a reasonable acquaintance with some important ideas in the philosophy of science.

The points alluded to above are not entirely novel and were recognized in the first edition of McGuigan's (1960) book, *Experimental Psychology*, which supplied the template for most subsequent methodology texts. Prior to McGuigan, methodology texts dealt with substantive psychological topics such as vision, memory, etc. The new vision for methodology texts outlined by McGuigan was as follows:

> The point of departure for this book is the relatively new conception of experimental psychology in terms of methodology, a conception which represents the bringing together of three somewhat distinct aspects of science: experimental methodology, statistics, and philosophy of science. (p. x)

The first two of McGuigan's three objectives, the teaching of the procedural aspects of experimental methodology and statistics, have been admirably achieved, both in his texts and in most recent research methodology texts currently available that follow in his tradition. However, the third objective, that of conveying the implications of the philosophy of science, or what we characterize as a variety of new investigatory procedures that better inform the theory and practice of contemporary science, has not been realized either in McGuigan's text or in any of the others that follow in its tradition. One intention in this text is to provide you, the student, with the background to become a more sophisticated methodologist.

The available undergraduate methodology texts in psychology, which follow in the McGuigan tradition, provide excellent introductions to the procedural aspects of experimentation, data collection, and analysis. These are laudatory and necessary aims, and it would be hard to imagine a student functioning adequately in psychology without the benefit of this training. However, as necessary and important as this training is, it does not encompass the totality of the considerations necessary to fully understand and apply particular methodologies. Thus, it is not enough for you, the student, to learn how to apply a particular methodology to a specific empirical or theoretical problem in the absence of learning the more general assumptions that underlie that methodology. Fledgling psychologists, if they are to become more sophisticated practitioners, must also learn how scientific methodologies arise initially and are ultimately justified or rejected. This, of course, is the primary purpose of this supplementary text. We realize that these objectives will present students with a considerable number of intellectual challenges because the ideas provided in the text are ones unfamiliar to most students.

Given the generally accepted understanding of science, it is impossible to separate more general considerations of theory evaluation from more practical methodological considerations. The reason for this is quite straightforward: *Science, as many view it today, is every bit as much an empirical enterprise as the empirical phenomena to which it is applied.* Many new empirical investigatory procedures are being applied to science itself. One of these attempts is to understand science by examining how specific scientific communities have practiced it in the past. This was the procedure employed by the celebrated philosopher and historian of science Thomas Kuhn (1962), who came to his conclusions about the nature of science by examining how it was practiced by specific scientific communities. We think that Kuhn was correct in his analysis of the relevance of history for understanding science. Since Kuhn, several additional empirical methods for illuminating science have been provided, and these have transformed our understanding beyond Kuhn's fondest hopes. Concerning these newer methods, Bechtel (1988), a prominent psychologist who has dealt at length with scientific issues, said in his book *Philosophy of Science: An Overview for Cognitive Science,* "There is beginning to emerge a cluster of practitioners from a variety of disciplines who take science as their subject matter. Increasingly, the term *science of science* is being used to characterize these investigations" (p. 2). The trend noted by Bechtel in 1988 has come to greater fruition in the subsequent years. This book is largely about these new investigatory procedures, and these provide a picture of science that not only increases our understanding of it but also contributes to the practice and application of science to the subject matter of psychology.

To aid readers, we have provided brief definitions of terms and descriptions of significant individuals in the glossaries found at the back of the book. The terms and individuals in the glossaries are indicated in boldface the first time they are mentioned in each chapter.

Part 1

MAJOR METHODOLOGICAL CHANGES IN SCIENCE FROM ANTIQUITY TO THE PRESENT

Chapter 1

UNDERSTANDING SCIENCE: THE ARMCHAIR VERSUS PRACTICE

Introduction

The goal of traditional research methods textbooks in psychology is to train students in the application of scientific methods to specific empirical and theoretical problems. Such training involves the various uses of alternative research designs, how to collect data and control for effects of extraneous variables, **hypothesis testing**, use of statistical methods to analyze data, how to conduct research with humans and animals in an ethical manner, and assorted related topics. These are worthy and necessary goals, and they contribute substantially to the student's ability ultimately to understand and conduct research. In the absence of a thorough grounding in the matters described in methods texts, neither individual practitioners nor the field would grow and progress. There can be little doubt that the training provided by available methods texts is as necessary as it is important.

What these texts deal with is the application of scientific methods to psychological problems. However, they say very little about the origins of science or of scientific methods and how these methods may have been invented and modified, and perhaps subsequently discarded, over the years. Methods texts do an outstanding job of conveying the specifics of experimental design, but they do not put these ideas in a broader framework. Using a tool metaphor, current texts are excellent at telling students how to use particular research tools. What they do less well is provide information about the origin of the tools, the justification for using a particular tool, why a particular tool might prove to be less useful than a new tool that may be invented, or how to determine if one tool is better than another for some purpose. It is well to realize, as we shall emphasize in subsequent chapters, that the psychological researcher is constantly being bombarded with newly devised methodologies. Often, these methodologies come accompanied by a variety of assumptions that may be difficult for the uninitiated to evaluate. Some of these assumptions may be highly controversial, and thus the methods to which they give rise may be suspect, a matter that will concern us in later chapters.

Methodology texts do not present a complete view of current methodological developments in contemporary science. As one example, experimental methods are under heavy attack by a substantial number of psychologists, who propose alternative methods. These psychologists reject experimentation and **quantitative methods** in general, favoring instead what are known as **qualitative methods**. A unique aspect of the present text is that we will identify and describe some prominent qualitative methods and the rationales their adherents provide for their use. We will also discuss what in our view are the strengths and weakness of qualitative methods, and by comparing the quantitative and qualitative methodologies, the reader will come to better understand both types of methods. Becoming increasingly acquainted with a wide range of methodological issues should enable students not only to become better researchers with reference to specific problems in psychology, but also to understand and appreciate more fully how contemporary science is practiced and how to practice science better themselves.

Justification of Methodological Practices

Core methodological beliefs and practices must be justified. We may ask, by what procedure would the typical working scientist want her or his core methodological beliefs and practices justified? As a specific example, what is the justification for suggesting, as has the philosopher Sir **Karl Popper**, that theoretical propositions should be falsifiable? Historically, two general methods have been proposed, but one is more compatible than the other with the attitude of working scientists. The historically older and certainly more typical procedure has been to justify core methodological beliefs and practices using intuition and logic. This approach has been described as **foundationism**. Any number of historical figures who have contributed substantially to our understanding of science, as currently practiced, have used intuition and logic as the foundation for their methodological conclusions. Some individuals have emphasized logic almost exclusively (e.g., Popper), whereas the scientific views of others have been shaped to some extent by experience as well as logic (e.g., **Francis Bacon**). It is perhaps because of the prevalence of this "armchair" approach to science that many working scientists and students seem to feel that conventional philosophy of science is irrelevant to the everyday practice of science.

Although this attitude is understandable, it is not altogether accurate. History reveals that many of the accepted, currently influential ideas about science that have had considerable impact on its practice were suggested originally by nonscientists using logical and intuitive criteria, that is, employing armchair evaluation of methods. The irony here is that the working scientist may nevertheless accept many ideas about how contemporary science is to be practiced that were developed employing a procedure with which he or she is uncomfortable, armchair theorizing about scientific methods. In other words, working scientists are often unaware that they are accepting methodological procedures whose original justification was on the basis of logic and intuition, approaches that they would not otherwise apply in other areas of science. As Losee (2001) has clearly stated, "The scientist who is ignorant of precedents in the evaluation of theories is not likely to do an adequate job of evaluation himself" (p. 3). Our primary aim is to provide the reader with the sort of information needed to better evaluate scientific methods.

The second major approach that has been employed to justify various methodological procedures in science is of relatively recent origin, and it may transform our understanding of science in many ways. Indeed, as a systematic approach this method of justification is less than 50 years old. This second method places much less emphasis on what a particular individual thinks science should be and attempts, rather, to determine how successful science is and has been actually practiced. **Thomas S. Kuhn** (1922–1996) may rightly be considered to be not only an outstanding practitioner of this particular approach, but also its popularizer and, in this sense, its originator. This approach, called **naturalism** in reference to natural science, treats scientific issues as it treats issues in any other area of inquiry and seeks to gather data relevant to determining how useful science is actually practiced and accomplished. There are many sources of data relevant to this approach. Perhaps the most obvious source is that employed by Kuhn, which is essentially to look at the historical record, determining and identifying the specific practices employed within particular successful historical movements. Other sources of empirical data relevant to the practice of science will be described later. For now it is enough to mention that there is a growing realization that the approach best suited to understanding scientific issues is the very approach that science itself uses

Table 1.1 Methods for studying science and scientists

Type of method	How used	Principal advantage	Principal disadvantage
Historical	Intense study of a particular group of scientists or historical movement.	Rich source of data as to how meaningful science was conducted.	Little constraint on interpretation of the data.
In vivo observation	Observing scientists as they attempt to understand their data and theorize about it.	Can learn directly about how scientists think and reason about their data. Can also observe the social psychological factors that may affect problem solving.	May have to learn about unfamiliar subject matter in order to understand the scientist at work.
Personal reports	Study of scientists' accomplishments via interviews, examination of diaries, notes, and correspondence.	Provides insights into how creative scientists solve problems.	Danger of a biased presentation by the scientist, and reasoning processes employed may not be fully accessible to the scientist.
Controlled experiments	Provide scientists and nonscientists with scientific problems in controlled settings, and observe their method of solution.	Precise cause–effect relations in problem solving can be isolated.	The situation is artificial and may not be indicative of real-world problem solving.
Computer simulations	Develop a computer simulation that solves a specific scientific problem.	Can develop a precise model of the reasoning processes employed by a scientist in solving a problem.	Represents a possible way in which the problem was solved but not necessarily the actual way.
Personality studies	Obtain demographic and social/personality data from successful scientists, less successful scientists, and laymen.	Provides insight into characteristics that make scientists successful.	The data are correlational and may not reflect cause–effect relationships.

to better understand the empirical and conceptual issues in specific scientific subject areas.

As may be inferred from the above, by employing naturalism the gap between philosophy of science and orthodox science itself is much narrower than it has been employing foundationism. Indeed, in some respects the gap between philosophy of science and science is seriously diminished employing naturalism. For example, the idea that specific methodological statements are empirical statements (similar to the empirical statement *grass is green*), and therefore should be subjected to empirical test in the same way as other empirical statements are tested (e.g., by determining if grass is in fact green), is completely consistent with accepted ideas about how science itself should be practiced. It follows from naturalism that a variety of empirical procedures should be employed to evaluate many aspects of scientific practice. Thus, not only does the understanding of science that is arrived at through naturalism have much to offer to psychologists, but due to their specific training, psychologists have much to offer science approached naturalistically.

One area in which psychologists can contribute to a better understanding of science is through studying the psychology of scientists, a relatively new area of investigation (see, e.g., Feist & Gorman, 1998, and Gorman, Tweney, Gooding, & Kincannon, 2005). Psychologists are in a good position to isolate and describe the cognitive processes scientists use when solving particular empirical problems or constructing theory. This point, made years ago by the outstanding philosophers of science, Willard Quine and Thomas Kuhn, has only recently come to command the appreciation it deserves. Feist and Gorman have divided the study of scientists into four major areas: developmental psychology (the study of scientific reasoning in children and its development), cognitive psychology (the mental operations scientists and others employ in solving problems), personality psychology (the psychological characteristics of scientists as opposed to nonscientists), and social psychology (how scientific practice is influenced by the presence of others). Although this area is young, and relatively few studies have been reported, many interesting findings have been uncovered. For example, in terms of personality characteristics, scientists, as opposed to nonscientists, among other things, appear to be more dominant, self-confident, and have greater impulse control. Many of the findings about scientists have implications for the philosophy of science.

Weaving together the study of science and scientists, Table 1.1 provides the breakdown of methods used to study both how science is conducted, and the characteristics of those who conduct it. The table describes the various naturalistic methods that have been employed to study science as an empirical endeavor (see, e.g., Dunbar & Fuselgang, 2005; Klahr & Simon, 1999). Although we shall deal with these methods in detail in Chapter 6, we will have occasion to refer to one or the other of them in various chapters of this book. The table is meant to be self-explanatory. For example, Table 1.1 shows that the historical method involves the intense study of a particular group of scientists or a particular historical movement, and that this method has both advantages and disadvantages. Its advantages include that it provides a rich source of data as to how meaningful science was conducted in the past. Among its principal disadvantages is that, as with all historical methods, the data are open to multiple interpretations. Close attention to this table will repay the reader in dividends later in the book.

In the remainder of the chapter, we will introduce several of the foundational ideas that have been proposed throughout the history of science and have been incorporated into the contemporary conception of science. As previously indicated, many of these ideas were suggested by people other than working scientists. Having examined these foundational ideas, we will then describe briefly the approach we favor, that of naturalism. Essentially, the remainder of the book will be most concerned with developing the implications of the naturalistic approach to understanding the conceptions and practice of science. Our core conviction, one shared by many others (e.g., Bechtel, 1988), is that naturalism provides an approach to understanding science that is superior to that of the more conventional armchair approach of employing primarily logic and intuition. As indicated, the naturalistic movement is the latest approach to understanding the practice of science. Thus, it is not surprising that the implications of naturalism are in an early stage development and that such development is undergoing continuous improvement in scope and depth.

Precursors to Contemporary Science: An Historical Overview

To understand contemporary science, it is helpful to understand some of the major conceptions of science that were offered historically. In considering these, we shall not provide a general history of science, but rather focus on several important earlier methodological developments. The purpose of this treatment is to provide some idea of how scientific methodology developed over the ages.

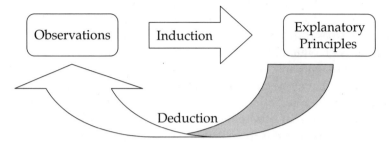

Figure 1.1 Depiction of Aristotle's inductive-deductive method, which suggests that observations lead to explanatory principles that in turn lead to deductions that give rise to additional observations (based on Losee, 2001).

Ancient views of scientific methodology

Aristotle (384–322 BCE) can be regarded as the first philosopher of science, and his views on science were accepted well into the 16th century. Much of Aristotle's proposal as to what constitutes true science is agreeable to a contemporary ear. As depicted in Figure 1.1, Aristotle suggested that science begins in observations, which give rise to generalizations (all crows are black), which in turn may be regarded as explanatory principles from which predictions are made, leading to further observations. A characteristic of Aristotle's approach was that scientific statements must necessarily be causal statements. For example, germs cause disease. These statements, according to Aristotle, either must be factually true or based on non-deducible "first principles" that are irrefutable. Each science contains first principles that cannot be deduced from the first principles of some other science.

Any discussion of the origins of science must recognize the important contributions of the atomists, Democritus (460–370 BCE) and Leucippus (480–420 BCE), which remain influential in contemporary science. Their major contribution was in suggesting that there is a reality behind the surface appearance, a reality that explains the appearance, a view that is widely accepted by scientists. In any event, the atomists attributed the underlying reality to atoms or monads, which were the smallest particles in nature because they were indivisible. It was the interaction of these invisible monads that was responsible for the appearance of things and how they behaved. The notion that there is a reality behind appearance is one of the more important ideas in all of science. As merely one example, **Gregor Mendel** (1823–1884), in order to explain the phenotypes of plants (e.g., their outward appearance), conducted experiments that ultimately led to genetics and the idea that the phenotypes of all organisms, plants and animals, have their basis in the genotypes (the mechanism that underlies the expression of outward appearance), which at the time were unobservable.

The **Pythagoreans**, or the followers of Pythagoras (approximately 580–500 BCE), may be credited with the view that what is real in science conforms to mathematical description. According to the Pythagorean view, anything that was real could necessarily be described in mathematical terms, and it is these mathematical relationships that comprise fundamental reality. Early scientific examples of this approach are as follows. Ptolemy (approximately CE 87–150), the father of the geocentric theory of planetary motion, formulated a series of mathematical models, one for each of the planets. Ptolemy's approach to astronomy, which suggested that the earth was the center of the then-known universe (geocentric view), survived until the 16th century. At that time, it became hotly debated due to Galileo favoring the Copernican model, according to which the sun is the center of the universe. The Copernican model ultimately replaced Ptolemy's geocentric system with its heliocentric system in which the earth and the other planets revolved around the sun.

The Enlightenment view of science

The **Enlightenment**, whose beginnings can be dated to Copernicus and Gallileo, broke with the idea that knowledge was to be found in the writings of the ancients, particularly the Greeks, and emphasized experience. Science in the era of the Enlightenment may be said to have begun with **Galileo** (1564–1642), who agreed with the Pythagoreans that mathematics is the language of reality. Dampier (1952) says of Galileo, "In a very real sense Galileo is the first of the moderns; as we read his writings, we instinctively feel at home; we know that we have reached the method of physical science which is still in use" (p. 129). Galileo's contributions were enormous. He was responsible for replacing the Aristotelian laws of motion with a more modern conception. He distinguished between primary physical qualities such as motion and secondary qualities such as the appearance of objects, for example, their color. Additionally, by defending the Copernican system, Galileo played a huge part in astronomy passing from the geocentric to the heliocentric system. Galileo tended to approach systems by assuming that they operate in an ideal manner. For example, rather than accepting the Aristotelian idea that an implanted force produced motion, he suggested that once a body was in motion it would tend to stay in motion until opposed by other forces. This is an idealized view about how motion should operate.

Sir Francis Bacon (1561–1626) is generally credited with the idea that the appropriate method in science is to proceed inductively, that is, to reach generalizations based on a painstaking analysis of specific instances. Bacon was reacting to the then prevalent notion that the way to gain knowledge was to study the writings of various Greeks such as Socrates, Plato, and Aristotle. Bacon recommended that knowledge should be generated by empirical observation. This point of view was furthered by **John Locke** (1632–1704), who felt that all knowledge came through the senses and is often mentioned in association with his idea of the *tabula rasa,* or the mind as a blank slate that is written on by experience. Another influence in the development of **empiricism** was Auguste Comte (1798–1857), who coined the term **positivism**. Boring (1950), in his well-known *A History of Experimental Psychology,* said of Comte,

> *Positive* for Comte carried the meaning of not speculative or inferential, of immediately observable, the immutable basis of fact which compels agreement because it is given prior to the inferences based upon it. Thus, *positive* means *basic, observational, preinferential, undebatable.* (p. 633)

The notion that **induction** was *the* method of science was accepted by **Newton** and was to predominate in science until the 19th century. The idea here was that proper scientific statements resulted from the accumulation of specific instances. One consequence of employing induction is that one does not go beyond what is directly observed. This tendency can be seen in Newton. For example, Newton's gravitational principle, that the force of attraction between bodies is directly proportional to their masses and indirectly proportional to the distance between them, is a descriptive rather than a causal statement. Newton was unwilling to speculate on the causes of gravitation. Because his gravitational principle was so important, entering into a variety of major deductions concerning phenomena, it laid the groundwork for the acceptance of the idea that scientific statements could be descriptive as well as causative, a major extension of the Aristotelian conception of science as only causal. With Newton, descriptive statements as well as causal ones came to be regarded as scientific. Prior to Newton, a necessary feature of a scientific system was that it was comprised of causal statements, and purely descriptive statements or systems were not regarded as scientific.

Three outstanding contributors to our improved understanding of science in the 19th century were John Herschel, **William Whewell**, and **John Stuart Mill**. One of Herschel's (1792–1871) major contributions was to distinguish sharply between the **context of discovery** and the **context of justification**. The context of discovery is normally thought to be psychological rather than logical, and is concerned primarily with the novel hypotheses that scientists may entertain and subsequently test. The context of discovery applies to all of those processes involved in the formulation of an idea, concept, or hypothesis. The context of justification refers to the various methodological procedures that scientists might use to confirm or justify their hypotheses and theories. In recent times, there has been some disagreement as to the importance of this distinction. On the one hand, philosophers such as Karl Popper think that the distinction is critical and that the gulf between the context of discovery and the context of justification is very wide indeed. On the other hand, philosophers such as Thomas Kuhn think that the distinction is quite overrated and that a sharp line cannot be drawn between the two. Losee (2001) credits Herschel with also being an early advocate of the idea that theories must survive crucial tests, not unlike that popularized later by Popper, as we shall see.

William Whewell (1794–1866) suggested the idea that there might be more to science than simple induction. According to Whewell, the proper method of science was to propose hypotheses and then attempt to test them by means of empirical observation. Whewell may be considered to be the father of the hypothesis testing approach to science. Another contribution of Whewell's was to suggest what has become known as the **consilience** of inductions. Consilience occurs when particular inductive inferences are supported by evidence from a variety of different sources. An example of consilience is the fact that the occurrence of evolution is supported by evidence obtained from the fossil record, embryology, and DNA testing, to name only a few sources. This consilience, as Whewell would call it, serves to increase our confidence that evolution actually occurred. Not surprisingly, perhaps, **Charles Darwin** was an advocate of consilience, as suggested by Whewell.

John Stuart Mill (1806–1873) argued that hypothesis testing, which has since emerged as one of the major methods of modern science, was not the only reasonable approach to science and proposed that theories that explained already existing phenomena (**explanatory theories**) were on a par, logically speaking, with theories that were produced through hypothesis testing (**predictive theories**). We think that Mill's view should be taken more seriously than it seems to be taken among

contemporary scientists, who seem to value predictive theori€
more highly than explanatory ones (see Laudan, 1996). As an ⁄
of the value of explanatory theories, one might consider that one oⅰ
the outstanding theories of current-day geology is that of plate tectonics,
which was suggested originally by **Alfred Wegener** in 1912 entirely
on the basis of already existing evidence. His theory of plate tectonics
brought all of the existing evidence together in a coherent and systematic
fashion, that is, it was exclusively an explanatory theory (see Oreskes,
1999). Of course, nothing prevents a theory from being a mixture of
the two approaches.

Science in the 20th and 21st centuries

In the 20th century, two major foundationist philosophies of science
emerged, **logical positivism**, developed by a group of philosophers
known as the Vienna Circle, founded by Moritz Schlick (1882–1936),
and **falsificationism**, developed by Sir Karl Popper (1902–1994). Logical
positivism became the dominant force in the philosophy of science in
the first part of the 20th century, and was extremely influential in experimental psychology, being especially compatible with behaviorism.
Although logical positivism is no longer the influential force it once
was, many suggest that it still continues to set the agenda for evaluating important developments in science (e.g., Bechtel, 1988). The two
terms describing the logical positivist's approach to science refer to the
following: Logical is meant to reflect the use of symbolic logic in the
formalization of scientific systems, and positivism is meant in the sense
of Comte to emphasize the central role of experience in science.

The logical positivists emphasized induction. According to this
approach, which emphasized verification, one sought additional con-
firmations of statements, and in this way statements became more
and more probable. For Popper (1959), confirmation was not critical.
What was critical for Popper was that a proposition could be disconfirmed or falsified. Consequently, Popper suggested that scientists
should deliberately attempt to falsify their theories. According to
Popper, the ability of a statement to be falsified was the demarcation
criterion between science and nonscience. Many scientists today think
of falsification as an indispensable feature of scientific theories.

Whereas the logical positivists and Popper emphasized a logical, or
foundationist, approach to science based on their ideas of how science
should be practiced, Thomas Kuhn recommended an empirical approach
in which the goal is to determine how science actually is practiced. In

particular, as noted earlier, Kuhn suggested that we could understand science and how it is created by studying the history of particular scientific practices.

In recent years, the general idea advocated by Kuhn has come into greater prominence. It is now widely, if not universally, accepted that science should be studied in much the same way as science itself studies other areas. As indicated, prior to the 1960s, our understanding of science was based to a considerable extent on a logical analysis of its methods and procedures. Kuhn suggested that to understand a particular scientific approach to a problem it was necessary to isolate and describe how a particular scientific community went about conducting science. In conducting such an historical examination, Kuhn suggested that insofar as possible, the attempt should be made to understand the particular scientific context of the given period. Kuhn's fundamental insights have been broadened in recent times to include other empirical approaches to understanding science. For example, one might examine the notebooks of a scientist who has made an important discovery or observe groups of scientists in laboratory settings, or one might devise experimental tasks to determine how scientists deal with specific types of problems. As indicated, this empirical approach to understanding science goes under the name of naturalism, the view that all problems are to be approached in the same manner that science uses to investigate empirical phenomena.

Research Paradigms, Programs, and Traditions

One of the interesting ideas that have developed in recent times is that there are scientific approaches that are more general than the specific scientific theories that they encompass. These broader approaches, called **paradigms** by Kuhn (1962), **research programs** by **Lakatos** (1970), and **research traditions** by **Laudan** (1977), essentially consist of assumptions and methodological commitments that give rise to specific scientific theories and research. Kuhn was the first to suggest that there are theoretical and methodological commitments that are broader than the theories they encompass. There are differences between Kuhn, Lakatos, and Laudan with respect to the characteristics of these more general commitments, which we consider in Chapter 3. Regardless of these differences, there are certain similarities among the concepts of paradigms, research programs, and research traditions. Each is concerned with what might be called ontological and methodological matters. **Ontology** refers to the sort of entities that a particular theory posits. For example, associative theorists might postulate associations between stimuli and responses as fundamental psychological entities. Methodology refers to the specific procedures favored by the paradigm – such as experimentation, systematic observation, and correlational investigation.

A clear example of a paradigm or research tradition in psychology is provided by behaviorism. The behavioristic tradition spawned a variety of theories, which though differing in a variety of respects, adhered to certain core propositions. The most fundamental assumption shared by this family of theories, which emphasized learning, was that the proper subject matter of psychology is behavior. This assumption was shared by theories as different as those of B. F. Skinner, Clark Hull, and E. C. Tolman. According to Skinner's radical behaviorism, the causes of behavior were in the environment and not in the organism. Hull, on the other hand, suggested that overt behavior was controlled by internal processes, but these internal processes were in turn behavior. Tolman suggested that behavior exhibited certain characteristics such as intention, which classified it as cognitive.

In addition to the behavioristic paradigm, psychology has had several other paradigms. A noteworthy example is the individual differences paradigm. Whereas the behavioristic paradigm emphasized the search for general laws, the individual differences paradigm did not. Sometimes this distinction is described as being between a *nomothetic* approach and an *ideographic* one. The nomothetic approach is concerned with general laws and processes, while the ideographic approach is concerned with differences such as those between individuals in intelligence, personality characteristics, and specific aptitudes. Whereas the behavioristic paradigm emphasized experimentation with animals, the individual differences paradigm allowed the use of nonexperimental methods (e.g., correlational methods) as well as experimental methods, and put a heavier emphasis on research with humans. Among the prominent individuals who may be regarded as pioneers of the individual differences approach are Sir Francis Galton (1822–1911), Karl Pearson (1857–1936), Alfred Binet (1857–1922), and James McKeen Cattell (1860–1944).

The postulation of paradigms has led to the recognition that a given scientific community may accept both theoretical and methodological propositions that are less immune to test than are particular theories. This appears to be one of the more important ideas about science to emerge in the latter part of the 20th century. As we shall see, much disagreement in psychology stems from the fact that different individuals adhere to different research traditions, or paradigms, and thus make fundamentally different assumptions, both methodological and theoretical.

Naturalism: A Brief Introduction

One of the great accomplishments of naturalism is that of revealing methodological statements to be empirical statements. Consider a contrary view by the distinguished philosopher of science, Sir Karl Popper, who is very well regarded among contemporary scientists. According to Popper, scientists should do everything in their power to falsify theories. Having falsified a theory, scientists should not attempt to rescue it by invoking auxiliary hypotheses. This view of Popper was based on his idea about how science should be conducted. According to the naturalistic turn of mind, however, the question of whether auxiliary hypotheses should be employed is an empirical matter to be determined as any other empirical matter is determined, that is, by how well it works in practice. What we should determine as naturalists is whether invoking auxiliary assumptions has had favorable or unfavorable empirical and theoretical consequences in the past, and under what circumstances. By a favorable consequence we mean that invoking an auxiliary hypothesis actually resulted either in new information or in saving the theory, and possibly improving the theory, in a non-arbitrary way.

Let us consider a significant historical example in which a powerful theory was rescued by invoking an auxiliary assumption (see Chalmers, 1999). Observations of the planet Uranus indicated that its orbit departed from that predicted on the basis of Newton's theory of gravitation. In an attempt to make Newton's theory consistent with the orbit of Uranus, two individuals, Leverrier in France and Adams in England, suggested that there might exist a previously undetected planet in the vicinity of Uranus. It was the attraction between the conjectured planet and Uranus that was to explain the departure of Uranus's orbit from that otherwise predicted. The approximate vicinity and size of the conjectured planet could be estimated. Once these matters were settled, it was possible to predict the possible region of the sky in which the new planet should appear. Employing this information, Galle sighted the new planet, which is now known as Neptune. As Chalmers (1999) indicates, "Far from being ad hoc, the move to save Newton's theory from falsification by Uranus's orbit led to a new kind of a test of that theory, which it was able to pass in a dramatic and progressive way" (p. 78).

What this historical example illustrates is that Popper's intuitions about how science should be practiced would have been counterproductive in this particular instance if they had been followed. That is, if we were following Popper's advice, Newton's theory would have been put in doubt and possibly rejected. Too, the discovery of Neptune would have been at the least delayed. Thus, postulating auxiliary hypotheses may not always be an ad hoc affair and may in some instances be positively useful. In this particular instance, the postulation of an auxiliary hypothesis was useful, perhaps because it not only rescued the theory but also had a testable implication. We are not suggesting that the postulation of auxiliary assumptions will always result in an outcome as positive as that described in the above example. In some cases, it surely will not. Our real point is the general one that methodological statements must be evaluated in the same manner as other empirical statements. It is impossible at present to state with any assurance the circumstances under which the postulation of auxiliary hypotheses will have a positive outcome. The reason for this is that methodological statements have for a long time been treated as logical, intuitive statements rather than empirical statements, and thus a systematic search of the particular conditions under which auxiliary hypotheses have led to positive outcomes unfortunately has not as yet attracted the attention it deserves from scientists. It is probably clear that what has been suggested above with reference to auxiliary hypotheses applies to all methodological statements, as for example, the methodological statement *prefer simple theories to complex ones*. Hopefully, with the appearance of naturalism on the scene, scientists will turn more and more to the evaluation of methodological statements by empirical means.

A major concern about naturalism is whether it can be prescriptive as well as descriptive. That is, can it tell us what scientists ought to do, thus going beyond describing what they actually do? Within the philosophy of science, there has been recognition since at least the time of Kuhn's (1962) work that there is a difference of opinion as to how we should arrive at how science should be practiced. Should we look at what scientists actually do? Or should we specify what they should do based on logical and intuitive arguments? Williams (1970) captured this distinction, noting that Kuhn based his system on what scientists actually *do*, whereas Popper based his system on what scientists *ought* to do. The idea that the naturalistic approach to science could be prescriptive as well as descriptive was emphasized by the philosopher Larry Laudan, whose position on this matter will be described at some length later in this book.

Remainder of Book

This chapter has served to provide an introduction to some of the major ideas in science from Babylonian times to the present. In the rest of the book, we will be elaborating many of the themes introduced in the present chapter. In addition, certain new topics not previously mentioned will be covered. The remaining two chapters of the first section describe in more detail the major changes in scientific methodology in the 20th century. Chapter 2 will deal with the agendas and controversies associated with the major figures in the development of science in the first two-thirds of the 20th century: the logical positivists, Karl Popper, and Thomas Kuhn. Kuhn is usually given credit for beginning the post-positivist era in the philosophy of science, which stresses naturalism. Chapter 3 provides a detailed exposition of naturalism's approach to science and examines the positions of three prominent postpositivists, Imre Lakatos, Larry Laudan, and **Ronald Giere**. Chapters 4–6 develop the implications of naturalism for science. Chapter 4 examines theory construction and testing, with particular emphasis on the strengths and limitations of induction, **deduction**, and hypothesis testing. Available methodological textbooks, although recommending hypothesis testing as the major methodological tool in science, examine its strengths and weaknesses in less detail than will be examined here. Chapter 4 also introduces **abduction**, which is a widely employed, extremely important method in science whose strengths and weaknesses are seldom explicitly discussed. Chapter 5 describes many of the criteria scientists use in evaluating theories, such as simplicity, and gives prominent real-life examples of how these criteria are utilized in practice. The chapter also provides a detailed exposition of the value of consilience as a goal in science in terms of evaluating hypotheses and theories. Chapter 6 describes and provides examples of novel procedures that have been recently developed for the evaluation and understanding of science that are consistent with the naturalistic perspective. These procedures are particularly relevant to psychologists because they embody empirical methodologies involving the cognitive capacities of scientists as problem solvers.

The final section of the book applies naturalism to contemporary methodological issues in psychology. Chapter 7 deals with some of the major criticisms of science from the perspectives of **postmodernism** and **social constructionism**. We provide a critical evaluation of these criticisms and show that, in our opinion, they are unwarranted. In Chapter 8, we present and describe the fast-growing approach to science involving qualitative methods. Our treatment includes thorough descriptions of several popular qualitative methods, as well as the rationales for their use. Chapter 9 provides a detailed analysis, discussion, and critique of the rationale for qualitative methods provided by their advocates. Chapter 10 pulls together various ideas from the preceding chapters and discusses in detail the concepts of internal and external validity. Examples of each type of validity are described.

Chapter Summary

We have shown in this chapter that from the time of Aristotle to the present, conceptions of science have been in a state of change and development. For the greater part of science's history, methodological procedures have often been justified by employing the armchair methods of logic and intuition. Recently, as a result of the efforts of Kuhn and those who followed him in placing emphasis on understanding science from an empirical point of view, naturalism has augmented logic and intuition as an important procedure for evaluating methodologies. According to naturalism, methodological statements are empirical statements and are to be evaluated on the same basis as any other empirical statement. Because naturalism is of recent origin, it is in the early stages of development, and it may be expected that a consistent application of naturalism will have a profound impact on our understanding and practice of science in the future.

Chapter **2**

MAJOR ISSUES TO EMERGE IN 20TH CENTURY APPROACHES TO SCIENCE

Introduction

We indicated in Chapter 1 that the philosophy of science went through several revolutionary changes during the 20th century, with three major movements having the predominant influence. These movements – **logical positivism, falsificationism,** and the **postpositivism** of Kuhn – had a substantial impact on science generally and the field of psychology in particular. In large part, they were concerned with how hypotheses were to be tested, what methodologies were to be used in testing them, and how concepts should be defined. Understanding the major ideas of these movements is of considerable importance because it will allow the reader to recognize which earlier scientific and methodological claims have been discarded and which newer ones have been incorporated into contemporary approaches to science. Psychology has been radically affected by each of these movements, particularly in terms of the methodological claims it accepts and rejects.

The initial major movement to emerge in the century was that of logical positivism. Logical positivism represented an extension of **positivism,** which is a view that is concerned with human experience, to include symbolic logic. This movement was extremely influential and successful in the first half of the 20th century. In experimental psychology, in particular, the influence of logical positivism and its close counterpart, **operationism,** was very substantial, leading to many methodological papers on how psychological research and theory should be practiced (Bechtel, 1988). In the period from about 1920 to 1950, methodological issues were at the forefront of many discussions in experimental psychology, thanks to the influence of logical positivism.

Although logical positivism was popular in many quarters, it was opposed within the philosophy of science by **Sir Karl Popper**. Popper's approach, which has been described as falsificationism, will be considered in detail later in this chapter. Popper became extremely influential within science generally and within psychology as well, and many would consider his approach to how science should be practiced to be better than that of the logical positivists.

With **Thomas Kuhn**, in the latter part of the century, the influence of positivism began to decline and the postpositivist era began. In this era, an emphasis on logic and intuition, so important to the logical positivists and Popper, was expanded to include an emphasis on an empirical approach to science. That is, Kuhn emphasized that science could best be understood through a detailed analysis of specific historical episodes (e.g., the historical developments leading up to Benjamin Franklin's theory of electricity). Kuhn's seminal work had a profound impact on the philosophy and history of science, on social science in general, and on psychological science in particular. To a significant extent, subsequent developments in the philosophy of science became a matter of either agreeing or disagreeing with Kuhn.

Logical Positivism

Logical positivism was primarily a European movement in the first half of the 20th century. The philosophy of science championed by the Vienna Circle used physics as its primary model of science. The model derived from physics was assumed to apply to all other sciences, a view that would be considered highly controversial today. Some prominent members of the Vienna Circle were Moritz Schlick, Rudolph Carnap, and Hans Reichenbach, among others. Among the non-continental logical positivists was the English philosopher A. J. Ayer.

The logical positivists saw **induction** as the central method of science. Induction is a reasoning process in which one progresses from particulars to the general. A classic example of induction concerns black crows (or, alternatively, white swans). On noticing that all particular crows so far encountered are black, one arrives inductively at the generalization *all crows are black*. The logical positivists distinguished between **analytic** and **synthetic statements**: Analytic statements are true by definition but lack empirical content, in contrast to synthetic statements, which are empirical. An example of an analytic statement is "all triangles have three sides," and an example of a synthetic statement is "grass is green." Statements that were neither analytic

21

(true by definition) nor synthetic (empirical) were considered by the logical positivists to be nonsense. **Metaphysical** statements fall into the nonsense category.

The logical positivists accepted Herschel's distinction, introduced in Chapter 1, between the **context of discovery** and the **context of justification** (e.g., Reichenbach, 1947). This distinction is concerned with that between the generation of theory (context of discovery) and the validation of theory (context of justification). The logical positivists focused almost entirely on justification, relegating discovery to psychology. According to this view, the scientist operating in the context of discovery is free to construct hypotheses and theories on any basis whatsoever. Unlike the context of discovery, the context of justification has to follow logical rules. That is, hypotheses and theories have to be justified using the methodological canons of science. From this view, science differs from other forms of intellectual activity in that, unlike them, it is justified on the basis of well-specified logical rules.

The logical positivists favored a verifiability theory of meaning. According to this view, the meaning of a statement is comprised by the set of conditions that would demonstrate the statement to be true. For example, the statement, "what I see before me is a blade of grass," may be verified by noting that what I see before me is green, that it contains chlorophyll, and so on. This verificationist view, as is perhaps clear, is consistent with the emphasis that the logical positivists placed on induction. That is, as a logical positivist, one would search for an increasing number of specific instances that would tend to confirm some general proposition. As the number of confirming instances increased, a proposition would be considered to be increasingly more likely, according to the logical positivists.

According to the inductivist view, as indicated, scientists note that all observed crows are black and thus arrive at the inductive generalization that all crows are black. A major difficulty with inductive generalizations of this type, first pointed out by the philosopher **David Hume** (1748/2000), is that there is no logical necessity for assuming that the next crow observed will be black. Contrary to Hume, the logical positivists thought that by collecting more and more evidence it became possible to increasingly confirm an inductive generalization. This suggestion has not met with approval from the scientific and philosophic communities at large. It is generally conceded that attempts to improve inductive logic so that it is permissible to derive universal affirmative statements such as *all crows are black* from a collection of particular instances have not been successful (Howson, 2000).

Despite this limitation of induction, scientists often propose universal statements on the basis of a series of specific observations. For example, in statements of Newton's law of gravitation, it is stated that all bodies attract each other with a force directly proportional to their mass. Although scientists clearly employ inductive inferences of this sort, in a strict logical sense, such inferences are impermissible. Given the limitations of inductive logic, we should always be prepared for the possibility that our inductive generalizations may fail when new observations are made.

A second limitation of the inductive method is that one's inferences are limited to the specific characteristics that one has observed. That is to say, the causal mechanism that is responsible for the inductive generalization is not given by the induction itself. To be specific, although one may arrive at the generalization that all crows are black, the reason for their being black is not given by inductive logic. This, of course, is a serious deficiency, because scientists attempt to go beyond describing observed characteristics of phenomena to postulating the underlying causes of the phenomena. For example, a psychologist wants to know not just that forgetting occurs, but why it occurs. The two deficiencies of induction, its inability to justify universal affirmative propositions and its inability to provide justification for any fruits of induction, suggest that the logical positivists placed too heavy an emphasis on induction as a tool for elucidating scientific propositions.

According to logical positivists, both explaining and predicting phenomena depend on the application of a general law, together with the specific conditions under which a phenomenon occurs. For example, to understand the force of gravitation between, say, the earth and the sun, we would need to have Newton's law of gravity plus information about the masses of the sun and the earth, and the distance between them. According to the positivists' view, there is no logical difference between explaining an already known fact and predicting a totally new one. This view has been criticized because prediction and explanation do not appear to have the considerable degree of symmetry suggested by the logical positivists' view. For example, it is a commonplace that a person's behavior in some area may be exceedingly difficult to predict but be perfectly understandable after it occurs. To select another example, physicists may not be able to predict precisely when a bridge will collapse, but they can give perfectly good reasons for its collapse after the fact.

Another difficulty with the logical positivists involves their distinction between analytic statements, synthetic statements, and nonsense.

Certain statements that make perfectly good sense would be classified erroneously as nonsense according to these categories. For example, before we were able to go to the moon, we would have had to say that any statement about the far side of the moon was nonsense. This is because the far side of the moon could not be observed and, therefore, any statement about it would not be a synthetic statement. Because the statement is also clearly not an analytic one, that is, one that is true by definition, we would have to say that it is nonsense. In other words, anything that is in principle observable, but not observable at a given time, would have to be classified by the logical positivists as nonsense, which does not seem reasonable. As a more contemporary example, physicists who postulate string theory as a means of bringing together relativity theory and quantum mechanics would be seen by the logical positivists as engaging in nonsense because, at the moment, there is no way that strings can be directly observed (Greene, 1999). Yet, few physicists would agree with this classification.

The logical positivists suggested that theory should be axiomatized, that is, presented in the form of logical propositions that are taken to be true. They were aware that many theories were not axiomatized, but suggested that this is an ideal that should be pursued. Euclidean geometry is an example of an axiomatized theory that would serve as a model for scientific theory. According to the logical positivists, when theories from different areas such as physics and biology were axiomatized, it would be easier to see relationships between them. This would allow the unity of science to become more apparent.

An example of a theory in psychology that embraced axiomatization is Clark Hull's (1943) theory of learning. We examine some propositions of Hull's theory in order to provide an example of an axiomatized theory in psychology. Hull was in agreement with the logical positivists, stating:

> It is evident that in its deductive nature systematic scientific theory closely resembles mathematics. In this connection the reader may profitably recall his study of geometry with (1) its definitions, e.g., point, line, surface, etc., (2) its primary principles (axioms), e.g., that but one straight line can be drawn between two points, etc., and following these (3) the ingenious and meticulous step-by-step development of the proof of one theorem after another, the later theorems depending on the earlier ones in a magnificent and ever-mounting hierarchy of derived propositions. Proper scientific theoretical systems conform exactly to all three of these characteristics. (1943, p. 7)

At a more specific level, Hull suggested that a scientific theory should stress conformation, and should be developed as follows:

> The typical procedure in science is to adopt a postulate tentatively, deduce one or more of its logical implications concerning observable phenomena, and then check the validity of the deductions by observation. If the deduction is in genuine disagreement with observation, the postulate must be either abandoned or so modified that it implies no such conflicting statement. If, however, the deductions and the observations agree, the postulate gains in dependability. By successive agreements under a very wide variety of conditions it may attain a high degree of justified credibility, but never absolute certainty. (p. 15)

An example of one of Hull's many postulates, and his deductions from it (corollaries), is concerned with the principle of reinforcement. According to Hull, in order for learning to occur an organism had to be reinforced.

> Postulate III Primary Reinforcement
> Whenever an effector activity (R) is closely associated with a stimulus afferent impulse or trace (s) and the conjunction is closely associated with the rapid diminution in the motivational stimulus (S_D or s_G), there will result an increment (Δ) to a tendency for that stimulus to evoke that response. (Hull, 1952, pp. 5–6)

In this view of learning, expressed above by Hull in formal language, an effector activity is a response (R), which becomes associated with a stimulus or stimulus trace (s). The "rapid diminution in the motivational stimulus" to which Hull refers is essentially reinforcement (e.g., eating would reduce the motivational stimulus of hunger).

Two corollaries about reinforcement that Hull deduced from the primary reinforcement postulate were *Corollary i. Secondary Motivation* and *Corollary ii. Secondary Reinforcement*. The first corollary is concerned with the ability of neutral stimuli to bring about motivationally charged stimuli, and the second corollary is concerned with neutral stimuli themselves becoming reinforcers. Proceeding in this manner, that is, axiomatizing theory, Hull provided a highly influential learning theory that attracted a great many followers. By the middle 1940s, for example, Hull, along with Tolman and Skinner, was clearly one of the major figures in all of experimental psychology. However, behavioristic theories such as Hull's are not as highly regarded today as they once were. Regardless of the fate of the particular learning theory that Hull established, it is clear that he is one of the major early figures in bringing mathematical theorizing, which is now common-place, into mainstream psychology.

Operationism

At about the time that logical positivism was becoming popular within psychology, another movement attracted the attention of experiment-alists, operationism. This view, originally suggested by the physicist Percy Bridgeman (1927), stressed **operational definition** of concepts. As a methodological device, many psychologists would advocate the use of operational definitions, as indicated by inclusion of the concept in most undergraduate methodology texts (e.g., Christensen, 2001). Bridgeman said of operational definition of a concept, "We mean by any concept nothing more than a set of operations; *the concept is synonymous with the corresponding set of operations*" (p. 5). As an example of an operational definition, Bridgeman used length. He indicated that there were various ways to measure length – by ruler, by trigono-metric triangulation, radar, etc. Each of these methods, according to Bridgeman, represents a different concept. An example of an opera-tional definition in psychology would be to define hunger motivation in two different ways. One would be a measure of how long ago an animal was fed, and another would be how much the animal was fed at some specified earlier period. According to Bridgeman, these two different measures of hunger motivation would represent different concepts. Bridgeman's purpose for introducing operational definitions into physics was to rid it of metaphysical concepts that, in his view, were responsible for the revolution in physics that occurred from **Newton** to Einstein.

Initially, operationism was widely accepted by the logical positivists, and it became very popular within experimental psychology, in part through the influence of logical positivism (Green, 1992). For example, Bergmann, a philosopher, and Spence, a psychologist, said in 1941, "No body of empirical knowledge can be built up without operational definition of the terms in use" (p. 2). Despite the popularity of opera-tionism within psychology, particularly in connection with behaviorism and sensory psychophysics, there was considerable disagreement as to what it meant. Green (1992) examined the interpretations of operation-ism provided by Bridgeman and by several prominent psychologists and philosophers, as expressed in a symposium sponsored by the journal *Psychological Review*. The participants in the symposium were the psychologists Edwin G. Boring, Carroll Pratt, and B. F. Skinner, the physicist Percy Bridgeman, and the philosopher Harold E. Israel. Green noted that the consensus on various aspects of operationism among the participants in the symposium was sparse. Summing up the views of the participants, Green concluded, "It is clear . . . that the adoption of operationism had not, as per its early promise, led to the rise of a united scientific psychology" (p. 308).

One of the basic disagreements between Bridgeman's conception of operationism and that adopted by many psychologists, such as Boring, Hull, and Tolman, concerned the type of concepts to which operationism was relevant. For Bridgeman, the purpose of operational definitions was to rid science of metaphysical concepts, which was also a major goal of the logical positivists, as we have seen, with their distinction between synthetic statements, analytic statements, and nonsense. However, for many psychologists, operational definitions were used for a different purpose, to justify the use of unobservable entities such as drive, intelligence and so on.

A major criticism of operationism is that it is impossible to completely define any concept. Indeed, it is suggested that such complete definition would lead to sterility, whereas openness of concepts may lead to scientific advance. Our own view here is that the various technical definitions of operationism and disputes about where it applies are not a focal concern. We suggest that in the interest of clarity one should attempt to define the operations used in connection with a particular concept as objectively as possible. It is often suggested that in defining a concept one should use what is known as the "physical thing" language. By this is meant definition in terms of physical measurement such as time and space. A major reason for doing so is to allow subsequent investigators to duplicate the conditions of an experiment as closely as possible. This allows replication of previous findings, if that is desired, or to use different procedures, if necessary, to determine their effects on the experimental results.

Popper's Falsificationism

The inductive approach of the logical positivists, whether in psychology or other sciences, was seen as deficient by Karl Popper, who became the most influential philosopher of science in the mid 20th century. One of the deficiencies of inductive logic, noted by Popper, namely that it is logically impossible to be certain of the validity of an inductive generalization, served as a springboard for him to create an entirely novel approach to science. Popper noted that some logical positivists, for example, Reichenbach, had attempted unsuccessfully to solve the problem of induction. Popper pointed out that no matter how widely used and accepted the principle of induction might be, "I should still contend that a principle of induction is superfluous and that it must lead to logical inconsistencies" (1959, p. 427).

Popper emphasized that an asymmetrical relation holds between induction and deduction. He indicated that although it is not possible to confirm an inductive generalization, it is possible to falsify it. Popper emphasized deductive logic. For example, if all Xs are Ys, and this instance before me now is an X, it follows logically that it must also be a Y. The proposition emphasized by Popper was that if the particular X turned out not to be a Y, then the general proposition all Xs are Ys is falsified and therefore must be rejected. On the basis of this observation, Popper suggested that the proper approach in science should be that of attempting to falsify hypotheses. Scientists, according to Popper, should deliberately try their best to falsify their hypotheses. An hypothesis that has undergone repeated tests of this type and has failed to be falsified (i.e., has passed all its tests) is said by Popper to be well corroborated. Note that corroboration is not the same as confirmation. Unlike confirmation, corroboration as used by Popper has no connotation of being increasingly more likely. According to Popper, all that we can hope for in testing hypotheses is that they become more highly corroborated. Some philosophers of science regard Popper's notion of corroboration as extremely vague. For example, Salmon (1988) indicated that Popper violates the distinction between confirmation and corroboration, because he treats corroboration much like others treat confirmation.

In any case, a good part of the appeal of Popper's view was the implication that a hypothesis that could not potentially be falsified is in no sense a scientific one. Three theories that Popper indicated were difficult, if not impossible, to falsify, were Marxism, Freudian psychoanalysis, and Adler's version of psychoanalysis. Popper noted,

> These theories appeared to be able to explain practically everything. ...Once your eyes were thus opened you saw confirming instances everywhere: the world was full of *verifications* of the theory. Whatever happened always confirmed it. (Popper, 1963, pp. 34–35)

Specifically, he indicated in connection with Adler,

> Once, in 1919, I reported to him a case which to me did not seem particularly Adlerian, but which he found no difficulty in analyzing in terms of his theory of inferiority feelings, although he had not even

seen the child. Slightly shocked, I asked him how he could be so sure. 'Because of my thousandfold experience,' he replied; whereupon I could not help saying: 'And with this new case, I suppose, your experience has become thousand-and-one-fold.' (p. 35)

Popper's complaints seem entirely consistent with that expressed by an anonymous author in the *Encyclopedia Britannica* many years before, in 1771. According to this author, the theory of ether, or aether [a medium theorized to fill the entire universe], could not be falsified:

Aether seems to be an exceedingly tractable sort of substance: Whenever the qualities of one body differ from those of another, *a different modification of aether* at once solves the phaenomenon. The aether of iron must not, to be sure, be exactly the same with the nervous aether, otherwise it would be in danger of producing sensation in place of magnetism. It would likewise have been very improper to give the vegetable aether exactly the same qualities with those of the animal aether; for, in such a case, men would run great risk of striking root in the soil, and trees and hedges might eradicate and run about the fields. . . . It is impossible to gravel an aetherial philosopher. Ask him what questions you please, his answer is ready: – "As we cannot find the cause *any where* else; ergo, by dilemma, it must be owing to aether!" For example, ask one of those sages, What is the cause of gravity? he will answer, Tis *aether!* Ask him the cause of *thought,* he will gravely reply, "The solution of this question was once universally allowed to exceed the limits of human genius: But now, by the grand *discoveries* we have lately made, it is as plain as that three and two make five: – *Thought* is a mere *mechanical* thing, an evident effect of certain motions in the brain produced by the *oscillations* of a subtle elastic fluid called *aether!"* (*Encyclopaedia Britannica,* 1771, p. 34)

Quite clearly, the problems that troubled Popper were bothersome to some others even centuries earlier.

Popper's approach to science and that of the logical positivists are quite different in suggesting how science should be conducted. If one is interested in confirming inductive inferences by the collection of more and more data, then the scientist should engage in the careful and painstaking accumulation of individual instances. However, this is not the way science should be conducted, according to Popper. In the Popperian tradition, one seeks to put forth hypotheses that are both bold and of great scope. Failing to falsify hypotheses with these characteristics leads to an enormous increase in knowledge.

As indicated, logical positivism exerted a strong influence on psychological research in the early part of the century (Bergmann & Spence, 1941, 1944), resulting in a strong reliance on data collection leading to proper inductive generalizations. A good example of this is to be found in the verbal learning tradition, whose primary concern was the learning and retention of verbal materials (words, nonsense syllables, etc.). This tradition followed in the footsteps of Hermann Ebbinghaus (1885/1964), who conducted many detailed experiments on himself in which he examined learning and retention of nonsense syllables as a function of a variety of factors. Ebbinghaus developed methods and measures of memory, and a strongly empirical approach, that undergirded the verbal learning tradition. This tradition was also influenced heavily by the functionalist school of thought in American psychology, which emphasized descriptive statements of results and minimized theoretical explanation.

The minimalist approach to theory was taken so far by the verbal learners that, according to Lachman, Lachman, and Butterfield (1979), "Verbal learning research could not be evaluated by the adequacy of the theory it generated, for it generated so little theory. It was evaluated instead by the quantity of additional research it stimulated" (p. 47). In other words, the primary criterion for research was its fruitfulness for stimulating new research, which resulted in the accumulation of masses of data concerning human learning and memory from which general principles were induced. Many psychologists concluded that the verbal learning approach was grounded too much in data collection and not enough in theory (Lachman et al., 1979), which was one reason for the shift to an information-processing approach, which emphasizes theory about internal processes, beginning in the latter half of the 1950s. As Lachman et al. note, when the verbal learners made the transition to an information-processing approach, "They lost their functionalist tradition and began to theorize forcefully" (p. 55). Many of the newer theories in cognitive psychology, for example, J. R. Anderson's (1996) ACT (Adaptive Control of Thought) theory, appear to follow more in the mold of Popper than of the logical positivists in that they are more theory driven than data driven.

It has generally come to be realized that Popper's emphasis on falsification has several weaknesses. One problem is that when it comes to questions of theory appraisal the falsification principle appears to be inconsistent with experience. As Kuhn has indicated on the basis of historical analysis, all theories at the time they are proposed are deficient in one respect or another and can be considered to be falsified. We previously gave the example of the planet Uranus and its relation to Newton's theory. Consider another example, **Charles Darwin**'s theory of evolution. At the time it was suggested in 1859, the known age of the earth was insufficiently long to support the complex process of evolution that Darwin was suggesting. In short, Darwin's theory required, for the sort of evolution being postulated, a much older earth than the then contemporary physics supplied. This could be considered a falsification of Darwin's theory. Darwin, of course, knew, on the basis of the contemporary physics of his time, that the earth was considered to be too young to support his conjectures about evolution, but nevertheless put forward his theory anyway. As it turned out, it was the physics that was wrong and not Darwin's theory. We now know that the earth's age of 4.5 billion years is old enough to support Darwin's theory. We will have more to say later about the various difficulties Darwin's theory had to overcome.

Another difficulty with falsification is that although it is straightforward and certain if one is dealing with a logical category, it is much less so if one is dealing with an empirical category. Consider logic first. If one suggests that *all Xs are Ys*, and then stipulates that this X before me is not a Y, then the general proposition that *all Xs are Ys* has been falsified. But, notice that in this example no empirical content is specified. Once one brings empirical considerations into the equation, the certainty that attaches to falsification in the logical realm is no longer applicable. For example, if the generalization is that all crows are black, and the specific instance is that this bird before me is a crow but is not black, one is obliged to demonstrate that the bird before me is actually a crow. Clearly, within the empirical realm, such a claim can be questioned. One might suggest, for example, that the bird before me appears to be a crow but is actually a member of a closely related species.

Kuhn (1970a) says of Popper, in this connection,

> What is falsification if it is not conclusive disproof? Under what circumstance does the *logic* of knowledge require a scientist to abandon a previously accepted theory when confronted, not with statements about experiments, but with experiments themselves? Pending clarification of these questions, I am not clear that what Sir Karl has given us is a logic of knowledge at all . . . Rather than a logic, Sir Karl has provided an ideology; rather than methodological rules, he has supplied procedural maxims. (p. 15)

In sum, what Kuhn is saying is that falsification applies to logic and not to empirical matters.

Popper was aware of these problems. To appreciate Popper's attitude here, it is necessary to recognize first of all that he was aware that his principle of falsification was what is known in philosophy as a convention. A convention is neither true nor false, but something adopted by agreement, for example, greeting people by saying "Good morning." As a convention, falsification was not based upon any empirical consideration and thus it could not be either true or false. Falsification represented Popper's idea of how science should be conducted, as Popper freely admitted. Popper also recognized that falsification in the empirical realm was subject to the sort of criticism listed above. He dealt with this by putting forward another convention. According to this additional convention, it was impermissible to attempt to rescue a falsified hypothesis by appealing to the sorts of considerations described above. But, of course, scientists do this on a regular basis, and sometimes it leads to improved theory. Examples of such improvement were offered above in connection with Darwin's theory of evolution and Newton's gravitational theory.

We can summarize Popper's position using his own words as they appeared in one of his papers:

> These considerations led me in the winter of 1919–1920 to conclusions which I may now reformulate as follows.
>
> 1. It is easy to obtain confirmations, or verifications, for nearly every theory – if we look for confirmations.
> 2. Confirmations should count only if they are the result of *risky predictions*; that is to say, if, unenlightened by the theory in question, we should have expected an event which was incompatible with the theory – an event which would have refuted the theory.
> 3. Every 'good' scientific theory is a prohibition: it forbids certain things to happen. The more a theory forbids, the better it is.
> 4. A theory which is not refutable by any conceivable event is non-scientific. Irrefutability is not a virtue of a theory (as people often think) but a vice.
> 5. Every genuine *test* of a theory is an attempt to falsify it, or to refute it. Testability is falsifiability; but there are degrees of testability: some theories are more testable, more exposed to refutation, than others; they take, as it were, greater risks.
> 6. Confirming evidence should not count *except when it is the result of a genuine test of the theory*; and this means that it can be presented as a serious but unsuccessful attempt to falsify the theory. (I now speak in such cases of 'corroborating evidence'.)
> 7. Some genuinely testable theories, when found to be false, are still upheld by their admirers – for example by introducing *ad hoc* some auxiliary assumption, or by re-interpreting the theory *ad hoc* in such a way that it escapes refutation. Such a procedure is always possible, but it rescues the theory from refutation only at the price of destroying, or at least lowering, its scientific status. (I later described such a rescuing operation as a *'conventionalist twist'* or a *'conventionalist stratagem'*.)

One can sum up all this by saying that *the criterion of the scientific status of a theory is its falsifiability, or refutability, or testability.* (Popper, 1963, pp. 36–37)

Popper's falsification principle is a version of **hypothesis testing**, which is a very popular procedure in contemporary science. In Chapter 4, we shall examine the strengths and weaknesses of hypothesis testing in much more detail.

Kuhn's Psychologism and Historicism

Kuhn's (1962) book, *The Structure of Scientific Revolutions*, represents one of those incidents in the history of ideas that is truly groundbreaking. In many respects, Kuhn's views have set the agenda for discussion and further elaboration both in science and in the philosophy of science. Kuhn's ideas represent a significant break with those that preceded him in the understanding of science. Whereas the logical positivists, Popper, and many who went before heavily emphasized a foundationist approach to science based on logical analysis, Kuhn's approach was much different. Kuhn proposed an original methodological approach to science based on empirical information, specifically that derived from historical analysis. **Quine** (1953) also suggested a naturalistic approach to science, based on psychology rather than history. However, Quine's influence was restricted primarily to philosophy and did not extend to other disciplines to anywhere near the extent of Kuhn's. This is perhaps because Quine's writings were targeted to professional philosophers, unlike Kuhn, who wrote for a more general audience.

In his usual felicitous style, Kuhn (1962) suggested in the very first sentence of his monumental book, "History, if viewed as a repository for more than anecdote or chronology, could produce a decisive transformation in the image of science by which we are now possessed" (p. 1). We shall show in detail later how Kuhn's methodological approach has had far-reaching implications for understanding the newer conception of science. In this section, we shall not emphasize Kuhn's methodology but focus, rather, on his specific view of science. That is, the conclusions about science that Kuhn reached on the basis of his historical examination of specific scientific movements are empirical statements which, like any other empirical statements, can be questioned.

Kuhn (1962) suggested on the basis of historical analysis that mature sciences such as physics come about through a series of historical changes. Kuhn distinguishes among pre-science, **normal science, revolutionary science**, and a return to normal science following revolutionary science. In the pre-scientific phase, there are many schools of thought around a particular topic, none of them dominant and each inconsistent in many ways with the other. In time, these many schools of thought are replaced by what Kuhn called a **paradigm**. As indicated in Chapter 1, a paradigm consists of a variety of factors, including one's basic beliefs about the entities contained in the world, various lawful statements, and ideas about proper methodological approaches to problems. According to Kuhn, a mature scientific community has only one paradigm. The beliefs constituting a paradigm are fundamental, so much so that they are immune from empirical test. Scientists when working within a paradigm do not attempt to test it, but rather postulate it in order to do scientific work. Once a paradigm is accepted, disagreement about fundamentals ceases, and members of the relevant scientific community attempt to solve a variety of problems suggested by the paradigm to be of importance. Kuhn described this as normal science. As an example of this in psychology, individuals in the behavioristic framework did not question the proposition that the fundamental data of psychology were provided by behavior.

According to Kuhn (1962), "Normal science . . . often suppresses fundamental novelties because they are necessarily subversive of its basic commitments" (p. 5), which is to work out various implications of the paradigm. When practicing normal science, the scientists' intention on the one hand is to fulfill the promise of the paradigm and on the other hand it is not to question any of the paradigm's major assumptions. The normal scientist, as conceived by Kuhn, is essentially a problem solver. Many philosophers of science were contemptuous of Kuhn's normal scientist. For example, Popper (1970) said, "The 'normal' scientist, as described by Kuhn, has been badly taught. He has been taught in a dogmatic spirit: he is a victim of indoctrination" (p. 53). Feyerabend (1970) is another individual who was critical of Kuhn's idea of normal science. Feyerabend stated,

> Every statement which Kuhn makes about normal science remains true when we replace 'normal science' by 'organized crime'; and every statement he has written about the 'individual scientist' applies with equal force to, say, the individual safebreaker. Organized crime certainly keeps foundational research to a minimum although there are outstanding individuals, such as Dillinger, who introduce new and revolutionary ideas. (p. 200)

Kuhn (1962) suggests that a normal scientist may encounter a problem that does not yield to the paradigm. The initial reaction to this might be not to question the paradigm but to redouble one's effort to solve the problem within the structure provided by the paradigm. Problems that seem at variance with the paradigm are perceived by the scientist as anomalies, or problems to be solved, rather than as counter-instances that call the paradigm into question. But as anomalous problems of this sort accumulate, there may occur over time some doubt about the paradigm's sufficiency to deal with the problems at hand. That is, what was formerly seen as an anomalous problem may come to be seen as a counter-instance.

Kuhn is not exactly sure of the processes that cause an anomaly to be seen as a counter-instance, but he suggests some possibilities, as for example, the length of time that a given anomaly has resisted solution within the paradigm. Kuhn also indicates that most anomalies are ultimately made consistent with the paradigm, so it is only the remaining few that become counter-instances. If these anomalies persist and so become counter-instances, and the number of them multiplies, a period of crisis may ensue in which adherents to the paradigm begin to doubt its usefulness. At this crisis stage, the rules of the paradigm are loosened, and scientific practice begins to take on some of the characteristics of pre-paradigmatic science. If the crisis becomes particularly acute, the community may search for a new paradigm. The work that leads to the demise of the old paradigm and its replacement by a successor paradigm is called revolutionary science. It is Kuhn's opinion that a scientific community will never abandon the old paradigm before a reasonable successor is identified. The old paradigm may be abandoned and a new one accepted by only a few individuals initially, but over time, as adherents of the old paradigm become fewer and adherents of the new paradigm more numerous, a successor paradigm may be born. Once a successor paradigm is adopted, the relevant scientific community tends both to perceive and conceptualize the world differently, and the process of normal science begins again.

In Kuhn's opinion, paradigm change does not necessarily imply advancement. That is, Kuhn suggests that successor paradigms are merely different from the prior paradigm and may in some respects be superior and in other respects inferior. In this connection, Kuhn likens paradigm replacement to evolution, which is not goal directed and successor species are not necessarily improvements over ancestral species but simply better adapted to the environment at hand. Kuhn also likens scientific revolutions to political revolutions. As is perhaps

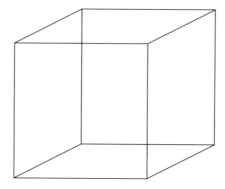

Figure 2.1 Necker cube reversible figure.

obvious, people on different sides of a political divide often fail to communicate with each other effectively. Kuhn makes a similar argument with respect to paradigms, which he describes as incommensurate. By incommensurate Kuhn means that the basic assumptions of the two views are sufficiently different that individuals who adhere to one paradigm may not be able to understand or communicate with individuals who adhere to another paradigm. In arriving at the idea of **incommensurability**, Kuhn often calls upon perceptual phenomena, particularly reversible figures that can be seen in different ways and examples of perceptual sets in which stimuli violate expectancies. For example, as shown in Figure 2.1, what is called a Necker cube can be seen in either one of two orientations that differ in terms of which square boundary is seen as the front and which as the back.

As regards incommensurability, Kuhn says,

> Therefore, at times of revolution, when the normal-scientific tradition changes, the scientist's perception of his environment must be re-educated – in some familiar situations he must learn to see a new gestalt. After he has done so the world of his research will seem, here and there, incommensurable with the one he had inhabited before. That is another reason why schools guided by different paradigms are always slightly at cross-purposes. (p. 111)

Another feature of paradigm acceptance suggested by Kuhn is that it corresponds quite literally to a religious conversion. According to Kuhn, "The transfer of allegiance from paradigm to paradigm is a conversion experience that cannot be forced" (p. 150). Kuhn adds, "Conversions will occur a few at a time until, after the last holdouts have died, the whole profession will again be practicing under a single, but now a different, paradigm" (p. 151). In Kuhn's view, although there may be some objective features responsible for the acceptance of a new paradigm, in the final analysis, resistance to change is always possible, and one is not required to abandon the old paradigm. The reason for this is that scientists are not in agreement on the criteria considered important for the evaluation of a paradigm. For example, one scientist may consider simplicity and parsimony to be the most important criteria of a paradigm, whereas another scientist may be more impressed by explanatory scope. If the successor paradigm is more parsimonious than the preceding paradigm but has less explanatory scope, the two scientists will disagree as to which is the better one.

It is this feature of Kuhn's analysis that has resulted in many critics characterizing Kuhn as a relativist. For example, Kuhn said that in accepting a novel theory, "An apparently arbitrary element, compounded of personal and historical accident, is always a formative ingredient of the beliefs espoused by a given scientific community at a given time" (p. 4). Moreover, Kuhn (1970a) said, "The criteria with which scientists determine the validity of an articulation or an application of existing theory are not by themselves sufficient to determine the choice between competing theories" (p. 19). Statements like these clearly give the impression that Kuhn was a relativist. In fairness to Kuhn, though, it is appropriate to mention that he denied being a relativist. He suggested that when people accept theories they do so for good reasons. And, according to Kuhn, these reasons are "furthermore, reasons of exactly the kind standard in philosophy of science: accuracy, scope, simplicity, fruitfulness, and the like" (1970b, p. 261). Although Kuhn resisted the charge of **relativism**, his defense is regarded as ineffective by many (e.g., Curd & Cover, 1998; Gholson & Barker, 1985; Laudan, 1996). For example, in listing accuracy, scope, simplicity, and fruitfulness as criteria for theory evaluation, Kuhn indicated in other places that individuals may evaluate each of these criteria differently and arrive at different conclusions. In any event, it is interesting to note that Kuhn's influence was profound on relativists and non-relativists alike, and he may be considered one of the major intellectual figures of our time.

The field of psychology itself was influenced very substantially by Kuhn, probably to a greater extent than by any other single philosopher. O'Donohue (1993) stated, "When psychologists talk about their science and clinical pursuits, they usually employ Kuhnian concepts and claims" (p. 267). In support of this view, O'Dononue cited the work of Coleman and Salamon (1988), who found 652 articles in psychology journals from 1969 to 1983 that cited Kuhn's (1962) book, *The Structure of Scientific Revolutions.* This number would be much higher today. An example of an analysis employing Kuhnian concepts is provided by the previously mentioned Lachman et al. (1979) text on cognitive psychology and information processing. Lachman et al. presented information processing as the dominant paradigm in experimental psychology, using Kuhn's definition of a paradigm. They presented various characteristics of the information-processing paradigm and compared them to those other paradigms such as neobehaviorism and verbal learning. In agreement with Lachman et al., Chen, Andersen, and Barker (1998; Andersen, Barker, & Chen, 1996) recently argued that many aspects of cognitive psychology are in fact consistent with Kuhn's model of science.

Chapter Summary

In this chapter, we detailed many of the prominent changes that occurred in the understanding of science during the 20th century. The beginning of the 20th century saw the rise of logical positivism and operationism, which became very popular in experimental psychology. For example, they extensively influenced the conduct of research in learning and memory. The logical positivist view came under considerable criticism from Karl Popper, who emphasized that scientists should attempt to falsify their hypotheses rather than seeking to confirm them, as the logical positivists suggested. With Kuhn in 1962, what has come to be called the postpositivist movement began and has since eclipsed both logical positivism and falsificationism. Kuhn's seminal book produced a virtual revolution in the practice and conduct of the philosophy of science and of science itself. Essentially, Kuhn could be agreed with or disagreed with, but his approach was such that it could not be ignored. As will be seen in the next chapter, there were two outgrowths of Kuhn's analysis.

METHODOLOGY IN THE POSTPOSITIVIST ERA

> For too long philosophers have debated how scientists ought to judge hypotheses in glaring ignorance of how scientists in fact judge hypotheses. (Ronald Giere, 1988, p. 149)

Introduction

In this chapter, we cover modern developments in the history and philosophy of science that are not ordinarily discussed in methodology texts. In our view, the material covered in this chapter is of considerable importance for evaluating many knowledge claims currently being made by a diverse array of psychologists, ranging from relativists and radical empiricists on the one hand to most academic psychologists on the other. Both relativists and radical empiricists reject the idea that science as it is normally practiced by most psychologists is capable of producing acceptable theoretical statements about phenomena. Consequently, they advocate employing methodologies that differ considerably from those accepted by most scientific psychologists. Informed evaluation of these methodologies and methodology in general requires an understanding of these matters, as will become clear in this and subsequent chapters.

The field of psychology has changed drastically since the first half of the 20th century. Among the changes is rejection of **logical positivism**, which was the predominant philosophy of science influencing experimental psychology in particular and psychology in general at that time. Although it is true that logical positivism is essentially outmoded, some psychologists, particularly those that espouse **qualitative**

inquiry (see Chapter 8), continue to suggest that psychology is still dominated by that view. Consider some recently expressed opinions concerning logical positivism and psychology. Although the quotes below use the word positivism, it is clear from their context that the writers intend to identify logical positivism as of considerable importance in contemporary psychology, a view with which we disagree. They say:

- "Positivism is still the dominant paradigm organizing the discipline of psychology" (Tolman & Brydon-Miller, 2001, p. 5).
- "To date, the relatively limited research on social factors [involved in eating disorders] has followed mainly the positivistic paradigm, which is widely accepted within the field of psychology" (Piran, 2001, p. 219).
- "If positivism remains the dominant paradigm that organizes psychology . . . , it is likewise the dominant paradigm that organizes and shapes the teaching of psychologists" (Maguire, 2001, p. 277).
- "The methodological viewpoint generally taken for granted within the natural sciences, and dominant also in the social sciences, is positivist" (Smith, 2003, p. 11).

These comments, in our view, are meant to imply that psychology follows an outdated philosophy of science. However, it is the case that psychology, along with science in general, has moved beyond positivism into a postpositivist era. This has come to be generally recognized, and, in our view, logical positivism is for all practical purposes a dead letter. One of the major figures in the postpositivist movement, and one who has had enormous influence in psychology, is Thomas Kuhn, whose views were described in Chapter 2.

Kuhn's work produced two major streams of thought, which ironically are incompatible with each other, that have defined issues concerning science in the postpositivist era for more than 40 years. One stream is **naturalism**, which is the primary focus of this book. The other stream is **relativism**, which is very much a part of the social sciences. One cannot appreciate and understand methodological and theoretical developments in current-day psychology without being conversant with both of these implications of Kuhn's theory. This chapter will emphasize naturalism, although it will also have a brief description of how relativism arose from Kuhn's positions. We will have more to say about relativism in Chapter 7.

Naturalism in Science

In the positivist era, as well as prior to it, considerable theorizing about science was based on logic and intuition (**foundationism**). In the postpositivist era, the tendency to call upon logic and intuition has been reduced, being replaced by a tendency to think about science in empirical terms. This tendency to emphasize **empiricism** when characterizing science is, as indicated, called naturalism. With reference to foundationism, which favors a priori methods, **Ruse** (2001) notes, "The naturalistic approach, to the contrary, feels that appeal absolutely must be made to the real world" (p. 73). **Giere** (1985) says of the naturalistic approach, "The main thesis is that the study of science must itself be a science. The only viable philosophy of science is a naturalized philosophy of science" (p. 355). The major difference between foundationism and naturalism is captured by Giere's characterization of the former as "top down," or theory driven, and the latter as "bottom up," or data driven. Naturalism recommends an empirical approach to science, the same sort of approach that it recommends to specific content areas of science such as psychology. As Giere (2001) notes, "Naturalism also rejects the imposition of *a priori* principles whose justification would have to appeal to something beyond human experience" (p. 54).

The distinction between foundationism and naturalism has many practical consequences in terms of how science and scientific methodology are to be evaluated. As one example, prior to Kuhn (1962) it was generally believed that a new theory displacing an older one was acceptable only if it solved all of the problems of the older theory plus some new problems. Kuhn demonstrated on the basis of the historical record that these methodological criteria were not met in practice in connection with any theory. As an example close to psychology, behaviorism became widely accepted in the early 1900s despite the fact that it did not deal with many of the problems of concern to introspectionist psychologists such as E. B. Titchener. Another example is Popper's suggestion that if a theory were contradicted by falsifying evidence, it was necessary to reject it. Kuhn pointed out, again on the basis of the historical record, that all theories at the time of their introduction suffer from one or more empirical inadequacies. **Lakatos** (1970) was to make a similar observation. In both cases, a more accurate understanding of how science is actually practiced contradicted what seemed to be intuitively obvious to individuals employing the foundationist approach. Naturalism necessarily implies that new and improved criteria for theory evaluation need to be isolated and understood. That essentially is what this chapter and the next one are about.

Willard Quine was one of the earliest individuals to take a naturalistic approach to scientific methodology. Quine (1953), in rejecting foundationism, came to think about scientific matters in psychological terms. Quine rejected all forms of foundationism, even considering logical statements (e.g., the principle of contradiction) to arise from experience. **Laudan** (1996) said that Quine believed that scientific methodology is "in effect a branch of descriptive psychology, merely recording how we have come to construct the bodies of 'knowledge' which we call the 'sciences'" (p. 133). As we saw in the previous chapter, Kuhn's naturalism was based not on psychology but on history. As was indicated in Chapter 2, the field of psychology itself has been influenced very substantially by Kuhn, probably to a greater extent than by any other single philosopher. Too, Kuhn was very influential in many other areas of science. Giere, another naturalist, says Kuhn was perhaps the most important critic of logical positivism. Giere states,

> One of the reasons why Kuhn became more important – in hindsight, Kuhn appears as the major figure; the other people paled – was that he also had a strong *positive* theory. He was not just criticizing logical empiricism. All his criticism was indirect. Instead he had an alternative view. The other people didn't really. (quoted in Callebaut, 1993, pp. 17–18)

Giere's assessment of why Kuhn became so influential is consistent with a theme echoed throughout this chapter and the next, that theory appraisal does not occur in isolation but rather occurs in relation to alternative theories.

Callebaut (1993), the author of a book titled *Taking the Naturalistic Turn or How the Real Philosophy of Science is Done*, indicates that naturalism freed the philosophy of science from the limitations of positivism. He says,

> As long as positivism reigned supreme, philosophy of science was really a philosophy of "rationally reconstructed" *physics* disguised as a general philosophy of science. Current approaches to science display much more diversity and heterogeneity in comparison. . . . Special philosophies of various special sciences now flourish. The philosophy of (evolutionary) biology and the philosophy of (cognitive) psychology in particular are booming. (p. 72)

Callebaut goes on to say, "One trend in post-positivist philosophy of science has been to argue against any would-be 'universal' picture of science and to argue instead that physics may be and in fact is different from chemistry, chemistry from biology, biology from the social sciences, and the like" (p. 75). A recent trend in evaluating theories of scientific practice is to consider such evaluation in relation to some particular science, for example, biology (Sober, 2000), the social sciences (Rosenberg, 1995), or neuroscience (Bechtel, Mandik, Mundale, & Stufflebeam, 2001).

In the remainder of this section, we will consider some of the very important ideas about science that stem from the naturalistic movement. Although there are many prominent naturalists (see Callebaut, 1993), we will emphasize the slightly different views of two prominent individuals, Larry Laudan and Ronald Giere. But, we begin by describing the views of Imre Lakatos, who is clearly in the postpositivist tradition but is not normally classified as a naturalist. However, in our view, for reasons that will become clear below, it is appropriate to treat Lakatos as if he were a naturalist.

Lakatos's Sophisticated Falsificationism

Lakatos was heavily influenced by Popper and his emphasis on falsification. Lakatos recognized that falsification as recommended by Popper had deficiencies. For example, as indicated in the last chapter, falsification makes sense when applied to logical statements, but it is less applicable to empirical ones. A criticism of Popper's position by Lakatos was that it applied only to the testing of a single theory. Popper's idea of a genuine test of a theory was for the scientist to do his or her best to falsify it. Note that Popper recommends that theories be tested in isolation. In contrast, **falsificationism** as employed by Lakatos always considered theoretical alternatives to the tested theory. An objective of Lakatos's was to retain some of the virtues of the falsificationist approach, while modifying it to take account of Kuhn's criticisms of the approach. Essentially, Lakatos wanted to marry Popper's position with Kuhn's, while avoiding the relativism inherent in Kuhn's approach.

In developing his novel views, Lakatos arrived at a position that he called sophisticated falsificationism. According to Lakatos, naïve falsificationism suggested that the minimal requirement for a theory to be scientific is simply that it be falsifiable. Sophisticated falsificationism suggests additional criteria for deciding whether a theory is scientific. One criterion is that a theory is acceptable or scientific only if it has better empirical support than its rivals. A second criterion of acceptability is that the theory leads to the discovery of novel empirical findings, not derivable from other theories. Although Lakatos referred to his view as a variety of falsificationism, we suggest that this characterization is inaccurate. In our opinion, Lakatos's position best can be characterized as a variety of a view called **inference to the best explanation**, which suggests that a given theory is to be accepted only if it is superior to its rivals. We will provide extensive discussion of the concept inference to the best explanation in the next two chapters. For now, it is enough to say of it that theories can differ along a number of dimensions as, for example, parsimony, consistency, explanatory scope, and so on, and scientists attempt to choose the theory that is superior on the whole to the alternatives.

Central to Lakatos's (1970) views is the concept of **research program**, which is similar in some respects to the Kuhnian idea of **paradigms** in that it accepts the idea that scientists have general theoretical and methodological commitments that are more fundamental than the specific theories to which they give rise. These fundamental propositions constitute the hard core of the research program, called the metatheory by Ketelaar and Ellis (2000). The hard core of a research program, or metatheory, consists of concepts that are more or less immune to empirical testing and not open to modification, because it is sheltered by a protective belt of auxiliary hypotheses. As an example, the hard core of **Darwin**'s theory of evolution consists of **natural selection**. The idea of natural selection is so fundamental to Darwin's theory that it is taken for granted and applied to specific problems. Failure to accept the hard core essentially means a failure to accept the research program.

The protective belt of auxiliary hypotheses is amenable to empirical test and may be modified over time. The protective belt consists of a number of theories that are consistent with the hard core but are not derivable from it. For example, Darwin's idea of natural selection has given rise to a number of specific theories, some of which have been disconfirmed and discarded, and others that have been retained because they produced hypotheses that, on the whole, have been confirmed. When a theory in the protective belt is disconfirmed and discarded, it may have few, if any, negative consequences for the hard core because other theories in the protective belt remain viable.

The research program gives rise to a succession of theories that are modified and appraised over time. As indicated, Lakatos suggests that it is not a single theory that is evaluated scientifically, but a succession of theories. Lakatos postulates what he calls a positive heuristic and a negative heuristic. The positive heuristic describes what a scientist should do within the context of a research program. The negative heuristic specifies what a scientist should not do within the context of the research program. As an example of the two **heuristics**, for a scientist faced with an anomalous problem, the positive heuristic would consist in an to attempt to solve it in terms of the protective belt, and the negative heuristic would consist of refraining from attempting to solve the problem by modifying the hard core. Research programs that lead to new and interesting predictions are said to be progressive. Research programs that do not lead to new and interesting predictions are said to be degenerative. Thus, the hard core is indirectly rather than directly evaluated. That is, rather than directly evaluating the hard core, it is theories in the protective belt that are evaluated, and depending on the results of those evaluations the hard core may be retained or discarded.

A specific psychological example involves the behavioral and cognitive research programs. The hard core of behaviorism, as alluded to in Chapter 1, is the view that all psychological phenomena can be described in terms of behavior. Theories in the protective belt of behaviorism include Clark Hull's methodological behaviorism, E. C. Tolman's cognitive behaviorism, and B. F. Skinner's radical behaviorism. Behavioristic theories were regarded as progressive by many from about 1915 to 1960 on the basis of the new experimental findings they generated and explained. Opinion about the progressivity of behaviorism began to shift around 1960, and many, but not all, psychologists turned to another research program, that of cognitive psychology or human information processing (Lachman et al., 1979). The hard core of the information-processing approach is that the human can be characterized as a communication channel, with information that comes in through the senses being represented and transformed by mental processes, resulting in an action being executed. As of today, the information-processing research program is regarded as progressive by many (e.g., Pashler, 1998). At the same time, there are some who have continued to work within the behavioristic research program (e.g., Follette & Hayes, 2000), as well as those who have worked in other research programs such as Gibson's ecological program (Heft, 2001). As regards behaviorism, on the basis of Lakatos's view, it is possible that opinion may shift again in the future and behaviorism may once again be generally regarded as progressive.

According to Lakatos, a research program that is degenerating for a period of time may become progressive again if it starts to yield new theoretical and empirical growth. Thus, in contrast to Kuhn, Lakatos suggests that at any given time more than one "paradigm" may be employed by the relevant scientific community and that one that falls out of favor may come to be highly regarded again at a later date. A good example of this from psychology is provided by what are called connectionist, or neural network, models (see Bechtel, 1988). These models, which attribute psychological phenomena such the masking of one visual stimulus by another to activation in networks of neurons (e.g., Francis, 2003), were popularized many years ago by Hebb (1949) and Rosenblatt (1962). However, they declined in popularity due to severe criticism by Minsky and Papert (1969) suggesting that neural network models were flawed and limited. More recently, neural network models have again come into prominence because they appear to solve a considerable number of theoretical and empirical problems, and neural network models can be found in many areas of psychology and cognitive science (e.g., Dawson, 2003).

Laudan's Research Traditions and Normative Naturalism

Scientists and philosophers have proposed many methodological rules that science follows. Some of these rules, as stated by Laudan (1996, pp. 131–132), are:

- Propound only falsifiable theories.
- Avoid ad hoc modifications.
- Prefer theories that make successful surprising predictions over theories that explain only what is already known.
- When experimenting on human subjects, use blinded experimental techniques.
- Reject theories which fail to exhibit an analogy with successful theories in other domains.
- Avoid theories which postulate unobservable entities.
- Use controlled experiments for testing causal hypotheses.
- Reject inconsistent theories.
- Prefer simple theories to complex ones.
- Accept a new theory only if it can explain all the successes of its predecessors.

How would we establish the validity of any of the above methodological rules? One way, of course, not looked upon favorably within naturalism, is to determine how well they comport with our intuitions.

As indicated, this was the approach taken by Popper in suggesting that scientists should seek to falsify their theories. A second way, one favored by naturalism, is to determine how well a rule has worked in practice. Granting the second approach, a further issue arises, namely, do rules of the sort considered above merely describe how scientists behave, as Kuhn would suggest, or do they prescribe how scientists should behave? That is, is an accurate description of what scientists actually do sufficient in itself to guide scientific practice? Laudan's answer to this question is that something further is required in order for a descriptive rule to become prescriptive. Let us examine Laudan's proposed solution to this problem. The position taken by Laudan is that descriptive methodological rules can be made prescriptive on the basis of empirical considerations, and so can be employed to suggest how scientists should behave.

Laudan's (1996) position is called **normative naturalism**, a view that is congenial to a variety of naturalists, as described in Callebaut (1993; see, particularly, pp. 97–105). According to Laudan, methodological rules should take the form of being hypothetical imperatives. By this is meant that methodological rules can be stated as follows: *If one's goal is Y, then one ought to do X.* Stated in this way, methodological rules should not be thought of as true or false, but as more or less useful for specific empirical purposes. Taking this view, methodological rules are empirical statements that have to be evaluated as any other empirical statements are evaluated, that is, in terms of how well they work in practice.

One way to evaluate methodological rules is as follows. If we say that in order to achieve our goal Y, we must do X, then we could determine in practice if X actually aids us in achieving Y and, moreover, if Y is achieved better using X than using some other method, Z. Laudan fleshes out this procedure in the following quote:

> If actions of a particular sort, m, have consistently promoted certain cognitive ends, e, in the past, and rival actions, n, have failed to do so, then assume that future actions following the rule "if your aim is e, you ought to do m" are more likely to promote those ends than actions based on the rule "if your aim is e, you ought to do n". (p. 135)

It is the case that the strategy recommended above by Laudan (1996) has, as a general rule, not been followed by scientists. This is because, until recently, science has been dominated much more by foundationism than by naturalism. Presumably, as naturalism becomes better known and more popular within science, justification of methodological rules will be based on empirical considerations.

Several aspects of **research traditions**, as conceptualized by Laudan (1996), differ from those of research programs, as conceptualized by Lakatos. Research traditions consist of "(1) a set of beliefs about what sort of entities and processes make up the domain of inquiry; and (2) a set of epistemic and methodological norms about how the domain is to be investigated, how theories are to be tested, how data are to be collected, and the like" (p. 83). According to Laudan, research traditions serve a variety of functions. Among others, these functions include indicating what assumptions can be taken for granted, helping to identify aspects of a theory that should be modified or abandoned, establishing rules for collecting data and testing theories, and posing conceptual problems for any theory in the research tradition that violates its claims. Research traditions apply to a cluster of theories that bear a family resemblance to each other and exemplify certain fundamental views about the world.

According to Laudan, the core commitments of a research tradition are not invariant over time but can change in response to empirical or conceptual advances. Laudan gives greater emphasis than either Kuhn or Lakatos to conceptual factors in modifying research traditions. As an example of a conceptual problem, a given theory within a research tradition may be shown to contain a contradiction or be inconsistent with accepted implications of other well-established theories. An empirical problem that a particular research tradition may face is that it fails to explain some phenomenon that is explained by another research tradition. Laudan, in agreement with Kuhn, thinks of a scientist as engaging in a problem-solving activity. Laudan suggests that we can determine whether or not a given research tradition is progressive by its rate of problem solving. He distinguishes between how well a particular research tradition is supported by the evidence and how progressive it might be. For example, a well-supported theory may not have solved many new problems for some time, and in that sense is not progressive. On the other hand, a less well-supported theory may be experiencing a rapid rate of problem solving, and thus is very progressive. In common with Kuhn, Laudan suggests that scientists may accept a theory that is progressive because it appears to have considerable promise for solving additional problems. Unlike many philosophers of science, in particular Popper, Laudan suggests that a scientist's evaluation of theory is more complicated than that of mere acceptance or rejection. For example, a scientist may hold a theory tentatively without necessarily accepting it, a common occurrence in science as it is normally practiced because scientists are almost always dealing with ambiguity.

According to Gholson and Barker (1985), behaviorism seems to be more compatible with Laudan's conception of simultaneously existing different theories than it is with either Lakatos's conception of theories within a research program changing over time or with Kuhn's conception of a dominant single paradigm that may come to be rejected and replaced by a successor paradigm. The basis of this view is that a variety of behavioristic theories such as those of Skinner, Hull, and Tolman existed simultaneously, rather than successively, and they were not modifications of each other, contrary to what Lakatos would suggest, and, of course, there was more than one behavioristic theory, in contrast to what Kuhn would suggest. Gholson and Barker (1985) conclude from their extensive analysis of various ideas about research programs that Lakatos's and Laudan's conceptions closely fit science in general and psychology in particular. Moreover, according to them, Laudan's research traditions and Lakatos's research programs provide a better analysis of how science is conducted than does Kuhn's paradigms. We have proposed that, in terms of the fit with psychology, Laudan's view of research traditions is superior to either that of Lakatos's research programs or Kuhn's paradigms (Capaldi & Proctor, 2000).

Because psychology had several paradigms operating simultaneously, it did not meet the definition of a mature science, according to Kuhn, who emphasized, as already indicated, that a mature science is characterized by a single dominant paradigm. However, according to both Lakatos and Laudan, a given scientific community can embrace several paradigms simultaneously, and thus according to their criteria psychology can be considered to be a science.

Giere's Cognitive Approach

Giere (1985, 1988), like other naturalists, places considerable emphasis on an approach to methodology based on various empirical methods such as those of history, cognitive psychology, and neuroscience. As is to be expected, naturalists who agree on a great many matters may nevertheless disagree among themselves in several respects. Some idea of similarities and differences among naturalists may be had by comparing some of Giere's views to those of Laudan (1996). Laudan and Giere, in agreement with Kuhn, feel that a naturalistic approach to science, which emphasizes the activity of scientists, should utilize and emphasize historical data. Moreover, Giere agrees with Laudan that methodology can prescribe as well as describe (Giere, 2001). They differ in that Giere's view of science places a much heavier emphasis than does Laudan's on psychology, particularly cognitive psychology. Giere (2003) says,

> Focusing on the *activity* of doing science, it is undeniable that an important aspect of this activity is *cognitive*. In particular, the activity is supposed to produce new knowledge of the world. This must be counted as a cognitive activity, no matter what one's general characterization of "cognitive activities" might be. (p. 1, downloaded file)

Giere also places much more emphasis than does Laudan on evolution and neuroscience as guides to constructing a view of science. Regarding understanding how to pursue a naturalized approach to the philosophy of science, Giere (1985) says, "I would suggest that evolutionary theory, together with recent work in cognitive science and the neurosciences, provides a basis for such an understanding" (p. 339). Giere argues that our perceptual and cognitive capacities have been shaped by evolution to be veridical, or objective, rather than subjective. He points out that many treatments of science begin with the assumption that our immediate perceptual experience is highly subjective. He rejects this approach as follows:

> Three hundred years of modern science and over a hundred years of biological investigation have led us to the firm conclusion that no humans have ever faced the world guided only by their own subjectively accessible experience and intuitions. Rather, we now know that our capacities for operating in the world are highly adapted to that world. (p. 340)

Giere's (1988) cognitive approach to science has been influenced heavily by studies of human decision making. Giere suggests that decision making in science is very similar to decision making in other areas of human activity. Having examined a number of approaches to decision making, Giere settles on a suggestion made earlier by **Herbert Simon,** a cognitive scientist who won a Nobel prize, as being the most promising approach. Essentially, he states that decision makers follow a strategy of determining whether there is a satisfactory outcome for the objective they desire to achieve; if so, they select that outcome. If the initial objective cannot be achieved, one's objectives are revised until a satisfying outcome can be achieved. This is the essence of what Simon (1983) called **satisficing**. Giere (1985) says, "My hypothesis is that scientists typically follow something approximating a satisficing strategy when faced with the problem of choosing among scientific theories. If this is correct, we have a good scientific explanation of theory choice in science" (p. 348). In many respects, Giere's suggestion is similar to that of other postpositivists such as Lakatos and Laudan in emphasizing that theory evaluation and choice involves a comparison of the theory chosen with other theories that have been rejected for one reason or another.

In addition to history, psychology, evolution, and neuroscience, other empirical means for understanding science have been suggested, as described in Table 1.1. Specific consideration of these various means for understanding science, and their implications, will be discussed in Chapter 6.

The Rise of Relativism

One of the major movements that arose out of the philosophy of science in the latter part of the 20th century was what is commonly known as *relativism*. In this chapter, we will briefly examine some of the major assumptions and characteristics of relativism, particularly as it relates to psychology. Although the current treatment will be brief, a more extensive examination and analysis of relativism will be provided in Chapter 7.

Thomas Kuhn's (1962) seminal work on the history and philosophy of science, which was responsible for an improved empirical approach to science (naturalism), was also responsible to a considerable extent for the rise of relativism, the antithesis of science as it is normally practiced. Relativism, as it is generally understood, denies that there is any privileged methodological basis for creating theory. It suggests instead that truth is created rather than found or discovered. **Richard Rorty** (1989), widely recognized as one of the leading exponents of the relativistic approach, traces some of its roots to the late 1700s, stating, "About two hundred years ago, the idea that truth was made rather than found began to take hold of the imagination of Europe" (p. 3). Rorty went on to contrast the views of conventional scientists with those of the emerging relativists, saying:

> Whereas the first kind of philosopher contrasts "hard scientific fact" with the "subjective" or with "metaphor," the second kind sees science as one more human activity, rather as the place at which human beings encounter a "hard," nonhuman reality. On this view, great scientists invent descriptions of the world which are useful for purposes of predicting and controlling what happens, just as poets and political thinkers invent other

descriptions of it for other purposes. But there is no sense in which *any* of these descriptions is an accurate representation of the way the world is in itself. (Rorty, 1989, p. 4)

Relativism, as it developed from Kuhn, had two major sources, **underdetermination** and **incommensurability**. Underdetermination, as defined by Capaldi and Proctor (1999), "is the view that a given body of evidence does not uniquely determine any particular theoretical position" (p. 137). Incommensurability "is the idea that it is impossible for individuals who ascribe to different theories to communicate effectively with each other" (p. 137). Statements such as the following by Kuhn indicate why it would be reasonable to interpret him as supporting underdetermination, and thus a relativistic approach:

[The] issue of paradigm choice can never be unequivocally settled by logic and experiment alone. (1962, p. 93)

Paradigm change cannot be justified by proof. (1962, p. 151)

Every individual choice between competing theories depends on a mixture of objective and subjective factors, or of shared and individual criteria. (1977, p. 325)

Regarding incommensurability, Kuhn said:

In the transition from one theory to the next words change their meanings or conditions of applicability in subtle ways. . . . Successive theories are thus, we say, incommensurable. (Kuhn, 1970b, pp. 266–267)

One of the leading varieties of relativism in psychology is **social constructionism**. According to **Gergen** (1985), "Social constructionism views discourse about the world not as a reflection or map of the world but as an artifact of communal interchange" (p. 266). According to this view, knowledge is placed within the social interchange among individuals, and "the validity of theoretical propositions in the sciences is in no way affected by factual evidence" (Gergen, 1988, p. 37). As should be clear, social constructionism is an avowedly relativistic position, gladly embraced by its adherents. For example, Gergen (1985) has stated, "Constructionism offers no foundational rules of warrant and in this sense is relativistic" (p. 273).

Another variety of relativism is **contextualism**. Not all varieties of contextualists are relativists, only those who can be described as philosophic contextualists (see Capaldi & Proctor, 1999). Many contextualists cite an

early work by **Stephen Pepper** (1942), which first described contextualism as major worldview. Capaldi and Proctor list five characteristics
that define philosophic contextualists:

- They reject the idea that general laws can be discovered.
- They accept the fact that novel events can appear at any time.
- They reject conventional science.
- They accept **radical empiricism**, meaning that they do not want to
  postulate any reality beyond the appearance.
- They tend to see experimentation as merely one context among many,
  and not a very representative one at that.

Postmodernists comprise another variety of relativists. The view known
as **modernism**, stemming from the period known as the **Enlightenment**,
accepted the idea that lawful relations could be discovered and that
sound methodology would ultimately be able to isolate the truth,
or at least approximations to it. These views are rejected by postmodernists. **E. O. Wilson** (1999), the founder of sociobiology and an
implacable foe of **postmodernism**, characterizes the views of postmodernists as follows:

> The philosophical postmodernists, a rebel crew milling beneath the
> black flag of anarchy, challenge the very foundations of science and
> traditional philosophy. Reality, they propose, is a state constructed by
> the mind, not perceived by it. In the most extravagant version of this
> constructivism, there is no "real" reality, no objective truths external
> to mental activity, only prevailing visions disseminated by ruling social
> groups. Nor can ethics be firmly grounded, given that each society
> creates its own codes for the benefit of the same oppressive forces.
> (p. 44)

It should be clear to the reader from this brief description that postmodernism, and other forms of relativism, are incompatible with
science as it is universally understood. Not surprisingly, the strongest
advocates of postmodernism are to be found in what may be called
the "softer" areas of study. It is very popular, for example, in English
departments. Among the sciences, it is more prominent in anthropology, sociology, and political science than in biology, physics, and
chemistry. In the field of psychology, it is rarely if ever found among
cognitive psychologists, neuroscientists, or experimental psychologists
generally. But, as we will see in later chapters, relativism is rapidly taking root in psychology. Because of this it is well to examine relativism
at some length in this book.

Chapter Summary

With Kuhn in 1962, what has come to be called the postpositivist movement began and has since eclipsed both logical positivism and falsificationism. Kuhn's seminal book produced a virtual revolution in the practice and conduct of the philosophy of science and of science itself. There were two outgrowths of Kuhn's analysis. One was to give us an improved picture of how science is practiced and how scientific propositions should be evaluated. This is Kuhn's naturalism. The other was to inspire various forms of relativism mainly, but not exclusively, because of the positions Kuhn espoused with respect to incommensurability and underdetermination. The last few decades have witnessed the rise of various forms of relativism that go under various names such as social constructionism, contextualism, and postmodernism. The assumptions behind these views are incompatible with those entertained by most scientists. For this reason, these assumptions are examined closely in later chapters of this book.

NATURALISM AND MODERN SCIENCE

THEORY TESTING

Introduction

The goal of science is not simply to amass a large body of unrelated facts. Rather, science seeks to provide elegantly simple explanations for phenomena and to provide highly specific predictions so as to uncover new phenomena and to develop theory. When science achieves these ends, it finds itself in the position to develop powerful new technological tools for the greater benefit of humankind. For example, as our scientific understanding of genetics increases, we are armed with powerful tools for benefiting people in a variety of ways, most notably, in preventing the occurrence of diseases that have a genetic basis. Another example, this one from psychology, is that as we come to better understand the thought processes of experts such as chess masters (e.g., that they rely primarily on recognition of patterns from their extensive experience; Ericsson, Charness, Feltovich, & Hoffman, in press), it becomes possible to develop powerful software tools, called knowledge-based expert systems (e.g., Leondes, 2002). These software systems mimic the thought processes of actual experts, with the idea being to provide expert guidance to the uninitiated.

In science, explanation ultimately involves the construction of theory. Some examples of theory in psychology include Piaget's (1929/1975) theory of cognitive development (that cognitive development progresses through several distinct stages), Gardner's (1983) theory of multiple intelligences (musical intelligence, spatial intelligence, social intelligence, and so on), and Festinger's (1957) cognitive dissonance theory (when reality does not meet expectations, people employ mechanisms to reduce the dissonance that is produced). The steps involved in the construction of scientific theories are one of the major concerns of this chapter. After saying a few words about the nature of scientific theory, we shall describe two major types of scientific theory, an explanatory type and a predictive type, and evaluate the role of **hypothesis testing** in each. We then will describe three logical processes that are intimately involved in the creation of scientific theories. Two of these, **induction** and **deduction**, mentioned in Chapter 2 in connection with the logical positivists and Popper, respectively, are well known and are often treated at length in methods texts and courses on logical reasoning. The third logical process is less well known but, we shall suggest, more important to the construction of scientific theory than the other two. This process goes under the name of **abduction** and, despite the fact that it is largely unrecognized, it is nevertheless often used by scientists, albeit often without awareness, in the construction of theory (Guttman, 2004; Hanson, 1958; Holcomb, 1998).

Scientific Theory

In everyday life, theory is often used as a synonym for idle speculation of dubious empirical validity. Many commonsense theories of human behavior are of this type. However, this is not the meaning of theory in science. In science, theory refers to well-confirmed laws that are tied together by common principles. Scientific theory has several functions. Theories tell us what sorts of phenomena are important, what sorts are unimportant, and how phenomena may be related or unrelated to each other. For example, in psychology, associative theories suggest that two events will become associated to the extent that they are contiguous in time. Associative theories emphasize the association between events, such as between stimuli and responses, and such theories may go on to say that associations can explain much or all of human thought and behavior. More cognitively oriented theories, although recognizing the importance of associations, may suggest that other factors such as information processing must be taken into consideration in the attempt to understand human behavior.

Too, theories, in addition to telling us what sorts of events exist, also tell us what sorts of events do not exist. For example, some associative theories suggest that understanding thinking does not require assumptions about information processing. As an example outside of psychology, once it became established that all life comes from life, biologists began to realize that spontaneous generation of life was impossible.

These matters about theory were put very aptly years ago by one of the giants of psychology, Neal E. Miller, who said,

> Pure empiricism is a delusion. A theorylike process is inevitably involved in drawing boundaries around certain parts of the flux of experience to define observable events and in the selection of the events that are observed. Since multitudinous events could be observed and an enormous number of relationships could be determined among all of these events, gathering all of the facts with no bias from theory is utterly impossible. Scientists are forced to make a drastic selection, either unconsciously on the basis of perceptual habits and the folklore and linguistic categories of the culture, or consciously on the basis of explicitly formulated theory. (1959, p. 200)

Of the many important points Miller makes in the quote above, one of the more noteworthy is the inevitability of theory. That is, even if one professes not to have a theory and does not explicitly acknowledge it, Miller is suggesting that some theorylike process is implicitly guiding the researcher's decisions. **Ruse** (2001), a philosopher of biology, makes a similar point, saying, "Simply going into the field, as it were, and looking for answers will not do. Unless one goes looking with some ideas or suggestions already at least partially formulated, one will get nowhere" (p. 74). It is the case that the points made by Miller and Ruse would be agreed upon by most scientists.

Theories in the beginning stages of a particular science often tend to be qualitative, that is, stated verbally. As a science matures, theories tend to become more and more quantitative, that is, stated mathematically, in the form of a computer program, and so on. Qualitative theories can be highly useful for a variety of purposes such as explaining and predicting phenomena. There are many useful qualitatively stated theories in psychology. For example, the theory that attention can be conceived as a spotlight has proved useful for understanding many aspects of visual attention and for generating predictions (Johnson & Proctor, 2004). According to this view, attention can be thought of as a beam that can be directed to different spatial locations independent of eye movements. Objects that are in the spotlight are attended to, whereas those falling outside of the beam are not. A prediction that follows from this theory is that performance should benefit more when a visual "target" stimulus occurs at a location that has been cued in advance than when it occurs in some other location. The reason for this prediction is that the cue can direct the attentional spotlight to the proper location, ensuring rapid processing of the stimulus. Thus, Posner, Snyder, and Davidson (1980) found that reaction time to identify a letter that appeared to the left or right of fixation was shorter when a cue presented 800–1,200 ms in advance validly precued the letter's location than when the cue was uninformative, and was longer when the cue was invalid (i.e., cued the incorrect location). These data are consistent with the idea that subjects shifted the attentional spotlight to the cued location and then had to redirect it to the other location when the cue was misleading.

Although qualitative theories such as the spotlight theory are valuable, scientists tend to seek more and more quantification. For example, Logan (2002) provides an instance theory of attention and memory (ITAM) that integrates several quantitative models of attention and memory to provide a unified account of many attention and categorization phenomena. ITAM is based on the idea that attention involves choice between competing objects in a display (i.e., attending to one and not the others), whereas categorization involves choice between competing classifications of display objects (e.g., as a square or circle), with the choice process being the same for both types of task. Quantification, as in Logan's theory, is desired because it offers a number of advantages. For one, it is easier to detect contradictions that might exist within and among theories. For another, as quantification increases, the precision of the deductions from a theory also increases. Too, complex implications of theories can be more easily identified as theories grow more quantitative. Essentially, one important aspect of what quantification does is to reduce ambiguity in a variety of ways.

Types of Theory

Historically, scientific theories have been of two major types, explanatory and predictive. **Explanatory theories** have tended to be more inductive (i.e., developed to explain known observations) than deductive (i.e., developed on the basis of testing inferences derived from general propositions), and **predictive theories** more deductive than inductive. Earlier in the history of science, theories tended to be explanatory. The general view among scientists prior to about 1850 was that theories were constructed mainly on the basis of gathering facts (the inductive approach), with theories being devised to explain a wide variety of related phenomena. As mentioned in Chapter 2, the great methodologist **William Whewell** in the 1850s proposed that theories should be evaluated in terms of their deductive consequences. Essentially, according to this view, one makes a prediction from a theory and then attempts to confirm the prediction empirically. Whewell

(1984, p. 256) was explicit on this point, stating, "It is a test of true theories not only to account for, but to predict phenomena." Note that what Whewell is saying is that a theory should not only be explanatory but predictive as well.

Another great methodologist, **John Stuart Mill**, became involved in a dispute with Whewell in suggesting that explanatory theories are themselves valuable. This dispute has continued down to the present day. It is probably the case that most current-day scientists value predictive theories over explanatory theories. Indeed, it may even be the case that at least some current-day scientists are suspicious of theories that are exclusively explanatory. The reason for this suspicion is the not uncommon belief that explanatory theories are post hoc and, therefore, carefully tailored to fit the known facts. Because theorizing of this type is believed to be unconstrained, at least some individuals think that constructing explanatory theories is of little value. Although we concur in the belief that predictive theories are valuable, and indeed that the ideal situation in science is to have theories that are both explanatory and predictive, we do not subscribe to the view that explanatory theories are necessarily of limited value.

Within science to some extent, and within the philosophy of science to an even greater extent, there has been much analysis concerned with the value of explanatory theories. We will attempt briefly to provide some of the major reasons for concluding that explanatory theories are valuable. In brief, some of the arguments that suggest that prediction is not always superior to explanation are as follows. Brush (1989), a physicist, suggested that explanation may be superior to prediction in certain instances. His argument is as follows. First, assume that some phenomenon has been known for a long time but has resisted explanation from a variety of theoretical viewpoints. Developing a theory that explains the phenomenon would be a scientifically important advance. In Brush's words,

> A successful explanation of a fact that other theories have already failed to explain satisfactorily (for example, the Mercury perihelion [the point at which Mercury's orbit is closer to the sun, which Einstein's theory ultimately explained]) is more convincing than the prediction of a new fact, at least until competing theories have had their chance (and failed) to explain it. (1989, p. 1127)

Brush supplied not only a logical argument in favor of explanation, but some empirical evidence as well. He examined the published comments of many physicists during the initial years after Einstein's prediction from the theory of relativity concerning the bending of light was confirmed. Brush found that this prediction was not more valued than relativity's explanation of the previously known fact that Mercury's orbit is not always identical. In short, he found that almost all physicists, in evaluating Einstein's theory of relativity, valued explanation of Mercury's orbit as much as prediction of the bending of light.

Snyder (1994) noted that evidence in science is objective in the sense that its evaluation or worth is independent of any particular individual or the time at which it was produced, either before or after the theory. Achinstein (1994) favors a position similar to Snyder's, except that he goes further. Achinstein suggests that explanation may sometimes be better than prediction, and vice versa. His essential argument reduces to this: The quality of the evidence for one may be better than the quality of evidence for the other, depending upon circumstances.

In addition to the arguments suggested above, it turns out that one of the most valuable theories in geology, that of plate tectonics, was originally devised in terms of explaining already known phenomena rather than predicting new phenomena. Plate tectonics is the explanation of continental drift that is widely accepted in geology (e.g., Lutgens & Tarbuck, 1998). According to plate tectonics, the continents are on giant plates that float and drift as a result of heat generated in the earth's interior. **Wegener**, who initially proposed plate tectonics, did so by showing that it was consistent with a wide range of already known phenomena. Geologists in the US rejected this explanatory approach to establishing a theory, placing emphasis instead on prediction. Oreskes (1999) examined the controversy over plate tectonics in detail in a recent book, stating:

> The thesis of this book is that American earth scientists rejected the theory of continental drift not because there was no evidence to support it (there was ample), nor because the scientists who supported it were cranks (they were not), but because the theory, as widely interpreted, violated deeply held methodological beliefs and valued forms of scientific practice. (p. 6)

According to Oreskes, the beliefs that were held by American geologists which resulted in them rejecting the explanatory theory of plate tectonics was a widespread acceptance of the idea that only predictive theories are worthwhile.

We have provided two sorts of reasons for the belief that explanatory theorizing can be valuable. On the one hand, there are logically compelling reasons for the view that explanatory theories can be as valuable as predictive ones under certain circumstances. On the other hand, it can be shown empirically that very valuable scientific theories have been constructed initially on the basis of explaining already known facts.

What the Wegener episode in geology illustrates is that different scientists employ different methodological and empirical criteria in accepting or rejecting theories. Methodology texts in psychology strongly imply, even if they do not state directly, that all scientists should use the same criteria in accepting or rejecting theories. One of the major criteria often cited is that of hypothesis testing. Hypothesis testing consists in deriving some implication of a theory and then attempting to determine if that implication is consistent with experimental findings that may be produced as a result of some scientific procedure such as experimentation. Note, if Wegener were a devotee of hypothesis testing in arriving at a theory, serious consideration of plate tectonics as a theory may not have occurred until a much later time.

The fact that different scientists employ different criteria in evaluating theories is highly useful in science. In addition to the Wegener incident, other considerations also illustrate this point. Consider two major examples. Scientists who put forward some novel theory long before it is generally accepted by the field as a whole are, justifiably or unjustifiably, employing criteria different from their colleagues. Often, such novel theories turn out to be incorrect, but sometimes they turn out to be both correct and highly useful. Another place in which it is evident that different scientists employ different criteria in the evaluation of different theories is in the rejection of theories. Well-established theories, when rejected, are not rejected simultaneously by all members of the relevant scientific community. Indeed, as Kuhn (1962) has pointed out, some members of the scientific community may continue to accept a theory long after the field as a whole has abandoned it. The lesson here seems obvious: *It is on the whole beneficial to science that not all scientists employ identical criteria for accepting and rejecting theories.*

Hypothesis Testing

Hypothesis testing, which was introduced into science relatively recently by Whewell, is one of the most powerful weapons in the arsenal of scientists. It is valued by practically all scientists, and understandably so. Many individuals value hypothesis testing to such a degree that they tend to identify the scientific method with hypothesis testing itself.

That is, according to these individuals, hypothesis testing gives science its unique approach to problems and is identified as *the* scientific method. Although hypothesis testing is an invaluable tool in scientific inquiry, it is our view that many individuals who extol its obvious merits often fail to recognize its limitations and that there are alternative scientific methods, alluded to above, that are valuable and useful in their own right. Moreover, many discussions of hypothesis testing found in standard texts are oversimplified. As the geologist Oreskes (1999) has said regarding hypothesis testing, "But is there such a thing as *the* scientific method? The answer is clearly no. . . . the methods of science are complex, variegated, and often local" (p. 5). Recognize that much extremely good and invaluable science was conducted prior to 1850, the approximate time at which hypothesis testing was explicitly introduced into science.

One of the things that makes hypothesis testing indispensable is that nature is far too complicated to be studied at random. This is not to say that observation, directed or undirected, is never valuable. It can be valuable under some circumstances, but like any other method, it has its limitations. The limitations of unconstrained observations of nature are precisely what hypothesis testing allows us to overcome. Hypothesis testing allows us to isolate and examine a complex set of phenomena that would not conveniently occur without direct attempts to produce them. Armed with a particular theory or hypothesis, we deduce some implication of that hypothesis and then attempt to produce the empirical conditions necessary to test the hypothesis. This may involve a variety of steps. For example, special apparatus may be required in order to produce the controlled conditions that must obtain in order for the hypothesis to be tested. Those conditions may be such as to allow us to reject alternatives to our hypothesis. To illustrate, by 1500, many observations had led people to believe that the earth is round, rather than flat, but nobody had demonstrated this directly. A direct test of the hypothesis that the world is round, and not flat, could be arranged by trying to circumnavigate the globe in a ship. Notice that successful circumnavigation would not only support the round earth theory but lead to rejection of the competing flat earth theory. Indeed, Ferdinand Magellan did successfully circumnavigate the globe in the years 1519 to 1522, supporting the round earth hypothesis. Although the example of circumnavigation is not a typical laboratory experiment, it nevertheless conveys quite well how a hypothesis, once formed, may be tested by empirical means.

However, hypothesis testing is also known among philosophers of science to have many limitations, but these are often not discussed much, if at all, among practicing scientists. Failure to consider these limitations results in hypothesis testing, important as it is, being overvalued and often equated with science itself. Some of the limitations of hypothesis testing are described in the following sections.

Immature hypotheses can be easily and inappropriately disconfirmed

One of the principal limitations of hypothesis testing is that it is easy to falsify hypotheses when they are in the initial stages of development. The principal reason why newly formed hypotheses can be disconfirmed so easily is that we know so little about the specific conditions under which they operate or the phenomena to which they are applicable. With experience, we may learn that a specific hypothesis is applicable to a particular set of conditions or phenomena and not to others. Early on, we may not know this and thus may attempt to apply the hypothesis to situations or phenomena to which it is not applicable. The danger here is that we could reject the hypothesis for irrelevant reasons.

The fallacy of affirming the consequent

A second limitation of hypothetico-deductive reasoning is the fallacy known as **affirming the consequent**. The essence of this fallacy is that because an empirical observation is consistent with the deduction from one's hypothesis it does not necessarily imply that that hypothesis is true. There may be many other hypotheses that would generate the same prediction. As an example of this, consider psychologists who study altruism (e.g., Rachlin, 2002). According to some, altruism consists in helping others for the benefit of the others and their benefit alone. That is to say, in performing an altruistic act, one gains no benefit for the self in any way whatever. A variety of other theorists suggest that altruistic acts are performed because the actor gains some benefit. One popular theory is that observing someone in distress produces a similar distress in the observer that can be alleviated by performing an altruistic act. Essentially, according to this view, by relieving the distress of another, we are reinforced because our own distress is alleviated.

Consider how we might go about testing these hypotheses. We can arrange for individuals to observe others in distress. We can also arrange for the observers to have the opportunity to leave the distressful situation. Too, we can offer the observers a way to help the distressed individual. Thus, there are two ways in which distress could be alleviated. One way is to help the individual in distress. The other way is for the observer simply to leave the situation. In the actual experiment, most people elected to help the individual in distress rather than to leave the situation. This finding, taken at face value, is consistent with the idea that true altruism exists. That is, helping others for the benefit of others is a basic human trait. But, notice that there are several alternative interpretations of the finding. For example, the observers may have felt that if they left the situation, the experimenter would form a bad opinion of them. The motive to have others think well of us is a strong one, perhaps stronger under the circumstances than the desire to leave the situation. Still another possibility is that leaving the situation might cause a person to feel guilty and thus oppose any tendency to flee. There are still other possible interpretations.

The point of this example is that consistency with a hypothesis, in this case as in all cases, does not establish the truth of the hypothesis. The philosopher of science who most emphasized this point was Sir Karl Popper. Remember, Popper suggested that, logically speaking, confirmation of deductive inferences merely establishes that the hypothesis is not rejected, not that it is confirmed.

The Duhem–Quine thesis

A hypothesis fails to be confirmed. Why? There may be many reasons: The apparatus used to test the hypothesis may have malfunctioned; a wrong inference may have been made from our hypothesis or theory; a minor correction may be sufficient to render the theory consistent with the data; and so on. Affirming the consequent, discussed in the previous subsection, deals with the case in which results are consistent with a hypothesis, but yet the hypothesis cannot be said to be true. The **Duhem–Quine thesis**, named for its initial advocates, the scientist **Pierre Duhem** and the philosopher **Willard Quine**, in a sense is concerned with the opposite problem, the logical problem of being unable to reject a hypothesis when obtaining a result that is not consistent with it, as in the above examples. Quine (1953) states that in a system of statements, reevaluating one statement may entail reevaluating a whole series of other statements. That is, the various statements of a scientific theory are not independent, and so any failure of one of the statements to predict correctly may be fixed by adjusting some other statement in the theory. As Quine (1953) puts it,

> Total science is like a field of force whose boundary conditions are experience. A conflict with experience at the periphery occasions readjustments in the interior of the field. Truth values have to be redistributed over some of our statements. Reëvaluation of some statements entails reëvaluation of others, because of their logical interconnections.... Having reëvaluated one statement we must reëvaluate some others, which may be statements logically connected with the first or may be the statements of logical connections themselves. But the total field is so under-determined by its boundary conditions, experience, that there is much latitude of choice as to what statements to reëvaluate in the light of any single contrary experience. (pp. 42–43)

The Duhem–Quine thesis is another instance in which much discussion has occurred amongst philosophers of science but, unfortunately, little has occurred among psychologists themselves. The textbook description of hypothesis testing is such as to suggest that if a finding is not consistent with a hypothesis, one automatically rejects the hypothesis. Of course, no scientist actually does this. Typically when hypotheses are disconfirmed, scientists may labor mightily to isolate a cause other than the failure of the hypothesis itself. A formal definition of the Duhem–Quine thesis recognizes that hypotheses are never tested in isolation but within networks of other propositions. For example, as indicated earlier, one assumes that the apparatus that gave rise to the observations is performing as it should. To be concrete, assume that you have the theory that persons with a particular personality trait such as honesty should behave in a particular way that is different from someone who does not have that trait. Assume that in testing this hypothesis, it is disconfirmed. It may be that the theory relating honesty to particular behaviors is not deficient but that the instrument used to measure honesty did not provide a valid measure of that trait. Other reasons that your hypothesis may be correct while being inconsistent with the data are that the data have not been recorded and analyzed appropriately, the deduction from the hypothesis was not a logically correct one, and so on. All of these possibilities can be, and should be, examined when the result is not consistent with the hypothesis. To do otherwise would not conform to good scientific practice. Other considerations that should be examined include whether some minor modification of the hypothesis, or of its sub-components, would render the recalcitrant finding consistent with the hypothesis. The point here is that it is not any easier, logically speaking, to reject a hypothesis than to accept it.

Our remarks here should not be construed as suggesting that hypotheses can never be tested. Of course they can. But it is not an easy task, and in many instances, a variety of possibilities have to be evaluated before one becomes reasonably confident about either retaining a hypothesis or rejecting it. There really is no algorithm for testing hypotheses. Under some conditions it may be relatively clear that a hypothesis can safely be rejected, or it can be retained because it is the best available. Under other conditions, it may be much more difficult, logically speaking, either to accept or reject a particular hypothesis.

What the above discussion amounts to saying, and what many scientists recognize as true, is that there is seldom a crucial experiment that settles an issue simply and directly. Matters are usually much more complicated than that, and it may take a number of experiments over decades to establish the acceptability of a particular hypothesis. A good psychological example from sensation and perception concerns the two major theories of color vision, trichromatic theory, according to which color perception is a product of three types of photoreceptors responsive to different wavelengths of light, and opponent process theory, according to which color perception is a product of a system in which red and green are coded as opposites in the same subsystem, as are blue and yellow. Both of these theories were proposed in the 1800s by Thomas Young (1802) and Hermann von Helmholtz (1852) in the first case, and Ewald Hering (1920/1954) in the second case. Following many experiments, it was only in the last half of the 20th century that evidence came to strongly support the contemporary view that the trichromatic receptor system is recoded into an opponent neural system, and that many color vision phenomena can be explained in this manner (see Hurvich, 1981).

Confirmation bias

A psychologist who holds a particular theory may attempt repeatedly to confirm it, even when initial findings are negative. This is called **confirmation bias**. Many people feel that confirmation bias is a serious limitation to hypothesis testing. Greenwald, Pratkanis, Leippe, and Baumgardner (1986) characterize confirmation bias as follows: "Researchers display confirmation bias when they persevere by revising procedures until obtaining a theory-predicted result" (p. 216). Greenwald et al., in common with a variety of others, suggested that confirmation bias leads to poor science and should be avoided. In our view, a generalization of this sort is unwarranted because it is not consistent in some instances with how good science is created. Consider some examples. In the early stages of theory construction, it is relatively easy to disconfirm a fledgling theory. The best strategy in these early stages is to attempt to confirm the theory to determine whether or not it has any possible worth. As we shall see later, **Michael Faraday**, a prominent physicist in the 1800s, followed just this strategy, which goes under the name confirm early/disconfirm late. Even with a reasonably mature theory, it is not inappropriate to attempt to confirm it under new and different conditions. Stressing one's theory in this manner could well lead to new insights of how the theory is to be applied in novel circumstances. These examples show that a confirmatory strategy can well produce positive benefits.

The negative consequences of confirmation bias, in our view, are much overblown. According to Greenwald et al. (1986), the primary negative consequence of a confirmation bias arises "when the researcher's primary goal is to test the theory. In testing a theory, the theory can dominate research in a way that blinds the researcher to potentially informative observations" (p. 217). Of course, it is possible that strong adherence to a theory beyond reason may blind a researcher. However, this is not the only outcome. Consider, for example, a theorist who pushes a theory toward confirming some inconsequential hypothesis. The damage done to scientific progress would probably be minimal because most scientists, including those who are not adherents of the theory, are reasonably capable of evaluating findings as to their worth. In short, we do not think that most scientists would be gulled into placing too much emphasis on minor, inconsequential findings.

But, there is an even more important reason why confirmation bias does not represent the threat to decent science that many suggest it to be. We are firm believers that no single individual, at any one time in the early stages of some investigation, can be truly unbiased. Of necessity, in such cases, a scientist must exhibit biases that may turn out in the long run to be incorrect but are entirely reasonable at the time they are entertained. Given such ambiguity, the individual scientist cannot know whether it is better to persist at pursuing some goal, which may turn out to be illusory, or to abandon attempts to attain the goal. Our view is that total methodological rigor, although not residing in any particular individual, can be at least an approximate property of the greater scientific community. That is, if a scientist reports a poor result as a consequence of confirmation bias, it seems likely that it will be ignored or evaluated as deficient by the more general scientific community. In practice, it is reasonable to assume that for every scientist seeking to confirm a pet theory there is at least one scientist, and possibly more, seeking to show its inadequacies. This view is captured in a quote by Moser, Gadenne, and Schröder (1988), who in a response to Greenwald et al. (1986) say:

> Even if scientists always tended to confirm *their* hypotheses, this would not render empirical criticism impossible. It is not always the same person who constructs a hypothesis and tests it critically. Assume that every scientist tries to demonstrate that his hypothesis is true. Let us further assume that there are competing hypotheses held by different scientists. We can conclude that these scientists are motivated to confirm their own hypotheses *and* to falsify the others. As is generally known, experiments are often designed in such a way that the results necessarily confirm one hypothesis and disconfirm another. This shows that confirming cannot be the only strategy used in psychological research. (p. 574)

Induction and Deduction

As indicated, three separate and distinct logical processes are employed in the construction and testing of theory. Two of these, induction and deduction, which are well known, have been discussed in previous chapters to some extent. We consider several aspects of these key logical processes here. We then provide a lengthier treatment of the third procedure, abduction, to emphasize its importance.

Induction

The inductive process, as described in previous chapters, is one that moves from the observation of a variety of specific instances to a general characterization of the observations. And, as indicated, many scientists are of the opinion that science can proceed inductively, a view that was generally accepted by scientists up until about 1850 and by the logical positivists in the 20th century.

In the initial stages of any investigation, when we lack necessary information, induction is a very useful method to employ. For example, when a biologist comes across a new species, she might want to determine whether all members of that species have a certain characteristic in common. Thus, it would make sense for the biologist to seek additional information by examining more and more members of that species, determining whether all members have the particular characteristic. Whether they do or do not have the characteristic might lead the biologist to collect still other data by inductive means. Thus, induction is a very useful procedure for gathering facts.

Despite the well-recognized usefulness of induction, it has two limitations, as indicated in Chapter 2. One is that induction does not necessarily assure us that any inference from it is necessarily true. We previously gave the example that having observed a number of black crows, there is no guarantee that the next crow observed will be black. To cite another example, a turkey which assumes that a farmer is being friendly because of the care provided throughout the year is due for a rude awakening when Thanksgiving comes. Essentially, induction cannot provide the basis for universal affirmative statements such as "all crows are black." The second problem with induction is that its scope is limited to the particular characteristics that are observed, that is, it tells us that crows are black but not why they are black.

As Guttman (2004) has indicated,

> Scientists do not use induction as classically described. They do not sit around their labs trying to establish generalizations about the color of crows or that the sun will rise tomorrow or that a turkey will continue to be fed every day. A little independent observation of scientists will show that, in fact, scientists engage in mystery-solving essentially like that of detective work. (p. 46)

The detective work that Guttman has in mind is that of abduction, which we will treat in some detail later.

Deduction

The deductive process is one in which specific predictions are derived from general premises. For example, from the general premise that all men are mortal, we may conclude that Socrates, being a man, is mortal. Some scientists follow Popper in suggesting that science should proceed deductively, as well as inductively.

Deduction, like induction, is a very useful tool in science. Whereas induction is more or less data driven, deduction can be characterized as being theory driven. That is, deduction can be used to derive predictions about the world from theory. For example, we may entertain hypothesis H that has the implication that all A's are B's. Employing deduction, we would arrange conditions that are capable of determining if the general premise that all A's are B's is indeed correct. There are two general outcomes in employing deduction: As indicated, the deduction from theory may be consistent or inconsistent with what we observe empirically. Consistency does not necessarily imply truth of the theory because the observation may be consistent with a variety of other theoretical premises. Inconsistency could imply that the theory is deficient in some respect, but, as indicated earlier in the chapter, this determination is not a simple one. Thus, in the final analysis, the best we can ever get from a deductive test is that the proposition of concern has not been falsified. This is not the same as knowing that the proposition is true.

Pigliucci (2003) suggests that deduction is truth-conserving (i.e., whatever is in the premises is preserved) but not truth-ampliative (i.e., it does not go beyond the premises). What he means by this is clear from the following quote:

> *If* the premises are true (and the deductive sequence is formally correct), then the conclusion is guaranteed to be true (i.e., the truth of the premises is conserved). However, a deductive reasoning does not augment our knowledge of the world (it is not ampliative), it simply makes explicit what is already contained in the premises. While the latter is often a valuable enterprise, it clearly is not the sort of thing that would help . . . a scientist make generalizations about the world. (p. 18)

In sum, although induction and deduction are necessary tools in science, they are not in themselves entirely adequate to generate useful theory. Holcomb (1998) summarizes the problems with induction and deduction, concluding that scientific theories are not based on induction and deduction alone.

Abduction and Theory Construction

If induction and deduction are not entirely sufficient to give us what we want, scientifically speaking, is there a logical process that does? A third logical procedure, called abduction (Peirce, 1940), described below, seems to provide a positive answer to this question. This procedure was initially made popular by the philosopher **C. S. Peirce** in the late 1800s and subsequently recommended by a variety of individuals, including the philosophers **N. R. Hanson** (1958) and H. Holcomb (1998). One of the virtues of abduction is that it can be employed in connection with a great variety of scientific statements, ranging from restricted hypotheses to general theories of either the explanatory or predictive type. Abduction has been used in several different senses by various writers, but our reading of the literature suggests that abduction can be described as involving three separate and interrelated ideas (see, especially, Holcomb, 1998).

Explaining patterns of data

Peirce's idea of abduction as a logical procedure was enthusiastically accepted by Thagard (1988), who says of abduction,

> Most people with an interest in inference have heard of induction and deduction, but Peirce's abduction is not widely known, although a few writers in both philosophy and artificial intelligence have studied it. Yet abduction is a pervasive phenomenon, both in science and in everyday life. (p. 52)

We heartily agree with Thagard's assessment that abduction is a commonly employed mode of inference but is seldom explicitly recognized as such. In advancing the idea of abduction, Peirce suggested that it involves surveying a number of phenomena, observing their pattern, and forming an explanatory or causal hypothesis. Essentially, the scientist is saying that if this generalization were true, then the world would be as she observes it. Notice that this is neither an induction nor a deduction. Induction is not involved because there may only be a small number of examples and the generalization is not about their shared properties but about their cause. Deduction is not involved either, for the generalization is not a derivation from the phenomena it applies to but rather is an explanation of them.

As some examples of abductions in this sense, consider the following. **Newton** suggested that the motion of the planets could be understood if they were exerting a force of attraction on each other, which he called gravity. Wegener suggested that similarity between the fauna of Africa and South America would make sense if it were assumed that the continents were once close to each other and moved apart because they were on plates that moved. Notice that Wegener's conjecture in no respect resembles either an induction or a deduction. It was a hypothesis that if true could explain a rather perplexing fact, why continents separated by thousands of miles had similar fauna.

Many scientists in forming an abduction employ analogy. One of the more famous analogies in science leading to the creation of an abduction was that employed by Rutherford and Bohr. According to them, the structure of an atom is very much like our solar system. In the solar system, planets orbit the sun. In the atom, electrons, for example, orbit the nucleus. The resulting Rutherford–Bohr Theory of Atomic Structure advanced our understanding of the atomic structure of matter. An example of an abduction formed on the basis of an analogy in psychology is that of the blank slate forwarded by **John Locke** in the 1700s. The idea here is that experience "writes" on the mind much as chalk writes on a blackboard. By carrying this analogy further, for example, by analogizing retention in memory to chalk remaining on the blackboard, one can subsume a variety of psychological phenomena. Other analogies employed to understand memory include a tape recorder, conveyor belt, and leaky bucket (see Roediger, 1980).

Entertaining multiple hypotheses

The second idea involved in abduction is to arrange a test of a hypothesis, but always in the context of competing hypotheses. It is difficult to evaluate a theory in isolation. For example, is a theory's inability to predict a certain known fact *F* a reason for rejecting it? It might or might not be, depending upon circumstances. On the one hand, the theory may explain a variety of other facts better than any of its rivals, while neither it nor its rivals can explain *F*. Under those circumstances, the theory would not be rejected. On the other hand, its explanatory capacity over a wide range of phenomena may be equaled by its rivals while they can also explain *F*. In that case, we might want to reject the theory. Of course, there are many other possibilities. But the general point is that *the evaluation of a theory is always a matter to be decided in relation to other theories* rather than in isolation. Laudan (1997) has suggested these ideas quite forcibly, stating, "Let us say explicitly what scientific practice already forces us to acknowledge implicitly, viz., that the evaluation of a theory or hypothesis is relative to its *extant* rivals" (p. 314). Essentially, when testing a theory, we are concerned with determining whether it has been severely tested, by which we mean that it has passed certain tests that its rivals have not passed. Laudan goes on to say of a theory, "We need not require it to have passed all the tests to which it has been submitted, thus acknowledging that all theories characteristically exhibit some anomalies. But we do demand of an acceptable theory that it exhibit no anomalies not afflicting its rival or rivals" (p. 314).

As an example of comparative theory evaluation, consider the following. If we wanted to test the hypothesis that, natively, all humans have identical facial expressions for identical emotions (biological hypothesis), we might test people from different nations and of different races. However, for this hypothesis to have any force we would have to rule out the possibility that the similarity in facial expression is due to a common learning experience shared by different cultural or racial groups (learning hypothesis). Ideally, what we would want to say is that our biological hypothesis explains a variety of phenomena that the learning or cultural hypothesis is unable to explain. It is probably apparent that confirming the biological hypothesis relative to the learning hypothesis provides us with a much more satisfactory outcome than confirming the biological hypothesis in isolation.

As another interesting example, it was believed for a long time that mastering certain general skills such as Latin, Greek, geometry, and logic produced learning that was generally applicable to a wide variety of situations (e.g., Angell, 1908). Much of our educational system is still based on this notion. A rival theory is that specific skills are learned, and they only transfer to similar situations and domains that use the same knowledge (e.g., Singley & Anderson, 1989). Each of these theories looked at in isolation provides what might be considered to be a satisfactory explanation of learning and transfer. It is by arranging tests that differentiate between them that we can determine which one better fits the data. In this case, a variety of recently obtained data have indicated that transfer of learning and knowledge is more specific than general, and the majority of current theories of expertise and knowledge acquisition tend to favor the specificity of transfer across situations.

John R. Platt (1964), a physicist, calls hypothesis testing of this sort *strong inference*. Platt's method sets up alternative hypotheses that have different consequences: H1 implies C1, H2 implies C2, H3 implies C3, and so on. Let us assume that an experiment designed to test these hypotheses produces the result C2. Under these circumstances, we are in a position to suggest that H2 is more likely to be true than either H1 or H3.

Note that this hypothesis testing procedure, as illustrated in the examples above, differs substantially from that recommended by Popper and that usually found in methodology textbooks. It differs as follows: It asks, not as Popper might suggest, that a hypothesis be tested in isolation to determine its validity, but rather that the hypothesis be tested in the context of competing hypotheses. In the case of the first example, the origin of facial expressions was tested by contrasting a biological hypothesis with a learning hypothesis. In the case of the second example, transfer general theories were contrasted with transfer specific theories.

Inference to the best explanation

The third element of abduction is as follows: We not only evaluate theories in the context of other theories, but we attempt to come to a global conclusion as to which of the theories best satisfies the evidence at hand. This procedure, known as **inference to the best explanation**, was first suggested by Harman (1965), although Thagard (1988) indicates that it was used informally for centuries before. Regarding the procedure of inference to the best explanation, Holcomb has said:

> Accept the hypothesis that provides the best possible explanation of the available evidence. If sufficient evidence is unavailable, the best explanation is accepted as preferable to alternative hypotheses. If sufficient evidence is available, the best explanation is accepted both as preferable and believable. (p. 315)

Laudan (1996) has put the matter somewhat differently but equally forcefully, as follows:

> The fact that a theory has a high problem-solving effectiveness or is highly progressive warrants no judgments about the worth of the theory. Only when we compare its effectiveness and progress to that of its extant rivals are we in a position to offer any advice about which theories should be accepted, pursued, or entertained. (p. 86)

Another naturalist who has not explicitly used the phrase inference to the best explanation, **Giere** (2001), suggests something quite similar to it. According to Giere, "An 'available' scientific explanation must be one that, relative to the science accepted at the time, is plausible enough that something not too different is likely eventually to prove correct" (p. 57).

In sum, just as one should not accept theories in isolation, one should not reject them in isolation. A theory cannot be rejected in absolute terms but only relative to some other theory. Even a bad theory, for which problems are known to exist, is better than a worse theory or no theory. Although this approach of arguing to the best explanation is seldom explicitly stated, we believe that it is observed implicitly in practice by most psychologists in particular and scientists in general.

What are the factors that constitute the best explanation? Many can be cited, and in the initial stages of theory development different individuals may have different preferences. Among the criteria that may be usefully employed to evaluate theories are the following:

- Fruitfulness: The ease with which the theory generates new predictions.
- Parsimony: How few assumptions the theory makes.
- Quantification: The extent to which a theory is quantified because, among other things, quantitative theories are more precise and less arbitrary than qualitative theories.
- Scope: The number of diverse phenomena that a theory explains.
- Progressiveness: Whether the predictions of a theory are novel and leading to progress in understanding the domain to which it applies.
- Internal consistency: The extent to which a theory is free of internal contradictions.
- External consistency: The extent to which assumptions of a theory do not violate assumptions in other, related theories.

In initial stages of theory development, some theories may be more adequate than others, as judged by subsets of these criteria. Say, for example, one theory may be fruitful and parsimonious, but not quantitative. A rival theory may be more quantitative but less parsimonious, and so on. What we should expect of a theory is that over time it should improve along the various dimensions mentioned above. To the extent to which this is true, its adequacy relative to other theories should improve. What the history of science teaches is that eventually the range of acceptable theories may be narrowed to only a few that satisfy most or all of the above criteria better than their competitors. Examples of such theories are provided in physics, where the theories of relativity and quantum mechanics have each proved very adequate in their respective domains, relativity over vast distances and quantum mechanics over exceedingly small distances. Consider, for example, the development of Einstein's theory of relativity. Like all theories when first proposed, it satisfied some of the above criteria better than Newtonian mechanics, which it was seeking to displace. Over time, as more information became available, the disparity between two views in terms of satisfying the above criteria became greater, leading to the widespread acceptance of the theory of relativity.

Interestingly, as adequate, theoretically speaking, as relativity and quantum mechanics are in their respective domains, some physicists remain dissatisfied because they seek a single theory that explains all physical phenomena, the theory of "everything," as Greene (1999) calls it. One attempt to unify these two theories involves the development of string theory, the idea that physical reality consists of exceedingly small vibrating strings. Whether or not this approach will prove to be successful is unclear at present and will depend on how well string theory is able to satisfy the above criteria. What we can be sure of is that physicists will compare string theory to relativity and quantum mechanics before making a decision whether to accept it or not. That is, they will argue to the best explanation available.

Chapter Summary

The hallmark of science is to construct explanations for phenomena that are called theories. A scientific theory consists of a set of laws tied together by common principles that explains a wide range of phenomena. It was indicated that theories are of two general types, explanatory and predictive. Explanatory theories are developed on the basis of already known phenomena, whereas predictive theories are developed in the main employing hypothesis testing. Hypothesis testing, which is sometimes equated with the scientific method, was shown to have weaknesses as well as strengths. We indicated that scientific theories of all types are developed and evaluated employing induction, deduction, and abduction. The most important of these three processes is that of abduction, which consists of recognizing a pattern in the data, comparing theories, and then selecting the one that provides the best explanation. One major conclusion of the chapter is that the construction of theories is an absolutely vital activity in science and that researchers should strive to make their theoretical assumptions as explicit as possible.

INFERENCE TO THE BEST EXPLANATION

Introduction

By what process do scientists come to accept or reject theories? According to some individuals, such as Popper, it is possible to reject theories if experiment reveals that they yield incorrect predictions. But, as Kuhn has shown, on the basis of historical examination, and as will be considered in detail later in this chapter, all theories at all times are faced with findings that they either cannot explain or that appear to contradict them. Kuhn, in considering this matter, suggested that scientists, in facing data that are problematical for their theories, did not necessarily consider them counter-instances to their theory, or, to put it differently, phenomena that called the theory into question. Rather, scientists could conceptualize the recalcitrant phenomena as problems that the theory might ultimately be able to solve. According to Kuhn, scientists could live with this sort of ambiguity for a very long time. Kuhn was not exactly sure of when a particular scientific community began to regard problematic data as counter-instances to the theory, rather than as problems that the theory could eventually solve. One of his suggestions was that this transformation might depend upon more and more examples of problematical data. Kuhn suggested that scientists would never abandon a **paradigm** before they had a new replacement paradigm in hand. Once the replacement was in hand, the shift to the new paradigm occurred very rapidly. On this model, it appears that what Kuhn is saying is that abandonment of a paradigm may take years, even decades, but change of allegiance to a new paradigm could occur exceedingly rapidly.

We think Kuhn was half right. On the one hand, Kuhn was correct in suggesting that scientists do not easily abandon successful theories and will hold onto them in the face of problematical data for a very long time. On the other hand, Kuhn was wrong in suggesting that new paradigms are accepted very rapidly by the relevant scientific community. The problems with rejecting a well-formed old theory are in some respects similar to those in connection with accepting a new theory. In both cases, there is considerable ambiguity concerning the proper course of action, whether to accept or reject a theory. Just as all the information necessary to reject a theory requires perhaps decades to amass, in the same way, the information necessary for accepting a theory may require decades to amass.

It appears that, in the case of well-formed theories, it would be a tremendous coincidence if all the information necessary to reject them were available at the time they initially encountered difficulty. At the same time, it would be an equally tremendous coincidence if all of the various information necessary for accepting a new theory were available at the time it was first proposed. In both cases, the accumulation of relevant information may require many years. It may involve the development of new technologies, the development of theory from other areas of science, new discoveries from a variety of different scientific sources, and so on. Due to Kuhn's influence, it has come to be generally recognized that well-formed theories are not easily rejected. What is less recognized, however, is that accepting new theories encounters many of the same difficulties as rejecting old theories.

In this chapter, we deal with four general matters relevant to theory choice. First, we list some of the salient criteria that may be employed in deciding that a particular theory is better than its competitors. Second, we discuss some of the problems associated with these criteria. Third, we provide two specific historical examples of **inference to the best explanation** employing theories of importance to psychology that are still in development. One is how our understanding of the functioning of the brain ultimately led to cognitive neuroscience, and the other is how our understanding of the mechanisms of evolution increased and how this led to evolutionary psychology. We show for each that over a long period of time, they were able to overcome many apparent difficulties that might otherwise be cause to reject them. Finally, we elaborate on the concept of **consilience**, first suggested by William Whewell in the mid 1800s and recently popularized by **E. O. Wilson** (1998), providing examples of how valuable consilience is in science.

Inference to the best explanation involves deciding which among several competing explanations is most consistent with our criteria of what constitutes a sound theory. Examples of such criteria might include which theory explains the data best, which is the simplest among several alternative theories, which theory is the most fruitful in the sense of generating a variety of interesting predictions, and so on. Sometimes it is relatively easy to decide which is the best among available theories. As one example, all biologists would agree that evolution is explained better by natural selection than it is by the Lamarckian proposition of the inheritance of acquired characteristics. As another example, no current-day physicist would argue with the proposition that Newton's theory of motion is better than Aristotle's. Within psychology, most psychologists would agree that cognitive psychology is an improvement over behaviorism, which in turn was an improvement over structuralism.

Some of the specific criteria for deciding which of two or more theories is superior are fairly straightforward. For example, who would quarrel with the idea that a theory that does not contain a contradiction is superior to one that does, at least in that respect? Unfortunately, however, the criteria for deciding which is the best among available theories are not always so straightforward. It was Kuhn's opinion that the criteria for selecting among theories were often ambiguous for one reason or another, leading others to believe that Kuhn was a relativist. We agree with Kuhn that there is ambiguity concerning these criteria in the short run, but, we suggest, such ambiguities have been, and can be, resolved by particular theories in the long run. It is the capacity of a particular theory in the long run to prove itself better than its competitors that allows science to avoid charges of **relativism**.

Evaluating Theories: A Critical Evaluation of Criteria

Consider a number of criteria that scientists in general, as well as Kuhn, consider desirable in a theory. Theories, it is said, should be fruitful, simple (or parsimonious), mathematical, non-contradictory, progressive (i.e., expanding into new directions and so on), broad in scope (i.e., explain a variety of different phenomena), and falsifiable. They should make surprising predictions and should not be inconsistent with similar theories in the same domain (e.g., theories of attention should not be inconsistent with neurophysiological information). Kuhn identified three broad classes of problems associated with employing the above criteria to specific theories. These are: rules in conflict, shifting standards, and rule emphasis.

81

Rules in conflict

A given theory may be superior to its rivals in connection with some of the criteria mentioned above, but inferior to its rivals in connection with others. Given this state of affairs, it would be difficult to conclude that one theory is superior to the other. To take some specific examples, the most parsimonious theory, in terms of having the fewest assumptions, may explain fewer phenomena than its competitors. As another example, a theory of wide scope may be less falsifiable than some of its competitors. As a final example, the most mathematical among available theories may be the least fruitful of the bunch.

Shifting standards

The problem here is that theories tend to judge their own worth in terms of criteria that are to some extent peculiar to themselves. This often gets expressed in terms of phenomena, though it could involve other considerations, such as methodological ones. As far as phenomena go, theorists of a given persuasion may feel that the particular problems solved by their theory are more important for one reason or another than the particular problems solved by another theory. For example, it is not unknown for theories that solve practical problems to consider themselves superior to theories that solve basic theoretical issues, and vice versa. Sometimes this involves methodological considerations as, for example, clinical versus experimental methods. In a later chapter, we will discuss **qualitative** versus **quantitative methods**, and the fact that some adherents of each consider their method superior to the other on the basis of their favorite criteria. The problem is that people who have different standards judge their intellectual products by their own standards, and, by definition, their products will be superior on that basis.

Rule emphasis

The problem here is that individuals may identify similar criteria for theory evaluation but disagree on their relative importance. For example, two people may both value parsimony and scope in theory evaluation, but one may place a greater emphasis on parsimony than scope whereas the other may value scope over parsimony. Thus, in a particular instance, two individuals who disagree over the relative importance of two or more criteria of theory evaluation may, in consequence, differ on which is the better of two theories.

Vagueness of criteria

In addition to the problems recognized by Kuhn, we would add vagueness of criteria. For example, it seems straightforward to say to prefer the simplest theory, but it is not. Simplicity may mean many different things to different people. Simplicity, or parsimony, is often cited by scientists as a reasonable criterion to employ in the evaluation of theories. However, there are two problems with simplicity as a criterion. One is that no convincing reason has been given as to why we should prefer the simpler of two theories. We suggest that the preference for simplicity that is often expressed may arise for aesthetic reasons rather than sound methodological ones.

Be that as it may, the second problem with simplicity is that we do not possess any reasonable definition of it. **Hempel** (1966), a philosopher of science, who has supplied a thorough analysis of the concept of simplicity, states, "Though, undeniably, simplicity is highly prized in science, it is not easy to state clear criteria of simplicity in the relevant sense and to justify the preference given to simpler hypotheses and theories" (p. 41). Hempel explores a variety of different meanings of simplicity, finding none of them to be persuasive as to the meaning of the term. Consider, for example, the idea that the simplest theory is the one that has the fewest assumptions and that we should prefer such a theory. But, as Hempel indicates, a given assumption may be broken down into several more basic assumptions, and contra-wise, several more basic assumptions may be combined into a single assumption. Given that this is the case, it would be difficult to decide which is the simpler of two theories. One might suggest that not assumptions, but number of concepts, be employed to evaluate the simplicity of a particular theory. However, as Hempel indicates, the same considerations that apply to assumptions also apply to concepts.

Resolution of Ambiguity over Time

According to Kuhn, in the final analysis, it is not possible to accept or reject theories definitively. It follows from this that Kuhn believes that inference to the best explanation is not, and cannot be, a feasible procedure for deciding among theories. The general reason for these views, as indicated earlier, is that Kuhn concluded that the various criteria for deciding among theories are indeterminate, either because they are contradictory or because they may be given different emphasis by different people, and so on. As indicated earlier, theory choice according to Kuhn occurs as follows. Problems with the old paradigm continue to multiply, and over time, the relevant scientific community begins to feel that the problems may be intractable. At this point, a search for a new paradigm begins. To the extent that the relevant scientific community believes that the new paradigm holds scientific promise, they will adopt it while simultaneously rejecting the old paradigm. However, at no point in this process is it possible to demonstrate definitively that it is necessary to replace the old paradigm with the new one.

We think that Kuhn's view of scientific progress is mistaken in this particular instance. Kuhn suggests that it is not only logically possible but not entirely unreasonable for individual scientists either to reject well-developed paradigms that are accepted by the relevant scientific community or to accept alternative paradigms. We think that the error in Kuhn's view lies in his considering too short a time frame for the development and evaluation of a theory. It appears, given sufficient time and an able scientific community, that scientists can come to isolate definitively a specific theory for acceptance while rejecting a variety of its competitors. History teaches that this process, like Rome, has seldom been completed in a day, and such prolonged theory evaluation is probably inevitable. When a theory is proposed initially, no matter what its eventual worth, there always will be reasonable reasons for doubting and questioning it.

Resolving these doubts and questions will require prolonged examination. The absolute amount of time required to discover and isolate a theory that eventually proves to be more adequate than its competitors no doubt depends on a variety of factors, such as how active, numerous, and able is the scientific community concerned with the problem. As an extreme example, passing from Aristotle's theory of motion to Newton's required many centuries, perhaps because there was a relatively small scientific community concerned with the issue. However, today, with larger scientific communities, greater technology, and better means of communication, the time required to isolate the best among a variety of theories appears to have been considerably shortened. Even in today's climate, definitive theory evaluation is not something that can normally be achieved in a few years. **Darwin's** (1859) theory of evolution by natural selection is a good example demonstrating the possibility of inference to the best explanation. Another example is increased understanding of how the brain functions. We consider evolution first and show below how its ultimate triumph over various difficulties required about a century.

Natural Selection

The theory of **natural selection** requires three things: variability, selection, and heredity. A predator that is faster than his comrades (variability) may enjoy greater success at hunting (selection), and if speed is determined genetically, running speed will be passed on to the offspring (heredity). During the century after Darwin's theory of natural selection was initially proposed, many alternatives to it and many problems in connection with it were disposed of. The theory of natural selection faced at least four problems at its inception. Most immediately, there was a rival to Darwin's theory of natural selection that was accepted, and continued to be accepted, by many in the relevant scientific community. That theory was **Lamarck**'s (1809) theory of evolution by the inheritance of acquired characteristics. Another difficulty was that Darwin lacked a mechanism for inheritance that was consistent with evolution by means of natural selection. A third problem was that physicists suggested that the earth was not nearly old enough for natural selection to work. A fourth problem was that there were phenomena that seemed to directly contradict natural selection. One of these contradictory phenomena was that some animals such as ants, bees, and termites had given up their own individual reproduction in favor of reproduction through a conspecific, for example, the queen bee. Another, related problem was that some animals appeared to have characteristics that were directly unfavorable to the idea that they had arisen through natural selection. A good example here would be the peacock's tail: The tail is heavy and puts the peacock at a disadvantage at avoiding predators. Darwin is supposed to have said, "I hate the sight of the peacock!"

Lamarck believed in two major causes of species change: a tendency for each species to progress and improve, and the inheritance of acquired characteristics. Darwin had no good theory of inheritance that was able to counter Lamarck's claim that evolution occurred via the heredity of acquired characteristics. Darwin believed that inheritance occurred through blending; thus if one parent is tall and the other is short, the resulting offspring would be of medium height. The blending mechanism is incapable of providing for the evolution of desirable traits through natural selection. For example, if there were a selective advantage in being tall, mating with a short individual would give rise to an individual of medium height, and thus tallness would be lost. There were two major occurrences that came to support Darwin's theory of natural selection. One was the discovery of the great German biologist, August Weismann (1893), that heredity occurs only through the germ line and not through bodily characteristics, contrary to Lamarck's view that bodily characteristics could be inherited. In a well-known experiment, Weismann cut off the tails of mice, observing that through the generations, all mice were born with tails.

As a result of Weismann's theory, **Gregor Mendel**'s earlier discovery of what came to be called genes was resurrected and became well known. In Mendelian inheritance, particular characteristics are preserved by the genes, such as tallness and shortness; we do not get blending. This is a much better mechanism for heredity than was the blending idea of Darwin's. Early on, evolutionists and geneticists viewed each other unfavorably, but eventually it was realized that the two belonged together, resulting by the late 1930s in what is called the modern synthesis in which the two were seen as highly related. By the late 1930s, Darwinism had triumphed over Lamarckianism, a matter that required about 75 years.

Given Darwin's theory of natural selection, an immense amount of time was required in order for the evolutionary process to go from relatively simple organisms such as bacteria to more complicated ones such as vertebrates. According to the physicists of his era, particularly Lord Kelvin, insufficient time was available for evolution to work via natural selection. Kelvin put the age of the earth at approximately 100 million years, much too short a time for Darwin's theory to work. Darwin was certain that Kelvin was wrong. Kelvin's view was based on the thermodynamic principle that energy always becomes less available and, hence, that hot bodies will eventually cool down. More specifically, Kelvin calculated how long it would take a body the size of the earth to cool down from a molten state. In 1868, he argued that the total age of the earth could not be more than 100 million years. Kelvin's estimate of the age of the earth was undermined by the revolution that took place in physics around 1900. Essentially, the discovery of radioactivity introduced a factor that had not been included in Kelvin's calculations. In 1903, Pierre Curie showed that the radioactive decay of elements such as radium produced a steady supply of heat. These elements are present throughout the earth's crust. By 1906, Lord Rayleigh had shown that the energy produced by radioactive elements more than compensated for the heat that the earth lost to space. Indeed, the rate of decay of some elements was so slow that physicists now calculated that the earth's heat balance could be maintained for billions of years. It is now agreed on all sides that the earth is about 4.5 billion years old. This, of course, is sufficient time for the sort of processes postulated by Darwin to work. Establishing that the earth was old enough to make natural selection feasible required about 50 years.

In 1871, Darwin suggested the idea that sexual selection occurred in addition to natural selection. There are two forms of sexual selection, intrasexual selection between members of the same sex and intersexual selection between members of the opposite sex. Intrasexual selection can explain why males possess many characteristics not possessed by females, such as large size and sharp horns. These characteristics arise because males compete with each other for access to females. As for intersexual selection, males possess features that are attractive to females, such as the large tail of the peacock. Although Darwin's hypothesis of selection was not popular when it was first suggested, recent research has indicated it to be one of Darwin's better ideas. It appears that males who have what appear to be outrageous characteristics, such as the peacock's tail, are in fact superior males, genetically speaking. Experiments have shown that peacocks with large tails have healthier offspring that survive better than the offspring of males with smaller tails. According to the current theory, supported by a variety of evidence, when females are mating preferentially with peacocks with large tails, they are essentially choosing better genes for their offspring. Better genes theory and evidence for it really did not become available until about 1970. So, the problem of why some features of animals seem to violate natural selection, such as the peacock's tail, was not solved until about a hundred years after Darwin's idea of sexual selection was first proposed.

Another problem for Darwin's theory was posed by the social insects such as ants and bees. It was difficult to understand within the context of natural selection why, for example, ants would give up their own individual reproduction in favor of reproducing through another individual, the queen. Around 1960, William Hamilton proposed that the unit of selection in evolution is the gene. This innocuous-sounding statement has many important implications. For one thing, it allows us to understand at least one major reason why human beings cooperate with each other. For example, when a parent aids his or her children, the parent in a real sense is engaging in self-help. This is because a parent and child have on average 50 percent of their genes in common. An interesting fact about some social insects is that they have 75 percent of their genes in common. This is because, unlike many other animals, they do not get 50 percent of their genes from one parent and another 50 percent from another parent. Instead, each individual inherits a full set of genes from the male and, thus, all of the females of the colony have the same set of genes from the male. But social insects, like us, receive half of their genes from the female. Thus, females of the colony have 75 percent of their genes in common. If they were to mate as we do, they would only have 50 percent of their genes in common with their offspring. Thus, genetically speaking, it is better to reproduce through the queen rather than to reproduce themselves. So, the problem that plagued Darwin's theory of natural selection in 1859, the peculiar reproduction of the social insects, did not receive a reasonable solution until about a hundred years later with the publication of Hamilton's idea.

The emphasis on the gene as the unit of natural selection has proved to be very fruitful in advancing psychological knowledge concerning cooperation and aggression. Among other things, it explains why we favor and cooperate with our kin. We act favorably to our mother, father, sisters, brothers, and children, with each of which, on average, we share 50 percent of our genes. The idea embodied in gene selection theory is that when we favor our kin, we are favoring ourselves, genetically speaking. Not only do we act favorably to our close kin, but we inhibit aggression against them as well. For example, Daly and Wilson (1988), using evolutionary reasoning, hypothesized that physical child abuse should be more common among stepparents than among biological parents. This is not to say that more than a very small fraction of stepparents are abusive to children, but it is the case that abuse, when it occurs, is far more common among stepparents than among biological parents. Interestingly, at the time that Daly and Wilson confirmed their evolutionary hypothesis, no other available hypothesis predicted differences between stepparents and biological parents in terms of child abuse.

James Watson and Francis Crick discovered the double helical shape of the DNA molecule in 1953. Since then, scientists have examined the genotypes of many animals. Similarity between genotypes of even distantly related animals, for example, human and earthworm, is such as to suggest that all life on earth is related. For example, humans have about 98 percent of their DNA in common with chimpanzees. We humans have much less DNA in common with more distantly related animals such as the horse. But, there can be no doubt that the DNA evidence is consistent with the idea that all life on earth is related because of a common heritage with either one or at most a few common ancestors.

So, over a period of 100 years, more or less, the theory of natural selection met and overcame many challenges. It deposed its principal theoretical rival, the idea of the inheritance of acquired characteristics. A view of inheritance was proposed, Mendelian genetics, which allowed natural selection to operate in a feasible manner. The objection of the physicists that the earth was not old enough to support natural selection was overcome by the discovery that elements produce heat when decaying. The ornaments of some males, such as the large tail of the peacock, which seemed counterproductive in terms of natural selection, were shown to favor evolution via sexual selection. The peculiar reproductive behavior of the social insects, which seemed to violate natural selection, was later shown to be consistent with that theory by an emphasis on the unit of selection being the gene.

So successful has Darwin's theory of natural selection been that it is generally recognized among biologists to be the only scientific explanation of the evolution of life on earth. If any theory proves that Kuhn is wrong in suggesting that inference to the best explanation is not possible, it is Darwin's theory of evolution via natural selection. This is not to say that the theory of natural selection is a perfect theory. No doubt, it can be criticized along a number of dimensions. For example, many people feel that an inadequacy of the theory of evolution via natural selection is that it is more explanatory and less predictive than they would like. Criticisms of this sort are probably always possible in connection with any theory. Remember, though, what inference to the best explanation promises is to identify the best of available theories. It does not promise theoretical perfection. There can be little doubt at present that natural selection is the best scientific explanation of how species evolved.

Brain Function and Cognitive Neuroscience

Cognitive neuroscience is an area of research that currently is attracting much attention in psychology. It rests on the idea that different parts of the brain perform different functions. But, how the brain actually functions required more than a century of research (Gazzaniga, Ivry, & Mangun, 1998; Kosslyn & Andersen, 1992). The major issue, as understood historically, was whether the brain functions as a single, integrated whole (globalist view) or is a collection of distinct organs each responsible for a separate ability (localist view).

Localization of function was suggested by the phrenologists Franz Joseph Gall and J. G. Spurzheim in the early 1800s. They suggested that more developed abilities were carried out by larger areas of the brain, and these could be recognized by bumps on the skull. Their characterizations of the functions of different areas of the brain were based on rather arbitrary criteria, and the phrenologists are generally recognized as being non-scientific. Pierre Flourens (1794–1867) is generally recognized as the first scientist to argue against the localization view. Flourens removed various parts of the brains of birds, observing their behavior after recovery. He claimed that, regardless of the area of the brain removed from the birds, the same set of abilities was lost. Thus, Flourens concluded that the brain operates as an integrated whole, and that specific abilities are not localized in different sites. It is generally recognized today that Flourens's experimental techniques were crude.

Soon after, Fritsch and Hitzig (1870/1960) reported evidence in favor of localization of function. They discovered that when they shocked specific locations of the cerebral cortex in dogs, specific sets of muscles twitched. Broca (1863) and Wernicke (1874) provided clinical evidence that aspects of language were localized to different portions of the brain. They found that when specific areas of the brain were damaged, specific language functions were lost. Broca's patients, who had damage in one area, now called Broca's area, had difficulty comprehending language, whereas Wernicke's patients, who had damage are in another area, now called Wernicke's area, had difficulty producing language. A major advance occurred with John Hughlings Jackson, who suggested that complex brain processes are regulated by multiple brain areas. In effect, Jackson claimed that multiple areas of the brain are involved in carrying out functions such as perception and action.

With Santiago Ramón y Cajal, the neuroanatomy of the brain began to be better understood. Cajal's theory was that the brain is made up of individual elements called neurons. He also showed that nerve cells are unipolar, that is, electrical impulses are transmitted along them in only one direction. While many other advances were made in understanding localization of function, Lashley (1929) provided evidence, now considered to be unsatisfactory, for a globalist view. Lashley removed various parts of rats' brains and found that rats were more impaired in learning, the greater the amount of cortex removed, and this was reasonably independent of the site of removal. The first of these findings Lashley called mass action, and the second was labeled as equipotentiality. Lashley's findings were found to be atypical. Following Lashley, many important findings were reported supporting localization of function. Perhaps the greatest technological advance in the period following Lashley was the ability of brain scientists to record from a single neuron. Research using this new technology was able to show that different aspects of vision may be represented in multiple locations in various parts of the brain. One of the latest developments in technology, which has fueled the widespread interest in cognitive neuroscience, is brain imaging techniques such as functional Magnetic Resonance Imaging (fMRI) which can be used within intact organisms. This technology, and others that allow examination of the brain in intact humans while various tasks are being performed, enables us to understand which portions of the brain may be carrying out which sort of cognitive activity.

As in the case of evolution, brain science required about 150 years to reach its current level of sophistication. It is important to emphasize that the rise in cognitive neuroscience has profound effects on how we study and think about cognition and behavior. Although neurophysiological approaches to psychology have been part of the field since its earliest days, through the 1970s and 1980s, most of the experimental research on human cognition proceeded independently of it. For example, in Lachman et al.'s (1979) book which provided a detailed survey of research on cognitive psychology and human information processing, the only discussion of neurophysiology and its relation to cognition is one of sensory physiology in the last chapter of the book, on pattern recognition. Nowadays, a large amount of research is devoted to trying to map out the structures and pathways of the brain that are involved in various aspects of cognition, such as the executive functions that control attention and working memory. As one example, the 20th volume of the prestigious *Attention and Performance* symposium series is devoted exclusively to functional neuroimaging of visual cognition (Kanwisher & Duncan, 2004).

What both these evolutionary and cognitive neuroscience examples show is that progress in better understanding some particular branch of science occurs slowly, and in a non-linear fashion, as ideas, theories, and technologies develop. In addition, developments in both cognitive neuroscience and evolutionary science have given rise to new approaches in psychology that seem to have great promise. It should not be overlooked that there are critics of both evolutionary psychology (e.g., Gould & Lewontin, 1979) and cognitive neuroscience (e.g., Uttal, 2001). We may expect that these new areas of psychology will require many years of careful study before we will be able to evaluate their benefits fully.

Consilience

An important aspect of theory evaluation is to determine how well a theory fits with theories from other domains. This aspect of theorizing is often considered to involve *consilience*, an important idea first introduced by the great methodologist William Whewell. According to Whewell (1840), *"The Consilience of Inductions* takes place when an Induction, obtained from one class of facts, coincides with an Induction, obtained from another different class. This Consilience is a test of the truth of the Theory in which it occurs" (p. xxxix). In other words, consilience is said to occur when a theory explains at least two different classes of data. Darwin, who was a big fan of Whewell's, regarded his theory as a consilient one because of its ability to explain diverse biological phenomena. For example, it explained why there were no inversions in the fossil record, namely, that animals that evolved later did not precede those that evolved earlier in the fossil record, and why an ancestral species of birds, finches, gave rise to many different species on each of the islands of the Galapagos. Regarding Darwin's use of consilience, the philosopher of biology, **Michael Ruse**, has said:

> Charles Darwin's *On the Origin of Species* truly was a watershed event. He changed . . . the status of evolutionary thinking. This was because of two things. First, Darwin provided a full and convincing argument for the very fact of evolutionary change. He did this by appealing to a unificatory or consilient type of argument (which incidentally he had learned from the philosopher-scientist William Whewell [1840]). He showed that, if one assumes evolution, then one can explain facts right across the biological board. Why for instance, it is that the finches of the Galápagos are very similar, but slightly different, and then again similar but different from the finches of the South American mainland? Why, for instance, it is that if we look at the fossil record we see a branching tree, roughly progressive from the simpler forms very different from those alive today? Why, for instance, it is that embryos of organisms very different as adults are significantly alike at the embryonic level? Why, for instance, it is that we see the isomorphisms, or homologies, between the bodies of organisms [e.g., why the bat's wing is homologous to the human arm], even though the parts serve very different ends or functions? All of these questions, and many more, can be given a simple and straight answer if one assumes descent from common origins. Conversely, argued Darwin, descent from common origins is made probable – to the point of overwhelming likelihood – by the convergence of all of these different parts of biology. (2001, pp. 83–84)

Note, too, that Darwin's reasoning, as described by Ruse, can be said to involve **abduction**, as well as consilience.

E. O. Wilson (1999) has been an ardent advocate of bringing the sciences, including the natural science and social sciences, together in a unified manner. According to Wilson, "Consilience is the key to unification" (p. 8). For example, he recommended:

> A balanced perspective cannot be acquired by studying disciplines in pieces but through the pursuit of the consilience among them. Such unification will come hard. But I think it is inevitable. Intellectually it rings true, and it gratifies impulses that rise from the admirable side of human nature. To the extent that the gaps between the great branches of learning can be narrowed, diversity and depth of knowledge will increase. They will do so because of, not despite, the underlying coherence achieved. The enterprise is important for yet another reason: It gives ultimate purpose to intellect. It promises that order, not chaos, lies beyond the horizon. I think it inevitable that we will accept the adventure, go there, and find out. (p. 14)

Wilson (1999) makes clear that he is not talking only about the natural sciences:

> Given that human action comprises events of physical causation, why should the social sciences and humanities be impervious to consilience with the natural sciences? And how can they fail to benefit from that alliance? It is not enough to say that human action is historical, and that history is an unfolding of unique events. Nothing fundamental separates the course of human history from the course of physical history, whether in the stars or in organic diversity. (p. 11)

Wilson emphasizes that consilience is not yet established and can become so only with the development of new methodologies. That is, in agreement with the approach taken in this book, Wilson recommends a natural science approach to consilience. In this connection, he said, "The only way either to establish or to refute consilience is by methods developed in the natural sciences – not, I hasten to add, an effort led by scientists, or frozen mathematical abstraction, but rather one allegiant to the habits of thought that have worked so well in exploring the material universe" (p. 9).

As we see it, there are two related but different types of consilience. In one type, a variety of different facts are related within a given field of study, such as physics. In the other type of consilience, emphasized by Wilson (1999), facts are related in different areas of study such as neuroscience and cognition. With regard to the first type, Thagard (1988), who regards consilience as an important procedure for evaluating scientific theories, gives the following examples of consilient theories from physics:

> An outstanding one is Newton's mechanics, which afforded explanations of the motions of the planets and of their satellites, of the motions of comets, of the tides, and so on. But the general theory of relativity proved to be more consilient by explaining the perihelion of Mercury, the bending of light in a gravitational field, and the red shifts of spectral lines in an intense gravitational field. Quantum mechanics far exceeds any competitor in that it provides explanations of the spectral frequencies of certain atoms, of the phenomenon of magnetism, of the solid state of matter, and of various other perplexing phenomena, such as the photoelectric effect and the Compton effect [the shift in wavelength upon scattering of light from stationary electrons]. (p. 80)

As Thagard notes, "A consilient theory unifies and systematizes" (p. 80), that is, it is more than a theory of broad scope. It unifies the several classes of phenomena it explains under common theoretical principles.

Tooby and Cosmides (1992) provide many examples of the second type of consilience, without naming it as such. Indeed, they suggest that, of late, conceptual unification has been the rule. Their remarks are worth quoting at length.

> Disciplines such as astronomy, chemistry, physics, geology, and biology have developed a robust combination of logical coherence, causal description, explanatory power, and testability, and have become examples of how reliable and deeply satisfying human knowledge can become. Their extraordinary fluorescence throughout this century has resulted in far more than just individual progress within each field. These disciplines are becoming integrated into an increasingly seamless system of interconnected knowledge. . . . In fact, this development is only an acceleration of the process of conceptual unification that has been building in science since the Renaissance. For example, Galileo and Newton broke down the then rigid (and now forgotten) division between the celestial and the terrestrial – two domains that formerly had been considered metaphysically separate – showing that the same processes and principles apply to both. (p. 19)

They go on to suggest that many other gulfs were bridged. For example, Harvey found that structures of the body such as the heart operated according to mechanical principles. Darwin, by attributing similar emotions to humans and animals, broke down the barrier between psychology and biology. Tooby and Cosmides say,

> The rise of computers and, in their wake, modern cognitive science, completed the conceptual unification of the mental and physical worlds by showing how physical systems can embody information and meaning. The design and construction of artificial computational systems is only a few decades old, but already such systems can parallel in a modest way cognitive processes – such as reason, memory, knowledge, skill, judgment, choice, purpose, problem-solving, foresight, and language – that had supposedly made mind a metaphysical realm forever separated from the physical realm. (p. 20)

The point Tooby and Cosmides are making is worth emphasizing: The conceptual distance between psychology and science in general, physical as well as biological, has been reduced to the point of irrelevance in view of a variety of modern developments.

Chapter Summary

In this chapter, we discussed criteria such as simplicity, quantification, and the like that may be employed in evaluating a theory relative to its competitors. According to Kuhn (1962), there are a variety of problems associated with these criteria in terms of deciding that one theory is better than another. We strongly disagreed with this assessment, showing in connection with two important theoretical developments, the theory of evolution by natural selection and cognitive neuroscience, that given enough time and effort, it became possible to establish the reasonableness of its assumptions. We traced the origin of the idea of consilience, or unification of knowledge, from its inception with William Whewell to its recent development and advocacy by E. O. Wilson and Tooby and Cosmides. We distinguished between two types of consilience, that which occurs within an area such as physics and that which occurs within different scientific areas such as, for example, uniting psychology with biology. It was indicated that consilience in science has not been strongly tested, and, as with other ideas that have to be established within a naturalistic perspective, its establishment as a fundamental objective requires further investigation similar to that done in particular fields of science.

6

THE NEW MEANS OF UNDERSTANDING SCIENCE

Introduction

Prior to the 1960s, for the most part, attempts to understand how science should be practiced relied on logic and intuition. As indicated, this is known as the foundational approach. Subsequent to the 1960s, due primarily to the influence of Kuhn (1962), the realization grew increasingly that science could, and should, be evaluated by employing various empirical procedures mentioned initially in Chapter 1 (see Table 1.1). This approach is known as **naturalism**. The intention of this chapter is to describe and elucidate in greater detail how these procedures can be used to better understand, inform, improve, and modify scientific practice. In describing the methods, we provide specific examples of their use in concrete circumstances and discuss some of the conclusions about the practice of science that have been reached by using them.

In addition to applying naturalism to scientific methodology itself, it has become customary to apply naturalism to the study of scientists as well in an effort to isolate the characteristics of successful scientists. It may be possible to utilize such knowledge to train better scientists in the future. As regards investigations of psychological characteristics of scientists, Feist and Gorman (1998) have provided the following definition, which incidentally stresses the naturalistic approach:

> The psychology of science applies the empirical methods of psychological investigation to the study of scientific behavior. In other words, it is the empirical study of the cognitive, biological, developmental, personality, and social influences of those individuals who are involved in the enterprise of science or who are simulating scientific problem solving. In this sense, the psychology of science is primarily descriptive, describing actual behavior, rather than prescriptive (describing ideal behavior). (p. 3)

A fundamental question that arises in connection with the psychology of scientists, and other naturalistic inquiry, is whether such knowledge can contribute to a better understanding of how science is best practiced. Another way of putting the question is, does a better description of the actual practice of science and psychology of scientists provide us with keys to understanding science itself? In our opinion, the answer to this question is a definite yes. As we attempt to show in this chapter, a better understanding of how scientists practice their trade, and of their psychology as well, can lead to a better understanding of science.

In this chapter, we will first provide a brief refresher of the various empirical procedures, introduced in Chapter 1, that have been employed recently to better understand how science is practiced. Following that, we will then describe in detail some of the major findings that have resulted from each of these procedures. These findings are not only of interest in themselves, but they also suggest improved scientific procedures for investigating psychological and various other empirical questions.

Empirical Methods for Better Understanding Science, Scientific Practice, and Scientists

Psychology is in a prime position to contribute substantially to attempts to better understand science empirically. Consider that psychologists have developed a variety of methods for studying cognitive processes in nonscientists, both in the laboratory (in vitro) and in the field (in vivo). These methods can obviously be applied to the study of scientists themselves, as was illustrated in Table 1.1. Likewise, social psychologists have created a variety of methods for studying social processes in a variety of settings, and these methods, too, can be applied to scientists. Methods devised by developmental psychologists may be employed to study scientific reasoning in very young children, and thus to determine how scientific reasoning develops over the life span.

The major approaches to the study of science and scientists that can be distinguished (see, e.g., Feist & Gorman, 1998, and Klahr & Simon, 1999, 2001) are:

- *Providing historical accounts of scientific discoveries*
  Historical studies have been conducted examining groups of scientists coalescing around a **paradigm** or a particular scientist developing a given theory.

- *Personal reports using the products of eminent scientists to examine how they solved problems*
  Scientists often leave records that provide clues as to how they solved problems. Among the products of individual scientists that have been examined to evaluate how a scientist solved problems are notebooks that the scientist may have kept, the scientist's correspondence with other scientists, laboratory records, and the comments of peers.
- *Controlled experiments observing scientists and nonscientists working on tasks related to scientific discoveries*
  In this procedure, scientists and nonscientists are taken into the laboratory, and an attempt is made to determine whether their solution to a particular scientific problem mirrors the original solution, and to examine the processes by which they arrived at their solution.
- *Observing ongoing scientific laboratories*
  A knowledgeable observer gains entry into a scientific laboratory and takes notes on the activities and interactions that occur within the laboratory, for example, at weekly meetings.
- *Characteristics of scientists in general and of eminent scientists in particular*
  A questionnaire may be provided to distinguished scientists to get their opinion as to what characteristics of scientists lead to the production of creative science. Another source of information is specific writings of distinguished scientists on this topic. Also, a wide variety of variables may be correlated with the attitudes of scientists versus nonscientists and of eminent versus average scientists. For example, are younger scientists more apt to accept a new theory than older scientists?
- *Computational modeling of the scientific discovery process*
  Computer simulation models are developed that are intended to mimic the steps that a particular scientist took in developing a well-known and important theory.
- *Analyzing the heuristics used by scientists to solve problems*
  Heuristics are rules of thumb used in an attempt to convert a complicated problem into a simpler one. As **Giere** (1988) has indicated, scientists tend to deal with complicated problems that overload the conceptual system. Such problems, in order to be tractable, have to be reduced to simpler, more manageable proportions.

We will describe each of these methods in more detail, characterize their strengths and weaknesses, and provide examples of their use in the section that follows.

Historical accounts of scientific discoveries

General characteristics. Perhaps one of the more major approaches to understanding how science is practiced is to examine communities of scientists historically, attempting to determine what their values and methods were in the construction of scientific theory. Within the social sciences, the individual best known for employing this approach is Kuhn (1962). He examined several different scientific communities from the point of view of determining their scientific objectives and their relations to other movements in previous and subsequent eras. Kuhn insisted that evaluation of a scientific community should be conducted within the context of its own aims and objectives, rather than those currently held.

In Kuhn's (1962) hands, the historical method led to the development of a naturalistic approach to science that was very general and very popular, with both scientists and philosophers of science. More recently, Laudan (1996) has used the historical method to show that scientists from earlier eras had a conception of science that was both similar to ours in some respects and different in others. An inference from Laudan's work is that our understanding of science, and how science is conducted, is a work in progress.

One strength of the historical method is that it is relevant to better understanding some of the major issues and events in science, as, for example, what scientists of various eras considered to be of importance in evaluating a theory. Another is the availability of a huge written record that in the case of some prominent scientists (e.g., Newton) provides a rather detailed and elaborate depiction of their thought processes in relation to specific scientific problems. Finally, because some scientific changes occur only over centuries, for example, the acceptance of atomism, and others occur over decades, for example, the acceptance of plate tectonics (see Chapters 1 and 4), these matters and their causes can only be known by examination of the historical record.

A weakness of the historical approach to science, as well as of an historical approach to anything else, is that multiple interpretations of the evidence are often possible. A common way of stating this limitation is that "there are no control groups" in history. Therefore, relying on historical data alone may not be sufficient to rule competing causal hypotheses in or out. Thus, historical data need to be supplemented with data of other types. This, of course, is typical of application of the empirical approach to other problems.

Donovan, Laudan, and Laudan's methodological approach. A volume edited by Donovan, Laudan, and Laudan (1992) contains a number of historical analyses of particular scientific communities and movements. In conducting historical analyses of science, there are a number of ways to go about it. Donovan et al. proposed a particular methodological approach that, though it may not be the only effective approach, strikes us as being a particularly good one. First, they suggested that they would select for examination particular claims of a given approach to science, for example, Popper's **falsificationism**. By selecting particular claims, what is meant is that they would not attempt to test an approach as a whole but rather to test its specific implications. The specific claims were derived from a variety of different approaches to science and treated as competing hypotheses. Donovan et al. then instructed the specialists who examined a given historical movement to gather evidence for or against the particular claims or hypotheses being tested.

Two examples of opposing hypotheses that were evaluated are as follows:

- Evaluate the following claims, that scientists convert from one paradigm to another all at once and rapidly, or that scientists modify their views gradually in a piecemeal fashion.
- Evaluate the propositions that scientists generally ignore anomalies that challenge their theories, or that they attempt to resolve these anomalies as they arise.

As we discuss later, the experts who examined particular historical periods, events, or prominent scientists were able in many instances to conclude in favor of one or the other hypothesis. In other instances, not surprisingly, the evidence regarding particular hypotheses was not conclusive. For example, Donovan et al. put forward the hypothesis that disconfirmations of a theory would tend to be recognized as such only after some other theory explained them. As they indicate, good evidence either for or against this hypothesis could not be obtained on the basis of the historical examinations reported in their book.

Additional instructions were given to the experts conducting the historical analyses to evaluate the hypotheses with respect to an outstanding achievement associated with either the specific historical period or a prominent scientist. One category into which the hypotheses were organized was the guiding assumptions employed in regulating acceptability of a theory. For example, "To what extent was the empirical accuracy of a theory a deciding factor in its acceptance?" Another category was to determine how the guiding assumptions of the theorist were affected when an anomaly, or disconfirmation, occurred. For example, "Did the scientist blame his own skills, or did he blame the inadequacy of his particular theory?" A third category was the role of innovation in acceptance of the guiding assumptions. For example, "Did scientists introduce new assumptions into their theory only when the old ones proved to be inadequate for one reason or another, or was this done prior to rejection of the original theory?" The final category concerned the effect of revolutions on the guiding assumptions. For example, "Do younger scientists accept a new paradigm more rapidly and readily than do the older scientists?"

Specific historical analyses. Finocchiaro's (1992) chapter provides a good example of how these various guiding assumptions were evaluated empirically. He was concerned with determining what aspects of Copernicus's heliocentric theory, that the earth revolves around the sun, convinced Galileo of its validity. In appraising Galileo's attitudes toward Copernicus's theory, Finocchiaro examined a collection of Galileo's writings that spanned his career, letters written by Galileo to other scientists, and secondary literature on Galileo. He partitioned Galileo's career into three periods:

1. The period of tentative pursuit, prior to 1609, in which Galileo was in the initial phases of making up his mind about the heliocentric theory.
2. The period from 1609 to 1616, which was one of full-fledged pursuit of establishing the heliocentric theory. Galileo's use of the telescope in this period was very instrumental in providing useful information that allowed him to embrace Copernicus's views.
3. The period after 1616, in which Galileo fell into conflict with the Catholic church.

In examining Galileo's work, Finocchiaro (1992) determined whether the evolution of Galileo's evaluation of the Copernican theory occurred on the basis of "empirical accuracy, general problem-solving success, predictive novelty, external problem-solving success, explanatory coherence, or simplicity" (p. 65). According to Finocchiaro, during the first period, Galileo evaluated the theory on the basis of its general and external problem-solving success in the physics of motion and in its explanatory coherence in astronomy. During the second stage, Galileo's judgments were based largely on the aforementioned criteria plus empirical accuracy. Importantly, Finocchiaro concludes, "At no time did he judge its acceptability largely on the basis of predictive novelty or of simplicity" (p. 65). So, it is clear, according to Finocchiaro, that Galileo regarded explanatory capacity as important for evaluating a theory. This is consistent with what we described in the previous chapter, with respect to plate tectonics, that accepting theories on the basis of their explanatory capacity and not only on their predictive capacity is an approach sometimes taken in science. In any event, Finocchiaro rejects the idea that Galileo's ideas about Copernicus's theory changed rapidly and totally. Rather, he says, "My evidence from Galileo's Copernicanism shows that this is not so, but rather his attitude toward it changed slowly, gradually and in a piecemeal fashion" (p. 65). Finocchiaro considers this finding to be a very important one.

Having seen how Finocchiaro used the historical approach in connection with Galileo, we are in a position to examine a number of other important conclusions about other movements in science reached by a variety of other specialists using procedures similar to those of Finocchiaro. Other authors' conclusions were consistent with Finocchiaro's analysis of Galileo's scientific approach, namely that he tended to rely on the explanatory capacity of Copernicanism. For example, Hofmann's (1992) study of Ampère's electrodynamics during the late 1800s convinced him that Ampère stressed the greater explanatory scope of his theory over that of his principle rival, Biot, and was not concerned with differential ability of the two views to make novel predictions. Likewise, Zandvoort (1992), who was concerned with the reception received by nuclear magnetic resonance after World War II, suggested that explanatory capacity of the theory was of most concern in evaluating it, with novel predictions being a secondary concern. Although the capacity of theories to make novel predictions is certainly important, it appears from these case studies that the explanatory capacity of a theory, at least in some instances, may play a bigger role in its acceptance than most scientists realize.

What does a scientist do, or what should the scientist do, when an apparent disconfirmation of his or her theory presents itself? According to one point of view, espoused by Popper, the scientist should immediately reject the theory and search for an alternative. According to another point of view, suggested by Kuhn, scientists ignore the apparent disconfirmation until such time as, for one reason or another, a crisis arises and the scientist is committed to rejecting the current paradigm. At the moment of crisis, according to Kuhn, the scientist must either resolve the discrepancy between theory and data or reject the paradigm. But, according to Baigrie (1992), who studied Newton's response to disconfirming data in some detail, neither of the positions outlined above characterizes how scientists seek to resolve disconfirmations. Rather, according to Baigrie, the scientist responds to anomalies as they arise without necessarily rejecting his or her theory and continues to keep the anomalies in mind while proceeding with its development.

Bechtel (1992), who examined early 20th-century biochemistry, came to the same conclusion as Baigrie. Bechtel suggested that scientists do not ignore anomalies or dismiss them as trivial. On the contrary, they seek to resolve them as they continue with their normal research activities.

Perrin (1992) evaluated the development of Lavoisier's oxygen theory, and came to a number of conclusions inconsistent with Kuhn's (1962) analysis of how science progresses. Contrary to Kuhn, according to Perrin, Lavoisier's ideas emerged slowly and gradually over a long period of time, much as Finocchiaro concluded was the case with Galileo's acceptance of Copernicanism. This analysis is consistent with that provided in the previous chapter relative to evolution and cognitive neuroscience. Too, this analysis is inconsistent with Kuhn's claim that new paradigms emerge suddenly and completely, over a short period of time. Contrary to Kuhn's claim that a new paradigm is accepted quickly by the relevant scientific community, Perrin shows that some chemists accepted the new oxygen view quickly, others slowly, and still others not at all. An influential view, suggested by Kuhn, is that scientists who work in different paradigms have great difficulty understanding each other, a problem you may remember that Kuhn called **incommensurability**. Perrin, who examined extensive discussions between Phlogistonists and oxygen theorists, found that they were perfectly able to understand each other and exhibited no signs of the incommensurability assumed by Kuhn. Mauskopf (1992), who was concerned with acceptance of Haüy's views on crystallography in the early 19th century, agrees with Perrin's conclusions concerning Kuhn. Briefly, not all scientists accept new theories when they initially appear, and some may hold out for decades while still being regarded as legitimate scientists.

Nicholas (1992) examined certain predictions of quantum theory to evaluate Kuhn's claim that a crisis precedes the rejection of the old paradigm and introduction of a new paradigm. He found no evidence for this view. Instead, he discovered that a variety of new assumptions at variance with the current paradigm were introduced prior to the rejection of the paradigm, and, indeed, the entertaining of new assumptions may be a pre-condition for rejection of the current paradigm. In effect, Nicholas is suggesting that Kuhn's analysis reversed the process that actually occurs when paradigms are replaced. That is to say, important elements of the new paradigm are introduced prior to, rather than after, rejection of the old paradigm.

A very important decision that scientists have to make is when to accept a new theory. A variety of historical research has isolated three conditions that particularly impress scientists in evaluating theories. It appears that scientists are more likely to accept theories that can take formerly disconfirming evidence and turn it into confirming instances of a theory. Another circumstance under which scientists are apt to be particularly impressed is when theories solve problems they were not explicitly invented or designed to solve. It appears that scientists are especially impressed by confirming instances of a theory that were to a greater or lesser degree unexpected. Moreover, if a theory is successful in solving problems, scientists will be inclined to accept it even if they have misgivings about it in several respects. For example, Rocke (1992) notes that Kekulé's theory of benzene was provisionally accepted by him and other chemists, despite obvious limitations and theoretical difficulties, because of its ability to solve chemical problems. Rocke noted, "The remarkable thing is that this contrast between the striking success and popularity of the theory on the one hand, and the seemingly insoluble problems of detail on the other, seemed not at all to disconcert the leading theoreticians" (p. 155).

The reader will undoubtedly have noticed that some of the conclusions reached by a variety of individuals on the basis of their historical analyses are in agreement with prior conclusions reached by Kuhn (1962), who may be considered to be the originator of the historical approach to science, whereas others are not. As an example of agreement, Kuhn suggested, contrary to the then prevailing view held by Popper and the logical positivists, that scientists would accept theories that did not solve all the problems solved by the predecessor theories plus additional ones. That scientists do not require that a new theory solve all the problems of its predecessor was noted by several of the contributors to the Donovan et al. (1992) volume. As one example of disagreement with Kuhn, whereas he concluded that new paradigms are quickly accepted by a great majority of the relevant scientific community, others have suggested on the basis of their historical analyses that new paradigms are developed slowly and are not always accepted by all members of the relevant scientific community, some holding out indefinitely. What should we think of these discrepancies? The key point to remember is that the study of science, either historically or by some other method, is an empirical endeavor. Like any other empirical endeavor, whether in psychology, economics, or physics, statements that may be accepted as facts at a particular time may later be disputed and, indeed, discarded in favor of alternative statements. When this happens in physics or some other science, no one is in the least bit surprised. Indeed, it is expected. On this basis, we should expect that the same will occur when examining science as an empirical endeavor. Disagreements of this sort should not only be expected, but they provide the opportunity for further study and analysis that should lead to a more accurate understanding of the nature of science. This is consistent with the spirit of naturalism.

Consider two areas in which historical studies of science have provided a much more accurate and precise description of how scientists practice their profession. For example, it is not unusual in contemporary accounts of science to stress that the basis of theory acceptance is prediction of new phenomena. We certainly agree that prediction occupies a prominent place in science. However, it is not the exclusive criterion for the acceptance of new theories. As we have seen, historical analysis reveals that many important theories were accepted on the basis of their explanatory ability, in addition to, or rather than, on the basis of their predictive ability. To take a second example, there seem to be two suggestions concerning how scientists do or should deal with disconfirming data. According to a widely accepted suggestion in textbooks and in Popper's philosophy, disconfirmations of a theory should lead to rapid, if not immediate, rejection of the theory. A second view, suggested by Kuhn, is that when scientists encounter a disconfirmation of their theory, they put it on the back burner, so to speak, ignoring disconfirmations until matters deteriorate such that a crisis occurs. Only at that point do scientists begin to worry about disconfirmations. Historical analysis, as we have seen, is relatively consistent in presenting a picture different from either of the two mentioned above. That is, rather than paying total attention to disconfirmations, or ignoring them entirely, what scientists appear to do is to keep working with their theory, with the disconfirming instances always of concern, but in the background of their minds. Over time, developments may suggest either that the disconfirmation is real, and thus that the theory should be modified in some fashion, or that the discrepancy with the theory is not a real one and thus that the apparent disconfirmation can be ignored.

Examination of the products of individual scientists

General characteristics. The conventional method of evaluating a scientist's approach to problems is, of course, to look at the various works of the scientist, such as journal articles and books. But as important as these scientific works are, there are other important avenues to exploring the methods and procedures of a particular scientist. These less conventional avenues are attracting increasing attention. They include diaries kept by the scientist that describe the day-to-day workings and thoughts of the scientist, autobiographies written by eminent scientists, laboratory notebooks that include notes about research and the generation of research ideas, correspondence with other scientists, interviews with scientists, and any other similar records. The emphasis is primarily with the problem-solving procedures employed by some outstanding scientist, rather than with the historical record as such.

The conclusions reached from studies of these products have high face validity because the products themselves are more or less directly related to particular scientific discoveries or ideas. It is also possible in some instances to infer from these products the social and motivational factors that were at work at the time of the discovery. A weakness of such products is that the scientist in recording observations may not recall them correctly.

Tweney's description of Faraday's hypothesis testing strategy. A good example of this approach is that of Ryan Tweney (1989, 1991), a psychologist, who examined of the notebooks of the eminent physicist **Michael Faraday**. Tweney constructed a detailed analysis of Michael Faraday's scientific problem-solving strategy. Tweney concluded that Faraday, certainly an eminent and successful scientist, followed a confirm-early and disconfirm-late heuristic. According to Tweney, who extensively examined Faraday's notebooks:

> When Faraday was working with a vague hypothesis that had not yet had a chance to be supported by much evidence, he was quite willing to ignore disconfirming evidence until later. Toward the end of a series, he paid much closer attention to disconfirming results, trying hard to find out why his earlier attempts failed, and considering serious ways to test and rule out alternative explanations. This appears to represent a consciously chosen strategy on Faraday's part. (1989, p. 355)

Tweney describes Faraday's conscious efforts here as employing a heuristic approach to the problem of **induction**, with a confirmation heuristic used early in **hypothesis testing** and a disconfirmation heuristic used later in hypothesis testing.

Essentially, Faraday argued for a procedure, which he often employed, namely, in one's first attempts to evaluate a hypothesis the optimal strategy is to attempt to confirm the hypothesis. The reason for this is fairly evident. In the early stages, when a hypothesis has not been particularly developed and is not incorporated into a network of other propositions, it is relatively easy to disconfirm, and such disconfirmation is not particularly enlightening. However, according to Faraday, once the hypothesis has matured, so to speak, it becomes appropriate to evaluate it by allowing attempts to disconfirm it. A good hypothesis should pass such tests. The strategy that Faraday recommends here seems vastly superior to that recommended by Popper, which is always to attempt to falsify one's hypotheses. If Faraday is correct, and we think he is, if we followed Popper's strategy, no new hypothesis would ever see the light of day because it would be falsified at birth.

Use of analogy in science. A variety of evidence indicates that employing analogy is very useful in solving scientific problems, with one line of evidence coming from historical analysis of the products of individual scientists. For example, when Rutherford attempted to understand the atom, as noted, he analogized it to the more familiar solar system. This use of analogy allowed Rutherford to apply what was known about the solar system to think more successfully about atoms. More generally, when a scientist employs an analogy, what she attempts to do is to employ relations in connection with a familiar problem (the base, or source) so as to better illuminate relations in a less familiar problem (the target), one that the scientist is attempting to understand. It would be helpful to the student to understand how scientists use analogy, given that it has been successfully employed by any number of scientists.

It is one thing to know what the characteristics of good analogies might be, and another thing to know how to go about creating good analogies. Holland, Holyoak, Nisbett, and Thagard (1986) have described several steps to be followed in forming good analogies:

- Construct mental representations of the base and target.
- Detect similarities between the two, and select the base as a potentially relevant analog.
- Map correspondences between elements of the problem, that is, determine which elements play similar roles in the base and target.
- Generate rules that can be applied to solve the target problem.

Rutherford followed steps similar to those described above in analogizing atoms to the solar system. According to Gentner and Jeziorski (1989), Rutherford:

- Set up a correspondence between two domains, the sun-nucleus on the one hand, and the planet-electron on the other.
- Mapped relations from the base to the target. For example, the sun is more massive than the planet was transposed to the nucleus is more massive than the electron.
- Sought relations that occur in the solar system and also in the atom. Most notably, the earth is not only less massive than the sun but also revolves around it, so too the electron is less massive than the nucleus and revolves around it.
- Disregarded irrelevant attributes (i.e., the sun is yellow) and isolated relations (such as that the sun is hotter than the planets).

Gentner and Jeziorski (1989) noted that these are examples of implicit rules that scientists use to form useful analogies. Some things they suggest should be done when attempting to come up with good analogies are:

- Avoid mixed analogies.
- Remember that analogy is not causation.
- Avoid using unnecessary relations, as, for example, noting that the solar system is made up of atoms.

Scientists and nonscientists working on tasks related to scientific discoveries

General characteristics. Problem solving and decision making have been studied extensively under controlled laboratory conditions. These methods may be employed, for example, to study either how laymen solve actual scientific problems or how scientists solve contrived laboratory problems. Laboratory studies of scientific reasoning are typically carried out under controlled conditions using standard experimental designs. Problems used have included discovery of the unknown function of a programmable device (Klahr & Dunbar, 1988), the discovery of arbitrary rules and concepts (Wason, 1960), and the simplification of real scientific discoveries.

Some of the advantages of laboratory studies are that they can be conducted in a minimal amount of time and yield fine-grained data regarding the problem-solving process. Disadvantages include the arbitrary nature of the task, the limited time available to solve them, and the restricted interactions of the problem solvers with other persons and materials. Additionally, because it is much easier to conduct laboratory experiments on lay people, there are relatively few studies employing experienced scientists.

Investigation of expertise in scientific reasoning. Two studies have compared scientific reasoning of persons with various amounts of competence in psychology, ranging from undergraduate students, to graduate students in psychology, to experienced psychologists in areas other than the content domain under study, to experts in that domain. One study, that of Shraagen (1993), presented a problem in sensory psychology, and the other, that of Schunn and Anderson (1999), a problem in memory. Shraagen asked participants to design a study to determine the taste people experience drinking Coca Cola as compared to drinking Pepsi Cola and an off-brand cola. Schunn and Anderson asked participants to design experiments in an attempt to test between two theoretical explanations of the spacing effect that were provided to the participant. The spacing effect is the phenomenon that spaced repetition of to-be-remembered items leads to better memory performance than massed repetition (see Kitao, 2002, for a review). In both studies, domain experts performed better than the other groups of participants, with the psychologists experienced in other domains of psychological research performing next best and considerably better than the students. In Schunn and Anderson's study, participants used a variety of heuristics to solve the problem, but the heuristics employed varied considerably across the different groups of participants in a manner to be described shortly. Before describing these, it will be helpful to have a clear idea both of heuristics and how they are employed in science.

As indicated, heuristics are rules of thumb that may simplify a complex problem and lead to an acceptable solution. For example, when asked to judge which of two cities has the larger population, people rely on a heuristic that is called availability (Tversky & Kahneman, 1974). That is, they will judge the population to be larger for the city for which they are able to retrieve easily the most instances of teams, events, organizations, and people associated with that city. In many instances, this heuristic will often lead to the correct answer (e.g., that Cincinatti, Ohio, is larger than Flint, Michigan, because Cincinatti has major league baseball and football teams), but not always (e.g., that Green Bay, Wisconsin, is larger than Newark, New Jersey, because Green Bay has a well-known major league football team).

Not only people in general, but scientists, in the evaluation of theory, may use a number of different heuristics. A major heuristic suggested by Ronald Giere (1988) to be useful in science is that of **satisficing**, mentioned in Chapter 3. The original impetus for devising satisficing was consideration of the behavior of ideally rational agents such as those in classical economics. An agent of this sort is rational in two different respects: The agent knows the options open to it, and it is able to calculate the expected utility (the consequences available for a course of action) for each option. The agent acts to maximize expected utility. Simon noted that such an ideal is not achievable by humans because of limitations in their ability to process information. For example, humans cannot calculate the expected utility for each possible outcome because this requires both more information and more processing capacity than is available. Under these conditions, lacking a perfect solution, people become satisficers. In satisficing, people distinguish between more and less satisfactory outcomes. In doing so, the behavior of the scientist is directed toward attaining

109

Table 6.1 General and domain-specific design heuristics examined by
Schunn and Anderson (1999)

General	Design experiments to test the given theories
	Keep experiments simple
	Keep general settings constant across experiments
Specific	Avoiding floor and ceiling effects
	Knowledge of variables likely to interact
	Choose variable volumes useful in the given domain

particular achievable goals. The major goal of satisficing, it should be noted, is to select from available possibilities that outcome or model that best satisfies the scientist's aim. Rationality, according to this approach, is evaluated in terms of how effective a particular behavior is in attaining the goals sought by the agent. Having produced a workable model of some phenomenon on the basis of satisficing, the scientist would then go on to subject the model to further scrutiny.

Returning to Schunn and Anderson's (1999) study, they identified a number of heuristics employed by their participants, some specific to the domain of human memory and some general in the sense that they could be applied to any domain of psychological research. Heuristics employed by the participants in the effort to design experiments to evaluate the spacing effect are shown in Table 6.1. The general heuristics were used equally effectively by both the memory experts and the psychologists who worked in another domain. The general heuristics were used much less effectively by the undergraduate students, regardless of whether they were of high or low ability. The specific heuristics were used effectively by the memory researchers and less effectively by the other participants. Interestingly, the psychologists for whom memory was not their domain of expertise were no better at using the specific heuristics than were the undergraduate students.

It will be helpful to examine the specific manner in which these heuristics were employed. Let us consider the general heuristics first. In devising experiments, both expert groups employed the theories provided by the experimenters, something the undergraduates failed to do. Another characteristic of the experts that differentiated them from the students was that the former kept their experimental designs simple and straightforward, whereas the latter did not. Also, in designing experiments, the psychologists were aware of the need to keep conditions constant across experiments, whereas the students were not.

With regard to the specific heuristics, from their experience of conducting memory research, the memory researchers, but not the other participants, avoided floor and ceiling effects in choosing variables. Such effects refer to performance being extremely high or extremely low, thereby precluding the opportunity for differences between conditions to manifest themselves. Knowledge of memory research also allowed the experts to select variables that would be likely to have interactive effects, which would help distinguish between the alternative theories. In particular, the memory experts but not the others varied the type of memory test (as, for example, recall of items versus recognition of items), in addition to simply manipulating variables designed to influence memory for items (as, for example, meaningfulness of items). The memory experts, but not the other participants, tended to isolate and identify ranges of the variables that would be more likely to influence the spacing effect.

One of the most provocative findings from Schunn and Anderson's (1999) experiment was the inability of undergraduates to distinguish between data and theory. This finding suggests that the ability to distinguish between data and theory is acquired through experience with scientific problem solving. Schunn and Anderson noted a failing of the undergraduates related to the inability to make the distinction between data and theory. They said, "That the undergraduates frequently relied exclusively on non-empirical justifications (i.e., personal beliefs) to support their conclusions suggests that these undergraduates have basic misconceptions about the role of evidence in scientific activity" (p. 368). The ability to distinguish between theory and observation is a skill that is fundamental and basic to the effective conduct of science. It is impossible to imagine anyone doing acceptable science in the absence of this ability. The ability to distinguish between theory and observation is one that can be acquired in general but is honed further as a consequence of experience dealing with problems in one's particular area of study.

Direct observation of ongoing scientific laboratories

General characteristics. In many branches of science, problems are solved and hypotheses generated within the context of group laboratory meetings in which issues are discussed in an effort to produce new hypotheses, reconcile old hypotheses with new findings, and so on. These laboratory meetings may provide rich insights into how scientists go about solving problems. To conduct an investigation of this type requires intimate familiarity of the subject matter of the particular scientific group being observed. The observer who employs this method might attend weekly lab meetings in which problems are discussed. At that time, the observer would record data that would later have to be coded and interpreted. The observational period may extend over a period of months or years.

Dunbar's investigations of scientific procedures employed in various laboratories. A prominent example of this procedure is Dunbar's (1997) investigations of molecular biology laboratories. Dunbar selected laboratories in molecular biology to study the behavior of scientists because molecular biology is a field that is going through rapid discovery and breakthrough. He identified leading laboratories in the United States. "My goal was to investigate the thinking and reasoning strategies that leading scientists use while conducting their research" (p. 463). More specifically, "The goal of this research was to identify the points in time at which innovative scientific thinking occurs, capture this thinking on audio- and videotape, and then analyze the processes involved in the scientists' thinking and reasoning" (p. 464). Dunbar selected four molecular biology laboratories for this purpose. The characteristics of the four laboratories were as follows: Laboratory A was run by a senior scientist with over 300 publications and numerous awards. His laboratory consisted of 22 postdocs, five graduate students, and four technicians. Laboratory B was run by a less senior, but highly accomplished scientist. He had three postdocs, five graduate students, and one technician working for him. Laboratory C was run by an associate professor who had made several important discoveries. His lab had four postdocs, two graduate students, and one technician. Laboratory D was run by an assistant professor who was nevertheless famous. His lab had four postdocs, six graduate students, and two technicians.

Dunbar's activities included becoming familiar with the scientists involved in the laboratory, staying in the lab during the day, attending lab meetings, interviewing the scientists in the lab, and reading grant proposals and drafts of papers. Dunbar states, "I discovered that the laboratory meeting is one of the central places in which new ideas and concepts are generated" (p. 464).

Dunbar found that the scientists developed much of their thinking through interactions with other scientists in the lab. He concluded that the lab meetings were the core source of data, and that interviews and papers were supplementary sources of information. An important finding was that scientists employ analogy in the discovery process. The analogies tend to be near analogies (i.e., using concepts from the same domain) rather than far analogies (i.e., using concepts from different domains). The majority of analogies are used to come up with explanations. Another use of analogies is to form hypotheses. He found that scientists tend not to have a **confirmation bias**. That is, they do not have a tendency to look for confirming instances of a hypothesis, ignoring counter-instances (see the discussion of this topic in Chapter 4). Instead of ignoring an unexpected finding (as distinct from a disconfirming one), when one was obtained it attracted a lot of attention and consideration. Another finding of Dunbar's was that the scientists used distributed reasoning. What this means is that they discussed issues and problems with each other, and by some means of agreement arrived at solutions. An interesting finding here was that the scientists had very little memory of what they or others might have said during the meetings that contributed to the final solution. This finding may have implications for how to interpret the recollections of scientists in recounting discoveries they may have made.

An interesting series of findings from Dunbar's observation of scientists in the laboratory concerns how unexpected findings are treated. Dunbar and Fugelsang (2005) found that the molecular biologists encountered unexpected findings frequently. Actually, about half of the findings they obtained were unexpected. The first reaction of the scientists to deal with the unexpected findings was to suggest that they might have resulted from some aspect of the method employed. However, after repeatedly obtaining the unexpected under a variety of different conditions, the scientists abandoned the methodological interpretation in favor of another. Under these circumstances the scientists attempted to generalize over the various findings obtained in an effort to develop a new hypothesis capable of explaining all of the data. At this point, the various members of the group advanced suggestions as to how to improve the model, with the plausibility of the different proposed hypotheses being evaluated. A characteristic of scientists is that they anticipate that negative findings will occur and have strategies to deal with them. One of the principal strategies is to anticipate the unexpected in the actual original design of the experiments. A key ingredient for isolating the unexpected is the expertise of the scientist involved. What is an unexpected finding to the expert scientist may not be recognized as such by the novice.

The question could be asked, "Are Dunbar's findings in connection with molecular biologists applicable to research psychologists?" This issue is one of **external validity**, the degree to which findings obtained in one area or setting can be generalized to others (see Chapter 10). Questions of external validity apply not only to Dunbar's particular findings but to any empirical finding. In any given instance, there is no way of knowing how generalizable the findings will prove to be, that is, how much external validity they possess. Although our conclusions concerning the external validity of Dunbar's findings must remain tentative, there is reason to believe that they are applicable to psychologists, particularly those who work in laboratory settings in groups and engage in similar experimental activities. In those cases, in particular, it is expected that psychologists, like the molecular biologists, would generate many useful ideas in the course of the laboratory meeting. Too, there is every reason to expect that psychologists, like molecular biologists, would come to understand their findings better by employing analogies, particularly near analogies. Consistent with this expectation, as indicated in Chapter 4, the use of analogy is widespread in psychology. It may also be strongly suspected that psychologists in laboratory meetings would tend to expend considerable energy in an effort to understand unexpected findings and, indeed, to design future experiments with an eye toward detecting and explaining such findings. One outcome of Dunbar's studies most certainly applies to psychologists and scientists in general: The tendency to isolate and identify unexpected findings increased along with the experience of the investigator. This outcome strongly argues for the value of intense, on-the-job training of young investigators in the specific procedures of their particular discipline.

Characteristics of scientists in general and of eminent scientists in particular

We now turn to research that is concerned with the characteristics of scientists. This research also compares scientists to nonscientists, and eminent scientists to less eminent scientists. The goal of this research is to determine what characteristics of scientists lead to progress in science. This has important implications for the training of scientists and also for determining how science is practiced.

General characteristics. One source of information about the characteristics of successful scientists is provided by distinguished scientists themselves. A few eminent scientists have written on the topic of how to be a successful scientist (e.g., Ramón y Cajal, 1897/1999; Watson, 2000). Another approach is to provide a group of distinguished scientists with a questionnaire to elicit their opinions as to what characteristics of scientists lead to the production of creative science.

A slightly different method for determining the characteristics of successful psychologists is to perform correlational analyses. For any subject groups that differ along various dimensions, as scientists do, correlational analyses can provide useful information as to which of the characteristics are most relevant. For example, scientists differ along dimensions such as age, gender, the thought processes they may employ, where they were educated, and so on. Knowing the correlation between some of these variables and successful scientific practice can provide insights as to how science itself should be practiced. For example, knowing that successful scientists employ reasoning processes that are not so regularly employed by unsuccessful scientists or nonscientists provides useful information to the student of science as to how science may be profitably practiced.

The weakness of any correlational method is that the correlation found between two variables may be due to some other variable. Thus, when working with correlational data, one must be cautious about inferring causality. In other words, just because successful scientists use certain reasoning processes does not necessarily mean that those processes are responsible for their success or that they will work effectively for other people. Of course, these matters can be determined by separate empirical investigations. The strength of the correlational method is that it can provide insights into certain matters such as the successful problem-solving strategies of outstanding scientists that cannot be gained with other methods. Despite the fact that correlation is not causation, under some circumstances additional information may serve to indicate that a particular causal interpretation of the correlation is warranted.

Characteristics of scientists. Thagard (2005) used two methods, the questionnaire method and that of reading the works of scientists on how to be a successful scientist, to arrive at a list of habits of successful scientists. The most important of these, in our view, are as follows:

- Develop a passion for your research.
- In attacking a problem, do not be easily deflected by failure; be intelligently persistent.
- Be open minded, read widely, and be involved in multiple projects.
- Select significant problems that seem to be solvable but to also have a high payoff.
- Attack problems using multiple methods.
- Do not be afraid to use other people as resources. This could vary from asking their opinions on particular matters to collaborating with them.

Comparing scientists to novices, still another successful strategy of scientists can be discerned. As noted earlier, scientists are better at evaluating theories than nonscientific adults because they have a greater

115

tendency to distinguish between the theory being evaluated and the evidence pertaining to the theory. Failure to make this distinction produces confusion and thus interferes with successful scientific reasoning. Similar findings have been obtained for children (D. Kuhn, 1989). When faced with evidence that disconfirms their hypothesis, children often distort the evidence, make selective use of it, or adjust the theory to fit the evidence. This is in sharp contrast to adult scientists who, as indicated, make a clear distinction between theory and evidence. The implication of the evidence gathered on children and young adults is that people need formal training in order to learn to think in scientifically constructive ways.

That formal training in science is important is suggested by the general finding that students who work with eminent scientists have a greater chance of making important contributions and becoming eminent themselves (Simonton, 1992). This effect appears to manifest itself at all levels of education. For example, having a strong mentor in high school and as an undergraduate in college is predictive of continuing in a scientific career. Going up higher, it has been found that scientists who train with Nobel laureates have a greater chance of becoming Nobel laureates themselves and are more productive scientifically by almost any measure than are other scientists (Zuckerman, 1977). As with any correlational studies, the causal effect could be in either direction, or even to a third variable. Applied to this particular case, it is possible either that students become better by working with more eminent scientists or that more eminent scientists attract more promising students, or both. Zuckerman in fact suggests that the causal influence probably goes in both directions.

Computational modeling of scientific discovery processes

Another approach to understanding how scientists think about and solve problems is to use computational modeling. A computational model is a computer simulation that, in this case, is intended to duplicate solution of a historical scientific problem. For example, Kulkarni and Simon (1988) created a simulation called KEKADA that duplicated Hans Krebs's discovery of the ornithine cycle. This cycle is a series of chemical reactions in living cells in humans and other higher animals involving the oxidative metabolism of pyruvic acid and release of energy. Kulkarni and Simon traced in detail the series of experiments Krebs and co-workers carried out between July, 1931, and April, 1932, the specific experimental strategies, and how their theory of urea synthesis emerged gradually. In constructing KEKADA, Kulkarni and Simon employed historical data from a number of sources: The recollections of Krebs concerning his discoveries, the accounts of those discoveries from published papers, and the diaries and laboratory notes generated in the course of discovery. There are certain limitations of these data. For example, human memory is fallible and unreliable, and is best considered a reconstruction of prior events (e.g., Neath & Surprenant, 2003). Thus, Krebs's recollections must be evaluated with a considerable degree of caution. Technical papers describe the discovery that was made, but rarely describe the thought processes of the scientist who made it. Laboratory notebooks have the advantages of recounting the ongoing process of discovery, before the conclusion becomes apparent. Consequently, Kulkarni and Simon relied extensively on the notebooks.

In constructing KEKADA, Kulkarni and Simon (1988) note that the system does not capture all of the details of the actual discovery process, "but it does represent a serious attempt to describe both the knowledge and the heuristics that Krebs used in his research" (p. 140). The heuristics (rules of thumb) were both general (applicable to a wide range of scientific problems) and specific (applicable to the particular content domain of organic chemistry). KEKADA was implemented as a production system. Production system models are composed of production rules, for which if a particular condition is met then a specific action is taken, and a working memory that contains current states. To use an example production rule provided by Anderson (1990):

> IF the goal is to drive a standard transmission car
> and the car is in first gear
> and the car is going more than 10 miles an hour
> THEN shift the car into second gear

The simulation proceeds in cycles, and on each cycle, a production is selected for action whose conditions match those of the current working memory states.

Employing KEKADA, Kulkarni and Simon (1988) were able to duplicate both the specific and general problem-solving techniques employed by Krebs in his discoveries. Moreover, the simulation showed that the process of discovery proceeded slowly and in small steps, rather than in a sudden, insightful fashion. Interestingly, this finding is highly similar to that obtained by the experts in Donovan et al.'s (1992) project who examined either particular historical periods in science or the discoveries of particular scientists. The name KEKADA is a Hindi synonym for Krebs and means "crab" in English. Rather poetically, in describing the results of the KEKADA simulation, Kulkarni and Simon say, "The process of scientific discovery is analogous to a crab crawling slowly to a destination" (p. 140). In agreement with much current work on expertise, the simulation suggested that it was the knowledge specific to the domain of chemistry that facilitated problem solution.

KEKADA is only one of many simulations that have been employed. The strength of a computer simulation is that it provides a formal routine that, if it works, actually generates the solution to the problem. Examining what is necessary for the simulation to duplicate the solution to an actual scientific problem can provide insight into how it may have been actually solved. The weakness of the simulation approach is that there may be a variety of simulations that differ in critical respects, all of which solve the problem. In modeling, this is often called the problem of identifiability.

Chapter Summary

In this chapter, we described and evaluated a number of naturalistic methods whose purpose is to increase our understanding of science. One of these methods, of course, is the historical analysis of the works of outstanding individuals such as Galileo or of particular historical episodes of importance. A novel approach to historical analysis was taken by Donovan et al. (1992). This approach consisted of suggesting specific hypotheses to experts in some area of science, asking them to determine if historical analysis would confirm or disconfirm the hypotheses. Another approach described was examining the products of individual scientists, such as their notebooks. Still another approach was to examine how certain eminent scientists went about creating highly novel scientific contributions: It became apparent that good scientists often use analogies in their work. A highly useful method is to study scientists in the laboratory situation, as for example in their group meetings, as they put forward hypotheses and attempt to solve problems. Finally, the chapter described a number of studies concerned with isolating and describing the personal characteristics of successful scientists. The use of all of these methods is in its infancy, and it seems likely that as their use is expanded and developed, they will contribute substantially to a better understanding and practice of science.

POSTMODERNISM AND THE REJECTION OF THE CONVENTIONAL CONCEPTION OF SCIENCE

> Enlightenment thinkers believe we can know everything, postmodernists believe we can know nothing.
> (E. O. Wilson, 1999, p. 44)

Introduction

Various views associated with **modernism**, which were developed during the period called the **Enlightenment**, are quite compatible with the scientific approach. According to these views, reality exists independently of the mind of the knower, and the purpose of science is to discover the nature of this independent reality. It is generally believed that although our scientific knowledge may be somewhat less than perfect, it is nevertheless possible to gain an increasingly accurate understanding of reality. This can be accomplished by the use of methods of various sorts, such as experimentation. It is believed that these methods, though not perfect, can be honed and modified through experience to better suit our purposes of gaining increased knowledge of the external world. These propositions cited above have been emphasized in the earlier chapters of this book.

Modernism and the view of science that accompanies it have been challenged throughout its history by various individuals. For example, Holzman (1999, p. 11), a recent critic of modernism and an adherent of **postmodernism**, has said,

Broadly speaking, from the postmodern perspective three core modernist conceptions – truth, reality and objectivity – are especially troubling. They are so deeply entrenched in our thinking and speaking, so embedded in our knowledge-seeking activities and so intertwined with modern science, that they have come to define what it is to know and understand. They are the modern gods and often function with a similar level of authority. To many postmodern philosophers and critics, it is important to expose the gods of modernism (its "grand narratives," its foundational pre-suppositions) for what they are – stories and myths.

Holzman is correct that truth, reality, and objectivity are cornerstones of modern science. But, the belief that they are "stories and myths" with which we can do without is a view that most scientists would dispute.

Clearly, if one adopts the view of the postmodernists, one would necessarily approach knowledge and its accumulation from an entirely different vantage point than that adopted by science. This has proved to be the case. Various postmodernists, as we shall see in Chapter 8, have rejected what they see as the major methodological approach in science, an emphasis on **quantitative methods**, and have in their place suggested a variety of new methods that collectively go under the name of **qualitative inquiry**. To understand the approach adopted by the advocates of qualitative inquiry, it is necessary to go more deeply into the various forms of **relativism** and postmodernism that were introduced in Chapter 3. In the absence of the sort of information contained in this chapter, one would be perplexed and befuddled by the methodological approach adopted by the advocates of qualitative inquiry, and the ability to evaluate what they propose and what they reject would be seriously compromised.

In this chapter, our initial concern is with two rationales that have been offered for challenging the objective nature of science, those of **underdetermination** and its close cousin, **incommensurability**. Following a treatment of these subjects, we then describe postmodernism and several of its varieties that have been embraced by many psychologists. The chapter concludes with a critique of postmodern approaches to psychology.

Underdetermination and Incommensurability

Underdetermination is the view that a given body of data is compatible with an infinite number of theories. Underdetermination has been one of the more influential concepts employed in the philosophy of science in recent years. Although some scientists of various persuasions have accepted underdetermination, it certainly has had its greatest influence in the social sciences, including psychology. For example, in a research methods book, two psychologists, Slife and Williams (1995, p. 187), stated:

> That experimentation cannot prove anything true has been known for a long time. . . . There are in principle an unlimited number of possible explanations for any experimental result. . . . This means, of course, that in addition to not *proving* a hypothesis, data cannot "tell" or "indicate" to the researcher which of many interpretations is correct.

In contrast with the view of Slife and Williams, Kitcher (1993), a philosopher of science, said the following:

> The notion that theories are inevitably underdetermined by experience has become a philosophical commonplace. Scientists, however, sometimes greet this allegedly mundane point with incredulity. "It's hard enough," they complain, "to find *one* way of accommodating experience, let alone many. And these supposed ways of modifying the network of beliefs are changes that no reasonable – sane? – person would make. There may be a *logical* point here, but it has little to do with science." (p. 247)

In what follows, we provide evidence that Kitcher's assessment is correct and Slife and Williams's is not. The point that Slife and Williams are making is merely a logical one that has very little to do with the reality of actual scientific decision making.

The problem with the thesis of underdetermination

Those who espouse the thesis of underdetermination, as do Slife and Williams (1995), are suggesting essentially that the failure of a set of facts to logically contradict some theoretical proposition is sufficient to imbue that proposition with acceptability. The incorrectness of that view (it has long been recognized that something that is logically possible is not necessarily true) can be illustrated with an example. It is logically possible that the world is inhabited by green men from another planet who are in our presence when we are not looking at them and disappear when we look at them. This is a preposterous proposition that few people would accept, although logically speaking it is possible. Notice that if we take the position that there is an unlimited number of statements of this sort that logically speaking are compatible with a particular set of facts, it is inevitable that the bulk of those statements will be as silly as the one suggested above. The points we are making here are these. As implied by Kitcher's (1993) quote above, *logical compatibility* of a set of facts with some proposition is not in itself sufficient reason for accepting the proposition. The basis for accepting some proposition is that it better fits the available facts than some other proposition. Logical compatibility alone is not sufficient to compel belief.

In addition to the above-described logical approach to underdetermination, there is another, which may be called the factual approach. According to this view, there is no particular empirical observation that can ever force us to abandon a theoretical proposition. This view has been associated with **Quine** (1970), a prominent philosopher of science, as noted previously. Quine has suggested essentially that if a theory is faced with some disconfirming finding, it can always be modified to escape disconfirmation by, for example, introducing some new assumption commonly called an auxiliary assumption. Quine has gone so far as to say that if it suits our purposes, we can deny accepted logical propositions such as the principle of contradiction, which states that things may not both possess and not possess certain properties at the same time and under the same circumstances. The problem with Quine's formulation is that it assumes that the modified theory will be an improvement over the original statement of the theory, else why make the modification? That there will be improvement is by no means obvious. Indeed, the modified theory may be less able than its original version to explain a wide variety of facts. This is not to say that introducing auxiliary assumptions is always to be avoided. We think that on some occasions it is both necessary and valuable to introduce auxiliary assumptions (see Chapter 5). But the point to be emphasized is this: Modified theories must meet the same challenge after they are modified as before they were modified, namely, do they explain the data better than available alternatives?

The sort of idea expressed by Slife and Williams (1995), and others, is as follows: All speculations that are compatible with a set of facts, that is, which are not contradicted by them, are equal. This is simply incorrect from a scientific standpoint. That is, for scientists to accept a theory, more than compatibility with a set of facts is required. The additional requirement is that the accepted theory explain the facts better than alternative theories, a central point of **abduction**.

The problem with the thesis of incommensurability

Incommensurability, the view that individuals who accept different **paradigms** are unable to communicate with each other, although closely associated with Kuhn (1962), was also widely accepted by the logical positivists. Kuhn appears to have accepted the idea from them that in order for individuals operating in different paradigms to communicate, they would necessarily require a common language comprehensible within both paradigms. For Example, Kuhn (1970b) has said,

> The point-by-point comparison of two successive theories demands a language into which at least the empirical consequences of both can be translated without loss or change. That such a language lies ready to hand has been widely assumed since at least the seventeenth century when philosophers took the neutrality of pure sensation-reports for granted and sought a 'universal character' which would display all languages for expressing them as one. Ideally the primitive vocabulary of such a language would consist of pure sense-datum terms plus syntactic connectives. . . . Feyerabend and I have argued at length that no such vocabulary is available. In the transition from one theory to the next words change their meanings or conditions of applicability in subtle ways. . . . Successive theories are thus, we say, incommensurable. (pp. 266–267)

We agree with Kuhn and Feyerabend that a common language equally applicable to two different paradigms, such as the theory of relativity and quantum mechanics, is not available. The issue, then, is whether such a language is necessary if incommensurability is to be avoided. Our view is that the absence of such a language in no way precludes scientists who work in different paradigms from communicating with each other. We suggest, for example, that Einstein, in expressing dissatisfaction with certain aspects of quantum mechanics, understood perfectly well the basis of his disagreement. After all, it is common knowledge that people who disagree with each other, even when those disagreements are fundamental, are perfectly capable of understanding what it is they disagree about. Laudan (1990) has suggested, "The *wholesale translation* of the claims of one paradigm into the language of its rivals *is not required to make rational choice between those rivals*" (p. 139). The choice between theories depends on more than having a common language: For example, the problem-solving effectiveness of a theory relative to alternative theories may be a factor in one's deciding to accept it.

It may be worthwhile to recap what has been said so far. It was made clear why underdetermination would lead to relativism. If every theory is as good as any other and no better than any other, and the data are not a decisive factor in choosing between the theories, then the idea that there is no theory better than any other on an absolute basis necessarily follows. In short, underdetermination necessarily leads to relativism. Because, as was demonstrated above, underdetermination can be rejected, it follows that underdetermination as the basis for relativism can also be rejected. As regards incommensurability, even if there were some degree of it, it would still be possible for scientists in different paradigms to understand each other by, for example, recognizing the problem-solving capacities of their respective approaches.

Postmodernism

Postmodernism is an approach that rejects many tenets of modernism such as that there is an independent reality that can be known by the application of objective methods. Guba (1990) is an individual who has espoused many positions common to postmodernists, such as that reality exists only in the mind and objective methods are not available. Describing some of Guba's positions will help in an effort to understand the views of postmodernists.

Guba (1990) is an avowed relativist who embraces fully the implications of the relativistic position. Guba states, "Realities exist in the form of multiple mental constructions, socially and experientially based, local and specific, dependent for their form and content on the persons who hold them" (p. 27, emphasis on multiple "realities" is his). Note that in this statement Guba is denying that there is a single reality that exists independently of the individual. According to Guba, the origin of these constructed multiple realities is in the social interactions that occur between and among people.

Guba (1990) also says,

> *Ontologically*, if there are always many interpretations that can be made in any inquiry, and if there is no foundational process by which the ultimate truth or falsity of these several constructions can be determined, there is no alternative but to take a position of *relativism*. . . . Realities are multiple, and they exist in people's minds. (p. 26)

By denying that there is any foundational process for discovering what Guba calls ultimate truth, he is denying that there is, or can be, any methodology that is any better than any other for addressing nature.

"Epistemologically," Guba (1990) says,

> The constructivist chooses to take a *subjectivist* position. Subjectivity is not only forced on us by the human condition . . . but because it is the only means of unlocking the constructions held by individuals. If realities exist only in respondents' minds, subjective interaction seems to be the only way to access them. (p. 26)

By a subjectivist position, Guba is denying that there is any hope for isolating objective procedures that are useful in making informed decisions about independent reality. If reality exists only in respondents' minds, as Guba asserts, then it follows that there is no external reality that can be known.

Guba (1990) also says, much like Slife and Williams (1995),

> No theory can ever be fully tested because of the problem of induction. Observing one million white swans does not provide indisputable evidence for the assertion, "All swans are white." There are always a large number of theories that can, in principle, "explain" a given body of "facts." Thus no unequivocal explanation is ever possible. (p. 25)

What Guba identifies in this quote is the so-called problem of under-determination, which, as described earlier in this chapter, is really a pseudoproblem.

Social constructionism

Within psychology, a prominent variety of postmodernism goes under the name of **social constructionism**. As mentioned in Chapter 3, a well-known exponent of social constructionism, **Kenneth Gergen** (1985), characterizes that view as concerned with realities that are created as a result of social interactions among individuals. Sentiments similar to those expressed by Gergen are also found in the writings of authors who advocate what is known as the strong program in the sociology of science. For example, Collins (1981), an advocate of that program, has asserted, "The natural world has a small or non-existent role in the construction of scientific knowledge" (p. 3). Similarly, Barnes and Bloor (1982) have stated, "For the relativist there is no sense attached to the idea that some standards and beliefs are really rational as distinct from merely locally accepted as such" (p. 27). Essentially, what these authors are saying is that, in so far as truth is concerned, it is general agreement among people that counts, rather than the correspondence of a statement with reality.

Social constructionists such as Gergen appear to agree with philosophers such as **Richard Rorty** that what we take to be objective problems arise merely from the way in which we use language. This view challenges the commonly accepted belief that the problems arise through observation of the natural world. For example, Gergen suggests that anger, which is normally considered to have its basis in biological processes, is in reality what he calls "a historically contingent social performance" (1985, p. 267). Understanding between people arises, according to this view, only as a result of cooperation between people in their relationships. In this connection, Gergen (1985) has stated, "The degree to which a given form of understanding prevails or is sustained across time is not based fundamentally on the empirical validity of the perspective in question, but on the vicissitudes of social processes (e.g., communication, negotiation, conflict, rhetoric)" (p. 268). Note the sharp contrast between Gergen's view and that of scientific **naturalism** advocated in this book and in science generally. Not too surprisingly, Gergen, who emphasizes communication between individuals as a means of establishing the validity of various questions, rejects various standard methodological approaches employed in conventional science and psychology. According to Gergen,

> Under modernism, methodology underwent a virtual apotheosis. Methodology was the means to truth and light, and thus to salvation. ... Under postmodernism, however, methodology loses its coveted position. Under postmodernism research methods in psychology are viewed, at worst, as misleading justificatory devices. They operate as truth warrants for a priori commitments to particular forms of value-saturated description. (1992, p. 24)

Social constructionists provide a characterization of science that is far removed from the conventionally accepted view. For example, **empiricism** is eschewed, along with "the Western conception of objective, individualistic, ahistoric knowledge" (Gergen, 1985, p. 272). It is stated that an alternative scientific methodology based on constructionist assumptions would take the following form: "Such a metatheory would remove knowledge from the data-driven and/or the cognitively necessitated domains and place it in the hands of people in relationship" (p. 272). Scientific formulations would be "the responsibility of persons in active, communal interchange" (p. 272). In other words, beliefs, including scientific beliefs, are arrived at solely on the basis of agreement among individuals. Methodologically, social constructionists have little to recommend. It is suggested that any method will do that fosters interchange among persons. According to Gergen, "Virtually any methodology can be employed so long as it enables the analyst to develop a more compelling case" (p. 273).

In a recent issue of the journal *Personality & Social Psychology Review*, an attempt was made to determine whether some sort of rapprochement between social constructionism and experimental social psychology, which practices conventional science, is desirable. In the target article, Jost and Kruglanski (2002) suggested that, indeed, it is desirable that there should be such a rapprochement. They say that the two views have been "oddly and unnecessarily estranged from one another" (p. 168) and that the views have more in common than is generally realized. They state, "Because social constructionists are fundamentally correct that human thought and behavior should be understood in relation to specific historical, cultural, and ideological contexts . . . , experimentalists will be in a better position to fulfill the distinctive mission of social psychology by embracing constructionist themes" (p. 169). Jost and Kruglanski raise the question of what is to be gained by merging social constructionism with experimental social psychology. They suggest that one thing to be gained is an escape from self-deception. In their words, "If social perceivers are constantly finding what they want or expect to see [as social constructionists say], what is to save the experimental social psychologist from a similar fate of self-deception?" (p. 172). Another purported benefit perceived by Jost and Kruglanski is that it would break down the barrier between science and ideology that is accepted by experimental social psychologists but not by social constructionists. They say,

> From this perspective, we have a professional obligation to weigh in on ideological issues, policies, and decisions. Furthermore, if experimental social psychologists insist on political aloofness, then we are bound to alienate and lose many young people who entered the field because of its potential for facilitating social progress and transforming political institutions. (p. 175)

Finally, Jost and Kruglanski suggest that experimental social psychologists, by adopting the methodology and **ontology** of social constructionism, can develop theories that are an improvement over current ones by being broader, less constrained, and more creative.

The reactions of other social psychologists to Jost and Kruglanski's (2002) suggestions are a rather mixed bag. Pratto (2002) finds the suggestions of Jost and Kruglanski to be extremely useful. Schaller (2002) sees virtue in combining the two approaches but is also of the mind that experimental social psychology could benefit from incorporating ideas from evolutionary psychology, which normally would be considered to be an enemy of social constructionism. Gergen (2002), however, although suggesting that the idea of rapprochement may be useful, is apparently ambivalent about the ultimate success of the approach. For example, he says, "One could argue that these differences [the ontological separation between social constructionism and experimental social psychology] are so fundamental and so radical that the kind of rapprochement favored by Jost and Kruglanski is quite beyond reach" (p. 189). The ambivalence of Gergen is amplified by Potter (2002) who takes the even stronger position that there is not much merit in combining the two approaches. He says, "Rather than reconciliation, which risks obscuring genuine points of metatheoretical, theoretical, and methodological conflict, I suggest that a creative rhetorical engagement would be most productive" (p. 193). Potter's view that engagement but not reconciliation is to be desired is closest to our own, for reasons we will describe later in the chapter. Generally speaking, it does not seem to be a good idea to attempt to combine incompatible positions: There is an old joke to the effect that what you get when you breed a crocodile to an abalone is a crock-of-baloney!

Contextualism

Contextualism is another prominent postmodernist view that has captured the attention of some psychologists. There are several varieties of contextualism, all of which trace their roots to a very influential book written by **Stephen C. Pepper** (1942) in which he identified four worldviews: mechanism, organicism, formism, and contextualism. Contextualism is the worldview embraced by postmodernists, with the worldviews of mechanism, organicism, and formism being rejected. Mechanism is the worldview normally associated with science, and it speaks of causal mechanisms. Organicism emphasizes the growing organism, and that growth is directed toward some goal or endpoint. Organicism is influential in developmental psychology as, for example, Piaget's stages of cognitive development. Formism is a worldview that emphasizes similarity and essences, for example, all oak trees are alike because they share a common essence. Contextualism, which is of most concern here, is based metaphorically on the historic event, that is, the unfolding of events in context.

We identified three varieties of contextualism (Capaldi & Proctor, 1999): philosophic contextualism, developmental contextualism, and functional contextualism. Of these, in our view, only philosophic contextualism represents true contextualism. The other two varieties, as discussed later in the section, attempt to embrace some of the tenets of philosophic contextualism while avoiding others. In this way, consistent with the recommendation of Jost and Kruglanski (2002), they hope to obtain what they see as some of the benefits of philosophic contextualism, while escaping some of its other more extreme positions such as relativism. However, our view is that, in the end, they bear a greater similarity to conventional science than to philosophic contextualism.

Philosophic contextualism. Philosophic contextualism rejects many of the standard assumptions of science. A defining characteristic of philosophic contextualism is its complete acceptance of what is known as **radical empiricism**. By radical empiricism we mean that one accepts events as they occur at face value, not attempting to interpret them in terms of underlying conceptualizations, as in conventional science. From this perspective, the philosophic contextualist asserts that there is no reality other than the reality that one directly observes. Slight changes in phenomena, according to the contextualists, may give rise to a totally different reality, characterized as a novelty. According to the philosophic contextualists, novelty is the rule rather than the exception. The prominent psychologist and philosopher, **William James** (1912/1976), who later in life embraced radical empiricism and novelty under the name of pragmatism, suggested that the pragmatist distrusts generalizations of any sort and attempts to describe the specific event observed and nothing else.

Understanding the role of novelty in contextualism is a key to understanding many of the contextualists' positions on important issues. Contextualists reject any procedure that restricts the range of variables that may be examined. Of course, this is exactly what experimentation does, and so philosophic contextualists reject experimentation as a reasonable method for advancing knowledge. The reasons for this rejection are quite straightforward. For one, an experiment represents only one of many contexts in which information could be gathered. For another, experimentation by its very nature demands that phenomena be restricted in some manner (e.g., through the use of experimental controls), and these restrictions can themselves influence in highly significant ways the nature of the phenomena observed. The contextualistic attitude toward experimentation, which is a mirror reversal of the attitude of conventional scientists, is well exemplified by words from Jaeger and Rosnow (1988):

While the experiment can play a role in describing certain relational patterns or identifying causal properties, by its limited and constraining nature it cannot accommodate the complexity of factors that simultaneously act upon or determine an event. Explanation of the event requires additional knowledge and information about its social, cultural, historical, and biographical context. Nor is the experiment well suited to describe the unfolding of an event and how the individual effects change in the course of the event. (p. 69)

Because contextualists expect that novelty can arise at any time, and because even a slight variation in conditions can produce a novel outcome, philosophic contextualists reject the possibility that lawful relations can be established. Some views of contextualists regarding lawfulness are as follows. Rosnow and Georgoudi (1986) are explicit in rejecting the possibility of isolating laws in psychology, stating,

The idea of contextualism intrinsically implies change and development as opposed to orderliness and stability (implied both by the mechanistic and organismic world views). Further, change is not something derivative but is basic or essential. . . . It is in this sense that contextualism implies that change is categorical and the search for absolute and immutable laws of behavior, chimerical. (p. 15)

Hoffman and Nead (1983) are in agreement with Rosnow and Georgoudi, suggesting that contextualism entails "rejection of the notion of 'universal law' " and "adoption of a notion of disorder" (p. 525). Blank (1986) offers a similar suggestion, saying that contextualism implies that "universal, transhistorical laws of personal behavior are impossible and the search for them fruitless" (p. 107).

The reader has probably gathered that philosophic contextualists are not in search of theories that more or less accurately describe a wide range of phenomena. There are multiple reasons for this: their radical empiricism, their idea that even slight changes in conditions will alter the phenomenon, and their view that the reality that exists today may change tomorrow. Instead of experimentation, philosophic contextualists favor alternative methodologies such as **narrative**, dramaturgy, and hermeneutics. An outstanding proponent of narrative and dramaturgy is the personality theorist Theodore Sarbin (1977), who has suggested:

The new scholars of personality will engage in a radical shift. Instead of looking upon 19th- and 20th-century natural sciences as models, they will explore the structure of identity and the means of identity transvaluation where these occurrences are most clearly presented – where the importance of context is continually confirmed – the world of literature, especially dramatistic literature. Shakespeare, Goethe, Thomas Mann, Kafka, Dostoevsky, O'Neill, Shaw, and Pirandello come immediately to mind as writers who could be perceived as authorities on identity shaping and on the contextual features that support the imputation or withdrawal of respect and esteem for role enactments. (p. 37)

Hermeneutics refers to interpretation. Originally, it referred to the rules and procedures for interpreting biblical texts. Its scope was then widened to include interpretation of works of a literary and scientific nature. Dougher (1993, p. 214) has made the relativistic aspects of hermeneutics exceptionally clear:

At its most basic level, hermeneutics refers to interpretive methodologies as they are applied to the human domain. More broadly, hermeneutics refers to a collection of approaches that stand in opposition to the application of natural science methods to the study of human behavior and experience. . . . In particular, hermeneutics rejects the positivistic, ahistorical, objective, and empirical nature of the physical sciences.

In a recent book, Lewis (1997), a philosophic contextualist interested in child development, describes several attributes of his position as follows:

1. An active self exists, one capable of thinking, planning, and having goals and desires.
2. These goals and desires are best understood within a meaning system occurring now; thus the emphasis on contextualism.
3. Earlier events need not necessarily determine later events; thus there is no need to think of development as a unidirectional, bounded process.
4. Finally, there is no need to postulate progress as an essential feature of the developmental process. In other words, there is no endpoint in the developmental process, no final state to be achieved. (p. 54)

Although the comments contained in points 2, 3, and 4 can be claimed to be unique to philosophic contextualism, the proposition expressed under point 1 certainly cannot. As we have indicated elsewhere (Capaldi & Proctor, 1999), a considerable variety of non-contextualistic psychologists postulate an active organism that processes information. In fact, most contemporary psychologists see organisms as, like Lewis (1997,

p. 54) claims, "capable of thinking, planning, and having goals and desires." Lewis's point 2 reflects the contextualistic belief that each context is unique and therefore has a unique effect. Point 3 expresses the contextualistic belief that novelty may appear at any point. His point 4 expresses the contextualistic view that there is only change; there is no single or unique direction of change, and no change is more significant than any other. Lewis's point 4 is in direct opposition to organicism.

To summarize, philosophic contextualists reject much of what is accepted in the conventionally accepted approach to science. The major point of agreement between conventional science and philosophic contextualism is the acceptance that observation is of importance. But, even here, differences arise. For the scientist, observation is the beginning of the enterprise that leads ultimately to laws and theories. For the contextualist, observation is to be taken at face value. At most, philosophic contextualists would expect that observed phenomena can be described reasonably accurately, at least from one perspective, a perspective that may differ from time to time and from person to person.

Developmental contextualism. Many people are attracted to contextualism because, in their view, as we shall see, it represents a broader approach to scientific problems than that of accepted science. An area in which this broader approach has been embraced with perhaps the greatest vigor is developmental psychology. About 1970, some developmental psychologists began replacing the mechanistic and organismic metaphors with the contextualistic metaphor. Contextualistic models seem to some developmentalists to hold more promise than the alternative worldviews to lead "to formulations that can integrate data about the plasticity and multidirectionality of and individual differences in developmental changes across the life span" (Ford & Lerner, 1992, p. 10).

Developmentalists who look favorably on contextualism soon realized that it was too unbounded to put any constraints on the direction of development. In other words, the possible directions that development could take were essentially infinite (see Lewis's point 4). A recent example of this reasoning is provided by Kagitçibasi (2000), who suggests that children may be influenced by a variety of different contexts. However, Kagitçibasi attempts to escape the relativism inherent in the philosophic contextualists' position by suggesting that because different contexts may nevertheless promote similar development, "a universalistic perspective appears to better predict the common patterns of change than a relativistic perspective" (p. 107). In order to evade the dispersive aspect of contextualism, developmentalists modified it in such a way as to constrain possible directions of development.

134

Essential characteristics of developmental contextualism are as follows (Capaldi & Proctor, 1999):

- Multilevel determination – Variables from a variety of different levels (biological, psychological, sociological, etc.) interact to determine human development.
- Reciprocal relations – There is no unidirectionality to the causal flow from one level to another. In simple words, level A influences level B and is influenced by level B.
- Active versus passive organism – Like true, or philosophic, contextualists, developmental contextualists adhere to the idea that organisms are not passive recipients of environmental and other factors. Rather, individuals actively select and transformation information.
- Nonreductionism – Developmental contextualists consider mechanists to be reductionists in the sense of attempting to explain psychology in other theoretical terms, for example, biology. The developmentalists consider all variables from all organizational levels (e.g., biology, psychology, sociology, etc.) to be equally important.

In summary, developmental contextualists do not share the major characteristics of philosophic contextualism, namely, radical empiricism and the rejection of theory. Indeed, it could be argued that developmental contextualists have almost nothing in common with philosophic contextualists. On the other hand, they have much in common with conventional scientists. If there is a difference, it is one of emphasis. For example, developmental contextualists may emphasize multilevel determination to a greater extent than some other psychologists. This difference and others are thus more quantitative than qualitative. In fact, in our view, the differences between developmental contextualists and other scientists are so small that developmental contextualists are not contextualists at all, but rather are better classified as a variety of conventional developmental psychologists.

Functional contextualism. This branch of contextualism arose within the operant psychology tradition associated with B. F. Skinner. Operants are responses that act on the environment, as for example pressing a bar to obtain food. The functional contextualists, like the developmental contextualists, shun the extreme dispersiveness of philosophic contextualism. A key assumption of the functional contextualists is that the goal one has in mind is of paramount importance and cannot itself either be justified or refuted. That is, if I say my goal is X, considerations that lead to the achievement of X are considered to be rational. It is by emphasizing goals that the functional contextualist gets around the problem of the extreme dispersiveness of philosophic contextualism. For example, Hayes and Hayes (1989), two principal exponents of functional contextualism, say, "Behavior analysis assumes that events are stable and open to direct investigation only because it works to do so with regard to behavior analytic goals, namely, prediction and control" (p. 37).

Several outstanding characteristics of functional contextualism, which emphasizes the concept of the operant, are as follows:

- The operant is a functional category – All operants that have the same effect on the environment are to be considered as members of the same functional category. For example, various responses that lead to the depression of a bar or key (depressing it with the left hand, right hand, etc.) are considered to be members of the same operant category.
- Behavior has a verb-like quality – Behavior is doing, running, jumping, swimming, etc.
- Context in the act – In studying the actions of the organism, it is not merely the action alone that is considered, but the context in which it occurs.
- The relation between the scientist and the world – The scientist does not stand apart from the world he or she examines, but rather is part of it.
- The truth criterion – Whereas most scientists view truth as correspondence with reality, functional contextualists view it as successful working. Whatever works in practice is assumed to be true.
- Radical empiricism – Functional contextualists, like philosophic contextualists but unlike developmental contextualists, are radical empiricists. That is, functional contextualists eschew theory and emphasize observation and the functional relationship between variables.

In summary, functional contextualists share some attributes with philosophic contextualists and others with conventional scientists (see Capaldi & Proctor, 1996). Like philosophic contextualists, functional contextualists are radical empiricists who eschew and distrust theory. Like conventional scientists, functional contextualists emphasize prediction and control, and thus rely heavily on controlled experiments. Also, like conventional scientists, functional contextualists emphasize functional relationships between variables, but unlike conventional scientists, they do not favor abstract interpretations of these relationships.

Our Critique

Our review of postmodern approaches to psychology raises several salient issues that we will consider in turn. The first of these is concern with whether philosophic contextualism and various other similar movements, such as social constructionism, that fall under the rubric of postmodernism, are in any sense scientific. Three general answers to this question have been given by individuals who identify themselves as some variety of postmodernist. One answer is that philosophic contextualism is clearly not a science and that scientific methods should be rejected in favor of others, such as narrative (described in Chapter 8). Sarbin (1977) clearly stated this position in describing his "prediction", described earlier, that psychology has more to gain from literature than from laboratory research:

> I am painfully aware that this prediction has an antiscientific coloring. I say "painfully" because I have construed myself as scientist for almost 40 years. When I look at the achievements of science (rooted in mechanism) in such areas as deviance, hypnosis, and imaginings, . . . and also language, moral development, teaching, and learning, I must admit that science may justifiably be called the false messiah – at least for problems that we identify as psychological. (p. 37)

Rychlak (2003) agrees with Sarbin, stating, "Psychologists have tried to stretch their scientific understanding of the material universe to cover human actions that simply cannot be captured in the same terms" (p. xi).

One can only wonder on what basis such statements by Sarbin and Rychlak can be made. We may rule out any a priori basis because one can determine whether science can be applied to a particular set of empirical phenomena only by attempting to do so. Their basis for concluding that psychology cannot be understood from a scientific standpoint must, therefore, itself be empirical. Unfortunately, neither Sarbin nor Rychlak ever reveals on what empirical basis they reject psychological science. Another deficiency of their analysis is that they overlook a very considerable body of evidence from various fields of psychology that scientific methodology has proved very useful in uncovering psychological phenomena. Apparently, many others agree with us, else why would Daniel Kahneman receive a Nobel prize in 2002 for his research with Amos Tversky on decision making? To mention some other examples, very little was known about either human problem solving in general or expertise in specific content domains prior to the work of Newell and Simon (1967) in the 1960s and subsequent research by **Herbert Simon** and his colleagues on expertise. Of course, many other examples could be cited. The general point we are making is that there is abundant evidence that psychology as a science is progressive in the sense suggested by **Lakatos** (1970). Blanket dismissals of the worth of science in psychology such as those of Sarbin and Rychlak are not to be taken seriously. Can the critics of psychological science provide a more convincing analysis of the shortcomings of the scientific approach to psychology? We have not seen such an analysis, and we doubt that one can be provided.

A second answer is that the scientific approach is but one of many approaches that may be employed, and it is in no sense any better than any of these other approaches at arriving at the truth, because there is no single truth. By this view, none of these approaches supplies truth in the sense that most scientists are concerned with. At best, all we have is agreement among individuals who adopt a common framework. Gergen (2001) expresses this view, stating,

> Empirical psychology represents a tradition of discourse, practice, and politics that has as much right to sustain its existence as any other tradition. The point of postmodern critique, in my view, is not to annihilate tradition but to give all traditions the right to participate within the unfolding dialogues. (p. 808)

Although this view sounds broad-minded, as Gergen portrays it, it in fact is not so because it involves a contradiction, which is as follows. The purpose of the experimental method as employed in empirical psychology is to produce basic knowledge. To suggest that one accepts experimentation while denying at the same time that it is capable of providing basic knowledge, as does Gergen, is perverse. Surely Gergen is aware that he denies that experimentation can accomplish what it is generally believed to accomplish by all scientists. We suggest that Gergen's position is incoherent.

The third view is that although philosophic contextualism is itself not science, it can be combined with other approaches, which are themselves scientific, to produce a better scientific approach to problems. This is the view of both developmental and functional contextualists, and it is also the view expressed by Jost and Kruglanski (2002) regarding the marriage of social constructionism with experimental social psychology. As noted, our position with respect to such marriages is closest to that of Potter (2002), who suggests that conflict, rather than cooperation, between views that entertain different fundamental assumptions is to be desired. In agreement with Potter, we do not think that a view, such as social constructionism, which suggests that truth consists of no more than agreement among individuals, can be reconciled with the conventional science view that truth is a matter of correspondence between our description of the real world and the real world itself. To take another example, what is the sense in combining Gergen's view that experimentation and similar methods are no better than post hoc justificatory devices with the conventional view of experimentation that sees it as serving the opposite role? The accepted view of experimentation, with which we agree, is that when used properly, it provides an independent assessment of our opinions and hypotheses, rather than serving merely as a justificatory device.

The idea that views such as modernism and postmodernism can be usefully combined was taken up decades ago by Pepper (1942), who, as previously noted, was highly influential in establishing contextualism in psychology and the social sciences (see, e.g., Hayes, Hayes, Reese, & Sarbin, 1993). He is widely quoted and recognized as an informed commentator on the various types of ontologies suggested by philosophers and scientists over the years. In attempting to combine diverse ontologies, Pepper says, "If world hypotheses are autonomous, they are mutually exclusive. A mixture of them, therefore, can only be confusing" (p. 105). He goes on to say,

> Yet it is a tempting notion, that perhaps a world theory more adequate than any of the world theories mentioned above . . . might be developed through the selection of *what is best* in each of them and organizing the results with a synthetic set of categories. . . . Our contention is that this method is mistaken in principle in that it adds no factual content and confuses the structures of fact . . . it is almost inevitably sterile and confusing. (p. 106)

We heartily agree with Pepper that combining modernism and postmodernism is a prescription for confusion. This is likely the reason why so few scientists would identify themselves as postmodernists. To put the matter simply, postmodernists are not scientists, and scientists are not postmodernists.

It is not our intention in this chapter to suggest that science, either in its early or later stages, is entirely devoid of cultural values. The question is, what role do cultural values play in science? We suggest that the approach taken by **Michael Ruse** (2001), below, supplies a reasonable procedure for investigating this problem. His approach is a naturalistic one. More specifically, Ruse has suggested that by employing the historical method, it is possible to decide whether changes in a given area of science, as it develops, are due merely to social factors or are due to methodological factors, or both. He applies this analysis specifically to the growth of evolutionary theory from roughly 1700 to the present. He begins by entertaining four hypotheses as to how any scientific area, and evolution in particular, may change as it develops from its earliest beginnings through becoming a full-fledged science. These hypotheses are:

- H1: Cultural values present at the time a particular scientific area is initially considered persist little, if at all, as the science develops.
- H2: Cultural values present at the time a particular scientific area is initially considered persist indefinitely as the science develops.
- H3: Cultural values present at the time a particular scientific area is initially considered slowly become less important, with scientific values becoming more important.
- H4: Cultural values present at the time a particular scientific area is initially considered change but are replaced by other cultural values.

Ruse notes that H1 is probably the view that would be accepted by most scientists, with H4 being the view that is most compatible with social constructionism.

Ruse examines these four hypotheses with reference to a specific cultural value, namely whether evolution is progressive, with later species being more complex and thus better than earlier species. He notes that in the early, pre-scientific days of evolution, prior to **Darwin**, the idea that biological evolution was progressive was applied to the social sphere, the idea being that societies become better over time. With Darwin's *On the Origin of the Species*, in 1859, evolution passed from being pre-scientific to being fully scientific, and thus it advanced epistemically. At the same time, many evolutionary-minded people still thought of biological evolution as progressive, thus justifying the idea that progressive societal change was possible. A major event in the history evolution occurred in 1940, when natural selection and Mendelian genetics were integrated into what is called the modern synthesis. This enabled evolution to become a more professional discipline in that it became more integrated with scientific work in universities.

Ruse sees two sorts of forces at work to mitigate the idea that evolution is progressive. One stems from the values of science itself, which tends to shun cultural values. The other stems from the desire of evolutionary practitioners to be viewed as scientific. Note that Ruse does not fully come out in support of H1, nor does he fully support H4. He suggests a fifth hypothesis, H5. According to H5, the historical record suggests that external cultural values diminish and epistemic values become more important as an area moves from being pre-scientific to scientific. However, it is not simply a case of the epistemic values pushing out the external cultural ones, although that occurs to some extent. Important to this process are the internal cultural values of science itself. That is, external cultural values are pushed out because of the desire of the practitioners of the science to become more professional.

Ruse's (2001) historical analysis applied to evolution can in principle be applied to any area of science, including psychology. Hopefully, as the naturalistic approach to science becomes more popular, the sort of analysis Ruse has applied to evolution will indeed be applied to other areas of science. Such application should provide a better understanding of the role of social and epistemic factors in various branches of science.

Chapter Summary

We began the chapter by contrasting modernism with post-modernism. Modernism is compatible with science as commonly practiced and postmodernism is not. It was indicated that acceptance of underdetermination and incommensurability lead to various forms of relativism, of which postmodernism is an example. Two other forms of relativism were considered, social constructionism and philosophic contextualism. It was shown that underdetermination, when properly understood, is not the problem for science that it is made out to be by various relativists, and the same is true of incommensurability. It was briefly indicated that one form of contextualism, developmental contextualism, does not imply relativism and is better considered as advocating a conventional scientific approach. Some have suggested that elements of conventional social psychology and social constructionism can be combined to provide a more complete approach to social phenomena. Although combining different worldviews of these sorts sounds appealing and broadminded, it really is not so. The problem is that combining these views produces, as one of the leading authorities on philosophic contextualism, Stephen Pepper, has said, incoherence. By this he meant that such views contain incompatible assumptions and therefore cannot be coherently combined. We ended the chapter with a method suggested by Ruse for evaluating the source of change in values as science develops.

Chapter 8

QUALITATIVE RESEARCH METHODS

Introduction

In recent years, there has been an upsurge of interest in what are called qualitative research methods. This new interest in qualitative research methods, as indicated in Chapter 7, stems largely from a relativist worldview that rejects experimental methodology and its undergirding assumptions. These **qualitative methods** are concerned with the lived experience of human beings. For example, a favored approach is to elicit from people **narratives** concerning their life experiences. Many adherents of qualitative methods suggest that the reported experience of people should be the most important, if not the sole approach, to psychological phenomena.

The popularity of qualitative methods is a relatively new phenomenon in psychology, one that is on the increase. The popularity of these methods occurred earlier in areas other than psychology as, for example, in anthropology. However, qualitative methods now occupy the full attention of many psychologists who strongly advocate that they are superior for most purposes to those traditionally employed in psychological research. The rationale for qualitative research methods is supplied by an approach that is sometimes called **qualitative inquiry**. Although qualitative inquiry is currently a minority methodological position in psychology, it is a rapidly growing and aggressive movement, as indicated by several factors. One is the considerable number of books on the topic that have been published in recent years, as for example, *Qualitative Psychology: A Practical Guide to Research Methods*, edited by Smith (2003). A second factor is that the American Psychological Association is lending support to the movement in various ways, as for example, publishing books such as *Qualitative Research in Psychology: Expanding Perspectives in Methodology and Design*, edited by Camic,

Rhodes, and Yardley (2003b), and sponsoring special interest groups devoted to qualitative methods, such as the *Teaching and Research on Qualitative Methods* group of the division of Counseling Psychology. Another is that numerous authors and contributors to works on qualitative methods hold faculty positions within colleges and universities. For example, of the 35 contributors to Camic et al.'s volume, 25 list university or college affiliations. A final indicator is the appearance of new journals devoted to qualitative methods such as *Qualitative Inquiry*, an interdisciplinary journal begun in 1995, and *Qualitative Research in Psychology*, a new journal begun in 2004.

Aside from the rapid growth of the qualitative research movement, there are several important reasons for closely examining its claims. On the one hand, many advocates of qualitative methods provide a particular rationale for their use. This rationale is widely accepted in certain quarters of psychology, and it differs substantially from that embraced by most psychological researchers. On the other hand, the advocates of qualitative methods provide a highly critical analysis of the approach to methodology embraced by most psychological researchers. An examination of the arguments pro and con of the qualitative researchers allows better understanding of the basis for the methodologies employed by most research psychologists, thereby allowing one to become a more sophisticated methodologist.

The rationale underlying qualitative inquiry is contrasted with that seen as justifying methods such as statistics and experimentation, which the qualitative researchers call **quantitative methods** (e.g., Camic, Rhodes, & Yardley, 2003b). Although the dichotomy advocated by individuals who label themselves qualitative researchers is supposedly between qualitative and quantitative research methods, it is really much deeper than that. It is between the worldview favored by qualitative researchers, described in detail later, and that embraced by most other research psychologists, regardless of whether they use qualitative or quantitative methods. Their fundamental assumptions as to how reality is constituted are then used as the basis for offering a unique methodological approach that embraces qualitative rather than quantitative methods. However, those who favor qualitative inquiry advocate the use of qualitative methods in a way that not only excludes quantitative methods but various conventional uses of qualitative methods as well.

Willig (2001), a strong supporter of qualitative research and inquiry, provides a treatment of methods that illustrates that qualitative researchers are not concerned with qualitative methods per se but only with that subset of such methods that is specifically relevant to their worldview. Willig distinguishes between what she refers to as "Big Q" and "little q" qualitative methods, a distinction originally suggested by Kidder and Fine (1987). Kidder and Fine define Big Q research as follows:

> Qualitative work with the big Q is field work, participant observation, or ethnography; it consists of a continually changing set of questions without a structured design. The big Q refers to unstructured research, inductive work, hypothesis generation, and the development of "grounded theory." (p. 59)

Willig indicates that Big Q methodology is "concerned with the exploration of lived experience and participant-defined meanings" (p. 11). According to adherents of qualitative inquiry, a characteristic of the Big Q approach is to regard the participant and the researcher as equals in the collection and interpretation of data. Willig says that little q methodologists, in contrast, tend to impose their own meaning during data collection, analysis, and interpretation. According to her, little q methodologists begin investigation with predetermined categories for the coding and analysis of data. In contrast, Big Q methodology is more fluid and inductive, and the researcher tends to develop its interpretive categories as the research progresses, with input from the participant. Whereas little q methodologists may be concerned with cause–effect relationships, Big Q methodologists are concerned with developing a deeper understanding of the participant's experience and not with prediction and control. Willig says of little q qualitative methodology, that it "is, in my view, not compatible with the spirit of 'qualitative methodology'" (p. 11).

Note that Willig's (2001) view, which is representative of the consensus among Big Q qualitative researchers, excludes not only quantitative methodology but also qualitative methodology that has aims and purposes different from those of Big Q qualitative researchers. Certainly there are cases in which Big Q methodology is appropriate, as, for example, when an anthropologist seeks to elicit information from members of a foreign culture or when a human factors professional interviews potential customers with the goal of improving the usability of software (e.g., Beyer & Holzblatt, 1998). It should be emphasized that in this chapter our emphasis is on Big Q qualitative methods, not little q qualitative methods. The two should not be confused.

Big Q methodology is seen by many of its advocates as replacing other methodologies, rather than as being part of a broad range of methodologies, each of which is appropriate under particular circumstances. In our opinion, this view of methodology is far too narrow.

We agree that qualitative methods of the type favored by advocates of qualitative inquiry do have a place in psychological research, but, as with all methods, they have their strengths and weaknesses. It is important to understand the strengths and weaknesses of all research methods employed in psychology if we are to be able to use them properly and to evaluate the results that they yield. Without such understanding, a researcher may employ an inappropriate method under particular circumstances, a tactic designed to produce failure.

Our major purpose in this chapter is to describe qualitative methods and the rationale for their use as advanced by their advocates. In the next chapter, we will provide our own critical evaluation of qualitative methods, the rationale provided for them by their advocates, and the criticisms of more conventional methodology provided by qualitative researchers. We shall also provide a justification for the rationale given for so-called quantitative methods.

Rationale for Qualitative Methods

As Camic et al. (2003b) note, "The vast majority of textbooks previously published in qualitative research has been in other disciplines such as anthropology, education, nursing, and sociology" (p. xiii). The term qualitative methods is used in contrast to quantitative research methods, the term used by advocates of qualitative methods to describe conventionally used methods in science and psychology, ranging from statistics through mathematics to controlled experimental studies. According to the qualitative methodologists Ponterotto and Grieger (1999), the difference between quantitative and qualitative methods can be illustrated through a variety of dichotomies, which they say, "stem from the writings of many scholars in the area and from our own interpretation and digestion of the variant paradigms" (p. 50). Among the differentiating characteristics of quantitative versus qualitative methods that Ponterotto and Grieger cite are the following (p. 51). The characteristics of quantitative methods are stated first, those of qualitative methods second.

- Natural science perspective versus human science perspective
- Positivism versus phenomenology, idealism, and constructivism
- One true measurable reality versus multiple realities, socially constructed and context dependent
- Deductive versus inductive methods
- Theory driven versus theory generating
- Hypothesis testing versus hypothesis generating

- Prediction versus understanding
- Quantification versus description
- Understanding laws and causes versus seeking meaning
- Objective and detached researcher versus involved and interactive researcher
- Experimental designs versus in-depth interviews and participant observation.

It should be clear from these dichotomies that the advocacy of qualitative methods extends well beyond issues of methodology per se and involves the acceptance of a worldview different from that prevailing among so-called quantitative researchers, or, in other words, the worldview commonly accepted by most scientists, including psychologists. More formally, advocates of qualitative methods embrace conceptions of **epistemology** and **ontology** different from those prevailing in typical science. This point is approvingly acknowledged by McGrath and Johnson (2003), advocates of qualitative methods, who state, "Most of the contemporary arguments urging the use of qualitative approaches are thoroughly embedded within a more general critique of the overall scientific paradigm as applied in our field [psychology]" (p. 31). The critique supplied by McGrath and Johnson overlaps with, but is not identical to, the dichotomies supplied by Ponterotto and Grieger (1999). We may summarize the various views of McGrath and Johnson as follows:

- Qualitative researchers suggest that facts and experimenters are interdependent (i.e., influence each other), whereas quantitative researchers (who they call positivists) believe that facts are independent of the experimenter.
- Qualitative researchers suggest that the researcher and the participant in the research project are also interdependent, whereas quantitative researchers believe that they are independent.
- Qualitative researchers see phenomena as embedded in particular contexts, whereas quantitative researchers attempt to remove phenomena from context.
- Qualitative researchers believe that science is not, and cannot be, value free, whereas quantitative researchers believe that science can, and should, be value free.
- Qualitative researchers believe that the experimenter and the participant are equals in the research process, whereas quantitative researchers see themselves as superior to participants in terms of accomplishing the research objectives.

- Qualitative and quantitative researchers seek different things. Qualitative researchers are concerned with seeking patterns of relations within phenomena in specific contexts; quantitative researchers, on the other hand, seek to isolate general laws.
- Quantitative and qualitative researchers entertain different ideas as to what constitutes progress in science. Whereas qualitative psychologists are concerned with understanding patterns of human experience, quantitative psychologists are concerned with prediction and control of action and performance.
- In terms of the direction of causality, qualitative researchers are concerned with reciprocal influence of cause and effect (effect acts on cause, as well as cause acting on effect). Quantitative researchers, it is asserted, are concerned with causation in one direction only, from cause to effect.

The listing by McGrath and Johnson (2003) of their view of the differences in beliefs between qualitative and quantitative researchers, though substantial, is not exhaustive. So, it will be helpful to briefly mention other differences between these two types of researchers suggested by other authors. Taking into account many sources, it is reasonable to conclude that the beliefs of many qualitative researchers also include:

- Qualitative methods should replace quantitative methods completely.
- Qualitative methods contribute to an understanding of psychology in a way that is more meaningful than that provided by quantitative methods.
- Qualitative methods are better suited to studying single cases than are quantitative methods.
- Qualitative methods provide descriptive data in the goal of understanding, whereas quantitative methods emphasize causal relations in the goal of prediction.
- Qualitative methods have their origin in literature and the arts, whereas quantitative methods have their origin in physics. In this regard, advocates of qualitative inquiry often suggest that quantitative researchers have "physics envy."
- Qualitative research is marginalized and considered inferior by quantitative researchers, and for this reason, is not taken seriously.
- Whereas qualitative research has **ecological validity** (applies to real-world contexts), quantitative research does not (cannot be generalized to the real world).

147

- Qualitative research studies real people in real-world contexts, whereas quantitative methods examine relations in stripped-down and antiseptic environments.

Notice that these ideas are similar to those presented in the previous chapter in connection with **postmodernism** and the various forms of **relativism**. This emphasizes that the issue is not simply one of which research methods to use but a concern with the more fundamental matters of ontology and epistemology.

Many of these views are reflected in the following opinions voiced by advocates of qualitative methods. We quote extensively from several authors of chapters in a recent publication of the American Psychological Association to convey their views of the differences between qualitative and quantitative methods. Regarding the status of qualitative methods, in the foreword to Camic et al.'s (2003b) book, Bamberg (2003) states:

> Something took place that contributed to my slow and gradual turn to qualitative methods as the preferred inquiry method in psychology. . . . What stood out for us at that time was our interest in singular cases and discursive processes that seemed to represent the individuality and subjectivity of experiences of our research participants – something that thus far had not been central to the social and humanistic sciences, not even in psychology. . . . To seek and to understand what was subjective in the experience and lives from the point of view of our research participants became the primary task. (pp. ix–x)

Camic et al. (2003a) provide their impressions of psychology's attitudes toward qualitative methods and how their worldview differs from that embodied in academic psychology and quantitative methods:

- "Although other disciplines (i.e., anthropology, sociology, education, marketing, program evaluation) have vigorously incorporated qualitative methods for a number of years, most of academic psychology has had an ambivalent relationship with qualitative methods" (p. xiii).
- "Moving from the negative stereotypes of qualitative research current in psychology to a more balanced approach will require a sea change in the field" (p. 13).
- "Overreliance on positivism and experimental method throughout the 20th century has hampered inventiveness, restricting the very nature of the questions that have been asked and the sources of data that have been considered legitimate. . . . Putting the methodological

cart before the horse has constrained our full understanding of psychological processes" (pp. 3–4).

- "Qualitative research questions whether an objective conception of reality can truly exist and suggests and that other forms of investigation are necessary to increase our understanding of the thing we are studying. . . . We may not find *the* answer to what is real, but the richness within the different realities may provide us with a better answer . . . Our realities may be different, depending on our cultural background, our gender, sexual orientation, our race, or age" (pp. 4–5).
- "As a profession, psychology has generally decided that numbers are more real than words and responses on paper-and-pencil tests more real (and valid) than interviews, conversations, and other complex forms of representation" (pp. 4–5).
- "Research that exist[s] outside of positivism and the experimental method are looked on as inferior and are not taken as seriously by journal editors, funding sources, doctoral dissertation committees, or faculty in psychology departments" (p. 5).
- " 'Objectivity' as taught in many psychology textbooks and class-rooms, is a myth" (Camic et al., p. 6).

Camic et al. (2003a) also indicate that, in their view, qualitative methods have several advantages. These include:

- Usefulness "as a tool for exploring a topic or problem that has not previously been researched" (p. 8).
- Seeking "to maximize the ecological validity of the data by gathering it in real-world contexts" (p. 8).
- The ability to supply a "holistic analysis of complex, dynamic, and exceptional phenomena" (p. 9).
- Usefulness in providing an "analysis of subjective meaning" (p. 10).
- A means for "analysis of the aesthetic dimension of experience" (p. 10).

Eisner (2003), who is rather contemptuous of experimental psychology, says that psychology took physics as its model and, in consequence, favored quantitative methodologies. Eisner says,

- Regarding psychologists' beliefs in experimental control, "These beliefs represented a kind of methodological catechism that was to be learned by aspiring researchers seeking tenure and needing to do really 'rigorous' research" (p. 19).

149

- Qualitative research, according to him, became popular in the 1960s and 70s with a "growing interest in pluralism: methodological, cultural, and epistemological" (p. 19).
- "Qualitative research is differentiated from what is commonly referred [to] as quantitative research by its form of disclosure. Qualitative research uses language and image to capture, describe, and interpret what is studied. The language it uses operates on a continuum extending from the literal to the literary, from the factual to the evocative" (p. 24).

Marecek (2003) gives three reasons why, in her view, qualitative inquiry is increasing in popularity: "First, qualitative inquiry embeds the study of psychology in rich contexts of history, society, and culture. Second, it resituates the people whom we study in their life worlds, paying special attention to the social locations they occupy. Third, it regards those whom we study as reflexive, meaning-making, and intentional actors" (p. 49).

Marecek (2003) describes what she sees as five myths about qualitative work that are held by quantitative researchers (myths 1–4) and some qualitative researchers (myth 5), but which she rejects:

- "Qualitative psychology and quantitative psychology are 'complementary methods'" (p. 52). According to qualitative researchers, qualitative methods provide their own unique understanding.
- "Qualitative work is an adjunct to quantitative research" (p. 54). Qualitative researchers believe that qualitative methods are adequate unto themselves, and the findings obtained with them do not require further exploration using quantitative methods.
- "Qualitative psychology is inductive; quantitative psychology is deductive" (p. 54). Although Marecek concludes that this distinction is a myth, many other qualitative researchers believe that qualitative methods are inductive rather than deductive. Moreover, it is not clear that quantitative researchers entertain the idea that quantitative research is exclusively deductive, whereas qualitative research is exclusively inductive.
- "Qualitative psychology is just 'psychology without numbers'" (p. 55). Although Marecek concedes that qualitative researchers tend to eschew numeric measurement, she suggests that this is beside the point. She goes on to say, "The heart of qualitative inquiry is its epistemological stance: its commitment to interrogating subjectivity, intentional action, and experiences embedded in real-life contexts. . . . Qualitative inquiry is not so much a different *means*

of doing psychology but an approach with different *ends*. It asks different questions and produces a different kind of knowledge" (pp. 55–56).

- "Qualitative approaches guarantee [politically] progressive outcomes" (p. 55). Marecek attributes this view to some feminists who advocate qualitative methods, but notes that any method can be used for various political ends.

The various quotes cited above are meant to convey the views of qualitative researchers, mostly in their own words, with minimal interpretation on our part. To summarize, the views of qualitative researchers include an emphasis on understanding rather than **causal analysis**, a belief that qualitative methods provide a sufficient approach to psychology in general, and a conviction that in terms of understanding real-world phenomena, qualitative methods are superior to quantitative ones. There is also the belief that objectivity, as understood by quantitative psychologists, is illusory and unattainable, or, as Camic et al. (2003b) put it, "a myth" (p. 6). The reason for this is that in the worldview underlying Big Q qualitative methods, there is no single reality but rather a number of realities determined by one's point of view.

Varieties of Qualitative Methods

The above comments and quotes provide the rationale for qualitative methods as seen by their adherents. Having considered the rationale that has been provided, we are in a position to describe specifically some of the leading methods that are employed by qualitative researchers. In many cases, similar rationales are provided for the respective methods. Rather than eliminate such redundancy, we retain it because to do otherwise would not make the rationale for the method clear. All of the methods listed below are described in Camic et al. (2003b), and can be found as well in a variety of other sources on qualitative methods (e.g., Kopala & Suzuki, 1999; Smith, 2003; Willig, 2001).

Narrative analysis

Narrative analysis is an approach concerned with the structure, content, and function of the tales that we tell both ourselves and others. Those who employ the narrative approach believe that it is through our own narratives that we understand ourselves and through the narratives of others that we understand them. As our personal narratives change, our understanding of our own identity undergoes a corresponding change. Thus, the function of narratives is to understand ourselves and others.

One of the functions of narratives is that they bring coherence into an otherwise disconnected world. Essentially, the narrative unites individual events into an understandable whole. According to Ricoeur (1991), emplotment is the process employed to bring elements into a meaningful configuration. The plot is what gives the narrative account its structure and coherence. Murray (2003) states, "The structure of narrative accounts is not fixed but depends on a variety of factors including the narrator, the audience, and the broader social and cultural context. . . . The story is constructed by the two or more parties to the exchange" (p. 99). Narrative therapists assume that psychological dysfunction occurs because people's narratives are insufficient to account for their everyday behavior. Narrative therapy consists of the therapist devising and suggesting to the client new narratives that are more in tune with the realities of everyday existence.

Narrative accounts are obtained primarily through interviews. The researcher seeks to encourage the participant to tell his or her story. This can be facilitated by the narrator getting to know the participant well before the interview begins. Too, the participant needs to feel that the stories he or she tells are valued by the researcher. If the participants are reluctant to tell their stories, there are several techniques the researcher can employ to overcome this resistance. One technique is to put the participant in a group situation in which he or she may gain confidence in relating their own narrative by listening to the narratives of others. Another technique is to get the participant to write his or her story.

Narratives are of several different types. For example, there is the life history interview in which the aim is to get a detailed account of broad aspects of the participant's life. A more restricted kind of narrative is sought in the episodic interview, in which the participant is encouraged to talk in detail about some specific aspect of his or her life, for example, how they reacted to some tragedy.

There are several procedures for analyzing narratives. For example, having heard the narrative, one might try to abstract a summary of it. In doing this the researcher might seek the core of the narrative, those aspects of it that exclude anything extraneous to the main story line. There are two methods employed to interpret narratives. One is the inductive approach in which the researcher avoids any specific set of theoretical assumptions. The second method is to employ a specific set of instructions. For example, one might interpret a narrative employing the assumptions of psychoanalysis. With either method, the goal is to come to an understanding of the person's life as they subjectively experience it.

Discourse analysis and discursive psychology

Discourse analysis is an approach within social psychology that began in 1985 (Litton & Potter, 1985). According to Potter (2003), "Discourse analysis is the study of how talk and texts are used to perform actions. **Discursive psychology** is the application of ideas from discourse analysis to issues in psychology" (p. 73). It is intended to provide not only a method for analyzing discourse but also "a perspective that includes meta-theoretical, theoretical, and analytical principles" (Potter, 2003, p. 73). This perspective is closely related to **social constructionism** and is intended to provide "a reworking of what psychology is" (p. 74).

Discourse analysis is applied to both conversational interviews between the researcher and a participant and to records of naturally occurring interactions such as the talk that might occur in a therapy session. The emphasis is not on causal influences of variables (i.e., what is the influence of X on Y), but on how particular acts are done. According to Potter, "This focus on how-questions leads to a focus on interaction rather cognition, a focus on concrete settings rather than abstract scenarios, and a focus on processes rather than outcomes" (p. 78). What Potter seems to be emphasizing is an emphasis on behavioral outcomes, for example, by what rhetorical devices does a speaker make his or her meaning clear to the listener?

There are relative merits to interviews and naturalistic observations as the basis for a discourse analysis. The type of interview method used in discourse analysis is focused on topics of concern to the researcher. The basic idea is to elicit from the participant matters that are of interest to the researcher. Potter notes, "Because of this aim, interviews in discourse work tend to be active and even argumentative" (p. 80). Potter lists three advantages and three disadvantages of interviews relative to naturalistic materials. We list the three advantages first:

- The participant's conversation can be focused upon certain pre-determined themes of interest to the researcher.
- The responses of all participants can be standardized by employing the same set of themes in the interviews.
- The interviewer can restrict the participant's verbal behavior to the specific themes of interest.

153

The disadvantages are:

- The interview may provoke the participant into providing responses that are more related to expectations, cognitions, and the like, than to action themes.
- The participant may reflect upon what is being said, which may be different than what they do in their real environment.
- If one is interested in a particular form of behavior, why not study it directly rather than asking about it?

The advantages of employing naturalistic materials, according to Potter, are as follows:

- Naturalistic materials are more direct.
- It is easier to capture the actions in the particular situations in which they occur.
- Reactions of the participant to general features of the setting can be studied.

Naturalistic materials do not allow the benefits of focus listed above for interviews, and there also may be ethical problems associated with employing them.

Most discourse analyses use a highly standardized transcription system that emphasizes interactionally important features of the conversation. Two interesting aspects of such transcription are as follows. One, it is extremely time consuming. According to Potter, it can take more than 20 hours to produce a transcript of one hour of interaction. The second is that it does not follow a fixed procedure but is "a craft skill" (Potter, 2003, p. 84) that can only be acquired through detailed experience with discourse materials.

Grounded theory

Grounded theory is an approach employing semi-structured interviews, case-study notes, and field observations that was developed by sociologists (Glaser & Strauss, 1967). By "grounded" is meant that the researcher begins the project with minimal preconceptions (more about this later), collects observations, revises his/her interpretation of the observations, repeating this process until a satisfactory theoretical explanation is achieved. According to Henwood and Pidgeon (2003), the researcher begins by coding the observations broadly, in a neutral manner, proceeding from there by looking for systematic patterns in the data, making new observations that generate new and more theoretically focused codes, and completing the process when no new theoretical insights occur. There is a slight difference of opinion as to how neutral the researcher can be in the initial stages of the investigation.

Henwood and Pidgeon (2003) say, "Our own experience of teaching grounded theory is that new researchers enthusiastically glean from the classic writings on the topic that they should approach their initial fieldwork and data analysis without any previous theoretical preconceptions or reference to earlier literature" (p. 137). However, even Glaser and Strauss (1967) indicate that it is impossible to achieve true neutrality. Glaser (1992) has continued to advocate an approach similar to that above in which the researcher remains as neutral as possible at the outset. However, Strauss and Corbin (1998) advocate a different approach. They suggest employing a variety of hypotheses at the outset that refer to the specific case under investigation. In summarizing these views, Henwood and Pidgeon note:

> Accordingly, we stress again our belief that there is no set way of achieving the most difficult task of all in grounded theory research: getting out of the maze of detailed and complex codings, deciding on the limits to making constant comparisons, and reaching theoretical closure or integration. (p. 152)

The listening guide method

The **listening guide** is a method whose purpose is to provide "ports of entry into the human psyche" (Gilligan, Spencer, Weinberg, & Bertsch, 2003, p. 157). Generally speaking, this is accomplished by listening to the distinctive voice possessed by each individual human being. The voice is not considered to be a singular entity but, rather, is polyphonic. According to Gilligan et al., "The *Listening Guide* method comprises a series of sequential listenings, each designed to bring the researcher into relationship with a person's distinct and multilayered voice by tuning in or listening to distinct aspects of a person's expression of her or his experience within a particular relational context" (p. 159). The steps of the successive listenings are as follows:

1. Listening for the plot – The first listening is broken into two parts, (a) listening for the plot of the stories that the participant is telling and (b) the listener attends to his or her responses to the interview.

2. I poems – The second listening involves isolating all of those instances in which the pronoun "I" is used. For example, the participant might say, "I went to the hospital." At another time, the participant might say, "I felt bad about seeing the patients." Each of these "I" lines is isolated and linked together to form what is called an I poem. An example of an I poem is given below:

> I went to the hospital
> I felt bad
> I went home

The purpose of the I poem is to focus on how the participant speaks about herself.

3. Listening for contrapuntal voices – This "offers a way of hearing and developing an understanding of several different layers of a person's expressed experience" (Gilligan et al., p. 164). The researcher reads through the transcript of the interview several times, "each time tuning into one aspect of the story being told, or one voice within the person's expression of her or his experience" (p. 165). "Some of these voices may be in harmony with one another, in opposition to one another, or even contradictory" (p. 165).

4. Composing an analysis – In the final step, "an interpretation of the interview or text is developed that pulls together and synthesizes what has been learned through this entire process and an essay or analysis is composed" (p. 168). Gilligan et al. conclude by saying, "The *Listening Guide* method offers a way of illuminating the complex and multilayered nature of the expression of human experience and the interplay between self and relationship, psyche and culture" (p. 169).

Participatory action research

Fine et al. (2003) define **participatory action research** (PAR) as "an epistemology that assumes knowledge is rooted in social relations and most powerful when produced collaboratively through action" (p. 173). PAR is usually practiced within some community with the aim of under-standing the impact of some social program within that community. The typical procedure is for the nominal investigator to involve the individuals being studied not merely as objects of study alone but as genuine and equal participants in the research process. This view that the participants are in fact participant-researchers is reflected by the fact that Fine has nine co-authors on her chapter, several of whom were prisoners who were the focus of the investigation. The fact that in the prison population study by Fine et al. the prisoners were not merely objects of investigation is indicated by the following statement:

> In the participatory research propounded here, the silenced are not just incidental to the curiosity of the researcher but are the masters of inquiry into the underlying causes of the events in their world. In this context research becomes a means of moving them beyond silence into a quest to proclaim the world (Gaventa, 1993). (Fine et al., 2003, p. 175)

The specific study reported by Fine et al. (2003) was concerned with the effects of high school and college courses on changes in prisoner attitudes and behaviors. The research was designed employing the input of a variety of individuals: the prison administration staff, the inmates, faculty, and volunteers. Fine et al. list eight methods that they employed in the study, seven of which would be classified as qualitative and one as quantitative. The qualitative methods included interviews (some of inmates, some of former inmates, some of corrections officers and administrators), focus groups (with inmates, children of inmates, faculty, and college presidents), surveys of faculty, and student narratives. The quantitative method employed was a statistical analysis of former inmates who attended college while in prison. Among the findings was that women who participated in college while in prison had only a 7.7 percent return-to-custody rate in contrast to a 29.9 percent rate for all female offenders released between 1985 and 1995. Another finding was that women with no college education were twice as likely to be arrested for a new crime than women with some college education. Women with no college education were 18 times more likely to violate parole than women with college education.

It was also found that women with college education underwent a transformation. This transformation consisted of a more positive feeling about themselves. They described themselves as different from their previous selves in being more self-controlled, more concerned with the impression they were making on others, caring more about whether their behavior would get them in trouble, being less angry, and so on.

Fine et al.'s (2003) interpretation of the findings described above was, "As these women testify, our quantitative and qualitative data confirm what other researchers and prisoners have found: Core elements of higher education, such as self-reflection and critical inquiry, spur the production of critical subjectivities, transformed and connected selves, and in turn transformed communities" (p. 186). One inmate-author-participant saw the following as advantages of PAR:

- Inmate-participants, prison staff, and administrators have inside knowledge of prisons and an understanding of prison life that is not accessible to outsiders.
- People in prison are more trusting of other inmates than of outsiders.
- Using prisoners as researchers provides a valuable experience beneficial to all participants in the study.

Among the weaknesses of the PAR procedure as applied to prison life are the following:

- Inmate-participants worry that being completely truthful about prison life may produce undesirable consequences from both other prisoners and administrators.
- The same difficulty was noted by the faculty researchers, i.e., speaking certain truths might produce difficulty for the inmate-participants.
- Power relationships among the inmate-participants and faculty-participants are inherently unequal and difficult to correct. However, Fine et al. indicate that over time distinctions between inmates and faculty diminished.
- Faculty researchers did not have complete control over the study. For example, the administration might decide to move one of the inmate-participants to another prison in the middle of the study. This is probably a general problem associated with more natural-istic types of research.

An avowed objective of many PAR researchers is not merely the gathering of technical knowledge. It is stated, "Empowerment, for example, is an avowed goal of participatory research, but it does not result from technical knowledge alone. Empowerment is realized through the experience in engaging in collective social actions" (Park, 1993, p. 4). Examples of such collective action are as follows:

> It is about rural black women in southern co-ops talking about loans for planting. It is about Latinas in New York City building their own literacy curriculum. It is about citizens of Korean descent in the United States or Canada taking political action. It is about community groups in Ontario proposing tax reforms. It is about people of the First Nations researching land rights. (Hall, 1993, p. xvii)

Portraiture

Davis (2003) defines **portraiture** as follows:

> The research portrait, a written narrative, is imprinted with the researcher's understanding of and relationship with the individual or site that is represented in the text. Like the artist, the research portraitist works to balance elements of context, thematic structure, relationship, and voice into an aesthetic whole that is so carefully constructed that every part seems an essential ingredient in the clarity of cohesive inter-pretation. (p. 199)

In portraiture, an important belief is that narratives, or stories, are the primary structures through which identities, both personal and pro-fessional, are organized. The ideal is to produce an authentic narrative that portrays the individual or individuals of interest. Coherence in portraiture is concerned with the coherence of the narrative that is developed. Portraiture is an interpretive technique in which the "portrait" emerges as a result of various conversations back and forth between the researcher and participant or participants. As Davis (2003) says, "portraiture relies on inductive rather than deductive analysis, the generation rather than testing of theories, and a humanistic deter-mination to speak through relevant voices" (p. 200). Note that Davis characterizes portraiture as being exclusively concerned with the generation, rather than testing, of theories. Portraiture as a research technique sees parallels between itself and what an artist does when creating a portrait. In both cases, authenticity is sought between the represented person and the portrait.

Elements that go into the creation of a portrait include the follow-ing. The researcher first seeks a general context for embracing the participants. This may include reading a variety of material such as newspaper articles and census reports. Other aspects of the context con-sidered important by Davis include the physical context, the personal context, and the historical context. The second element is group voice. A group voice refers to a perspective that is not just that of a single researcher but that of a group of researchers. In Davis's (2003) words, "Group voice is simply the agreed on parameters that lend harmony and coherence to the individual voices of team researchers as they meet various in their portraiture research" (p. 207). A third element is relationship, which refers to the relationship between the researchers on the one hand and the various participants on the other. In seek-ing a portrait, the participants let the researchers "know what, if any, erroneous information [they] may have included and where, if any place, [they] may have inadvertently offended" (p. 209). Emergent themes are a fourth element. The basic idea is that through a series of portraits certain themes will emerge, leading to a new understanding. The final methodological element is that of an aesthetic whole, which drives the entire research process. That is, the ultimate goal is a coherent portrait, with all of its various features balanced, and this goal determines what is done at each step in the process.

Ethnographic methods

Ethnographic methods were originally employed by anthropologists and sociologists, and more recently were adopted in the fields of psychology, communication, and education. Ethnographic methods are concerned with a special class of meaning, meaning that is structured by culture. According to Miller, Hengst, and Wang (2003), ethnographic methods, which arose originally in the study of different cultures, had the goal "to understand a particular culture on its own terms, to represent the meaning of actions and institutions from 'the native's point of view' (Malinowski, 1922)" (p. 219). There is a great variety of ethnographic methods that have some commonalities, which is what we will emphasize here.

In dealing with culture, what we would consider to be a modal approach in ethnography has the following characteristics. It is a socially constructed, interpretive view; it suggests that part of the research question is generated by the complex relationship between the researcher and the participant; knowledge is defined in terms of ways that make sense to both the researcher and the participant. These methods suggest that the actor's point of view should be a privileged one. In terms of some more specific procedures, Miller et al. (2003) suggest:

> Ethnographic research involves taking up a rigorous program of scientific inquiry marked by repeated and varied observations and data collection; detailed recordings of, and reactions to, such observations; a skeptical stance by the researcher that forces as many questions from the continuous interpretation of the data as it provides answers; and the presentation of ongoing interpretations to the larger scientific community. (pp. 222–223)

Ethnographic inquiries have the following characteristics:

- A sustained engagement with the participants by, for example, living among them.

- In trying to take the perspective of the participant, the researchers attempt not to mistake their own cultural understanding for the understanding of the culture being examined.
- In examining individual actions and events, the ethnographer attempts to interpret them within the context of the culture being examined.
- The ethnographer must be prepared to revise and extend his or her interpretations as new information becomes available as a result of continuous contact with the participants.

The psychoanalytic interview

Kvale (2003) is a strong defender of qualitative methods and suggests that quantitative methods may, under certain circumstances, be misleading. He certainly feels that this is true of the **psychoanalytic interview**, for which he says:

> One may speculate that if tape recorders had been available in Vienna in Freud's time, there would have existed no powerful psychoanalytical theory today; instead there might perhaps remain a small sect of psychoanalytical researchers reading and categorizing their transcripts, and discussing their reliability, rather than attentively listening to the multiple layers of meaning revealed in their embodied therapeutic interactions. (p. 288)

Kvale suggests that the psychoanalytical research interview, appropriately modified, can serve as a powerful qualitative research method. He bases this suggestion on noting an affinity with other postmodern developments: "The mode of understanding in the psychoanalytical interview is in important aspects close to conceptions of knowledge developed within existential, hermeneutical, and postmodern philosophy" (p. 277). Kvale notes a number of characteristics of the psychoanalytical interview and subsequently described how these can be modified to serve the purposes of research rather than therapy. These characteristics are as follows:

- Use of individual case study
- An open mode of interviewing in which the patient is free to express whatever thoughts come to mind
- Interpretation of the patient's statements by the psychoanalyst
- Extension of psychoanalysis over a considerable temporal period

- Reciprocal personal involvement between therapist and patient
- Emphasis on irrational behavior
- Goal of changing the patient.

Kvale goes on to indicate that some characteristics of the psycho-analytical interview with patients are not transferable to the psycho-analytical interview with research participants. One of these is the temporal period, which will typically be much shorter in research than in clinical practice. Another is that the intense emotional interaction between therapist and patient in clinical practice is simply not appropriate in the research setting. In the research setting, unlike the psycho-analytical interview, we are not seeking to change the participant.

According to Kvale (2003), the psychoanalytical interview technique, employed as a research method, is objective in four different senses:

- It is free from partisan bias as a result of the intensive training of the therapist or researcher.
- The method allows intersubjective agreement between therapist and patient, and among therapists.
- The method reflects the nature of the object researched by allow-ing the object to speak for itself.
- It also allows the object to object, by which Kvale means that the participant's views are taken into account.

Summary

The aims of the methods described above were summarized succinctly by Willig (2001), a strong advocate of qualitative research. She says,

Qualitative researchers tend to be concerned with meaning. That is, they are interested in how people make sense of the world and how they experience events. They aim to understand "what it is like" to experience particular conditions (e.g. what it means and how it feels to live with chronic illness or to be unemployed) and how people manage certain situations (e.g. how people negotiate family life or relations with work colleagues). Qualitative researchers tend, therefore, to be con-cerned with the quality and texture of experience, rather than with the identification of cause–effect relationships. They do not tend to work with "variables" that are defined by the researcher before the research pro-cess begins. This is because qualitative researchers tend to be interested in the meanings attributed to events by the research participants them-selves. Using preconceived "variables" would lead to the imposition

162

of the researcher's meanings and it would preclude the identification of respondents' own ways of making sense of the phenomenon under investigation. The objective of qualitative research is *to describe* and possibly *explain* events and experiences, but *never to predict*. (p. 9, emphasis ours)

We can summarize Willig's views by indicating that qualitative methods are inductive, rather than deductive, and emphasize individual experience over universal principles or laws, understanding rather than causality, description rather than prediction, and what is unique rather than what is common to people.

Chapter Summary

Qualitative inquiry is an approach to research that is rapidly becoming very popular in psychology. Adherents of the qualitative approach supply a rationale for their use that differs substantially from that embraced by most psychological researchers. In this chapter, we have tried to convey the central elements of the qualitative approach. One way in which this was accomplished was to supply differentiating characteristics of qualitative versus quantitative methods. As one example, whereas quantitative methods emphasize prediction, qualitative methods emphasize understanding. Another way in which we conveyed the elements of the qualitative approach was to describe several specific qualitative methods currently in popular use, such as narrative, discourse analysis, and participatory action research. Based on our coverage of the differentiating characteristics of qualitative and quantitative methods and our descriptions of various qualitative methods, the reader should have a good grasp of the major and fundamental differences between the qualitative and quantitative approaches to research. In the next chapter, we provide a critical analysis both of qualitative inquiry and its relation to more conventional approaches to psychological research.

CRITICAL EVALUATION OF QUALITATIVE INQUIRY'S APPROACH TO QUALITATIVE METHODS

> I actually think that the well-publicized tension between quantitative and qualitative approaches has a greater ring of truth when formulated as a problem in ontology rather than as a problem in method. (R. A. Shweder, 1996, p. 177)

Introduction

As is perhaps apparent from the **qualitative methods** described in the previous chapter, **qualitative inquiry** is primarily, if not exclusively, concerned with reports of human experience in real-world contexts. In this chapter, we will make clear why this approach is adopted by advocates of qualitative inquiry and why we think it is too narrow to be a fully adequate approach to psychology.

As emphasized throughout the book, our approach to scientific methods is that of **naturalism**. With regard to methodology, naturalism is the position that methodology should be evaluated as other matters in science are evaluated, empirically. This means that in evaluating a specific method, say, experimentation, we would evaluate it not in isolation but in terms of its ability to solve scientific problems relative to other methods applied to particular problem areas. For example, although experimentation may be among the best available methods for studying problems of learning and cognition, it may not be one of the best methods for dealing with certain gender differences because gender, unlike learning, cannot be varied experimentally.

Consistent with above, in specific instances, working scientists evaluate particular methodologies in terms of the desirable outcomes they produce. As one example, Krueger (2001) recently defended the use of null hypothesis testing statistics in psychological research on empirical grounds. Even some individuals who are committed to the use of qualitative methods agree that methodological issues should be decided on pragmatic grounds, that is, on which particular method works best under which particular circumstances. For example, Weinberg (2002), in his recent edited book, *Qualitative Research Methods*, which contains readings from the areas of anthropology and sociology, states, "My basic argument, then, is that the scientific validity and importance of qualitative research methods can only be sensibly decided within the context of specific *dispute domains*" (p. 2). That is, the issue of which methodologies are appropriate to a particular area of investigation is to be decided on the basis of a variety of specific and testable considerations. Weinberg goes on to say,

> The upshot of this approach to scientific method is this: it is only by explicitly granting that our ideas are *always* contestable, and endeavoring to discover, anticipate, and respond effectively to the precise ways in which they are contestable, that we might give our ideas whatever scientific legitimacy they may come to possess. (p. 3)

This statement is completely consistent with the spirit of naturalism recommended in this book.

Weinberg (2002) also notes, "Since, in practice, we cannot for long dispense with comparative evaluations of the truth of different ideas about the world, we might as well think seriously about how best to go about making them" (p. 4). Weinberg's position is, "On any actual occasion of dispute, there will be resources at hand, sufficient for all practical purposes, to determine the most adequate among competing accounts" (p. 13). Weinberg cautions qualitative researchers as follows: "We must not forget that the scientific legitimacy of qualitative research methods is to be achieved in no small part through direct dialogue with the specific critiques that have been arrayed against them" (p. 16). Note that Weinberg's position is consistent with naturalism and that it differs from that of most qualitative researchers in psychology, who advocate evaluating qualitative methods on other than empirical grounds.

Given the above position, it is clear that we are open to determining the circumstances under which qualitative approaches may be more effective than **quantitative methods**. Determining these circumstances is a legitimate area of scientific inquiry. We agree with the philosopher **Giere** (2001), who says, "Scientific explanations are the obvious exemplars for naturalistic explanations, but I would not want to rule out historical explanations in the form of narratives expressed in every-day concepts, or, indeed, every-day explanations themselves, so long as they make no overt appeals to a transcendental realm" (p. 54). Consistent with Giere's suggestion, we agree that qualitative research methods are widely valued tools that can be used effectively for certain purposes. That we are not alone in this view is indicated by the fact that virtually all undergraduate psychological research methods texts, which, of course, emphasize quantitative methods, also include discussions of qualitative methods and the conditions under which they are useful. Moreover, as far as we are aware, no quantitative researchers would discourage the use of qualitative research methods where they are appropriate. This would certainly include determining the wants, needs, and aspirations of people in order to improve their living condition, as is the case with **participatory action research** and user research for product development.

Consider some examples. The **narratives** of individuals can be of considerable usefulness in understanding their life situations, their hopes, aspirations, and problems. Too, listening to individuals who have specific experience with some system can be helpful in isolating problems of the system. In the process of designing systems for certain purposes, such as in the development of a product, and in the beginning stages of many inquiries, it is obviously useful to gather data, opinions of people, and the like, in the absence of strong preconceptions. In this regard, the noted naturalist **E. O. Wilson** (1987) states, "Words, as opposed to equations and data, are especially important in the early stages of exploration of a subject" (p. 10). At the same time, though using qualitative methods, nothing prevents the investigator from forming hypotheses for later test. These may include noting quantitative relations between variables, gathering additional data, and/or employing new and novel research procedures.

Despite our view that qualitative methods are useful in a wide variety of circumstances, we do have three differences with the modal positions of qualitative researchers on various issues. The major difference has to do with the criteria qualitative researchers employ to justify the use of qualitative methods. A second difference centers around various misunderstandings that qualitative researchers have of **logical positivism** and its influence in current-day psychology. The third type of disagreement has to do with the methodological and ontological assumptions that qualitative researchers adopt. Our misgivings about the qualitative approach seem to be shared by at least some of its advocates. For example, McGrath and Johnson (2003) state, "The assumptions of the alternative positions [those of qualitative inquiry], if fully adopted, make a shambles of the usual meanings of the scientific enterprise. Such a potential lapse into a solipsism that denies the value of systematic efforts to understand human behavior – that is the *dark side* of qualitative research." (p. 46). We could not agree more with these statements.

Justification of Qualitative Methods

The ultimate argument used by most qualitative researchers to justify the use of qualitative methods is that they employ a different **paradigm** than that embraced by researchers who use quantitative methods (see, e.g., McGrath & Johnson's, 2003, quote in the previous chapter). According to this view, the paradigm employed by qualitative researchers necessarily implies that qualitative methods are to be preferred, usually if not always, over quantitative methods. The reasoning is that because their paradigm has a different **ontology**, it necessarily implies that science be practiced employing both methods and aims different from those of quantitative researchers. Contrary to this view, we suggest that the paradigm employed by qualitative researchers, with its emphasis on individual experience of persons, does not rule out quantitative methods, nor does the paradigm employed by quantitative researchers rule out qualitative methods.

In examining the justification for qualitative methods employed by qualitative researchers, it is important to realize that the justification is based on other than empirical considerations. As the quote that begins this chapter, from a well-known qualitative methodologist, Shweder (1996), states, the distinction between qualitative and quantitative methods, in the view of qualitative methodologists, is really an argument over ontology rather than method. Essentially, in framing the difference between the two approaches, qualitative methodologists have based the distinction on ontological considerations rather than empirical ones. That is to say, qualitative researchers have not attempted to show that qualitative methods are superior to quantitative methods in the many cases in which both can be used. It should be noted that our view is that qualitative methods may be more appropriate than quantitative ones under some circumstances, and vice versa. This is not the view we are quarreling with here. Rather, our disagreement centers on two points suggested by qualitative researchers: that qualitative methods are always superior to quantitative ones, and that methods are to be justified on grounds other than empirical ones.

The view of justification adopted by qualitative researchers appears to stem from the specific view of science suggested by Kuhn (1962) in his influential book, according to which a change in paradigm always involves a change in methodology. That is, Kuhn argued that methodological assumptions are subservient to the more inclusive epistemological and ontological assumptions of a particular paradigm. In Kuhn's words, "Paradigms differ in more than substance. . . . They are the source of the methods, problem field, and standards of solution accepted by any mature scientific community at any given time" (p. 102). Kuhn goes on to say, "In learning a paradigm, the scientist acquires theory, methods, and standards together, usually in an inextricable mix" (1962, p. 108). According to Kuhn, a worldview consists of ontology, methodology, and values. As emphasized by Laudan (1984), Kuhn's position regarding scientific change is that a paradigm change from one worldview (WV1) to another (WV2) involves a change of all three simultaneously, as indicated below:

WV1 (ontology 1, methodology 1, values 1)
shifts to
WV2 (ontology 2, methodology 2, values 2)

It is important to realize that Kuhn offered little or no historical evidence for his position that methodology is dependent upon the particular paradigm in which it is embedded. To the contrary, the historical record indicates otherwise. Kuhn's student, Larry Laudan, has performed detailed analysis of the historical record and found many cases inconsistent with Kuhn's analysis. Contrary to Kuhn, the historical record indicates that the belief that distinctive methodologies require distinctive ontologies and epistemologies is incorrect. That is, the historical record indicates that methodology, ontology, and **epistemology** can each change independently of the other. The basis for the sort of incorrect analysis offered by Kuhn, according to Laudan (1984), is that historians and philosophers tend to emphasize major transitions between paradigms, which may occur over exceedingly long periods of time. In focusing upon the beginning and end of some major scientific epoch, historians and philosophers tend to miss the fact that the complete transition was produced by a variety of piecemeal changes that occurred over the long intervening time period. It is only at the end of the time period that all aspects of a worldview (ontology, methodology, and values) have changed.

Laudan (1984) demonstrated using historical material that changes in ontology, methodology, or values can each occur independently. In contrast to Kuhn's model:

WV1 (ontology 1, methodology 1, values 1)
can shift to
(1) (ontology 2, methodology 1, values 1)

or

(2) (ontology 1, methodology 2, values 1)

or

(3) (ontology 1, methodology 1, values 2)

Note in the three examples given above, that methodology can change independently of either ontology or values, and each of these can change independently of the other. Over time, WV1 may change into WV2 by a cascading of independent changes in the three aspects, as shown in the example below:

WV1 (ontology 1, methodology 1, values 1)
shifts to
(1) (ontology 1, methodology 2, values 1)

which shifts to

(2) (ontology 2, methodology 2, values 1)

and then to

WV2 (ontology 2, methodology 2, values 2)

Laudan (1984) offers historical evidence that each of the three aspects can change independently. We will consider the case in which methodology underwent very substantial change in the absence of change in either ontology or values. Among the trends that Laudan cited in support of his view was that, from **Francis Bacon** onward, scientists subscribed to the idea that science was to be advanced employing **induction**, that is, by the accumulation of specific instances that supported some general statement. The rule for scientists in this period was to carefully collect facts, eschewing as far as possible any and all prior hypotheses. In other words, the scientist was enjoined to keep an entirely open mind. This approach was embraced by scientists for about 200 years. By about 1850, the view that science was totally inductive was replaced by the idea that hypothetical entities could indeed be postulated and their justification was to be achieved by hypothesis testing. In other words, whereas scientists had previously subscribed to the idea that science was to be advanced by the painstaking accumulation of specific information, they now believed that science was best advanced by making bold guesses as to the hidden causes of observable reality. This shift, which may well have been the greatest single methodological change in all of science, was not accompanied by any change either in the ontology science embraced or in its scientific values (see Laudan, 1984, for details). Similar historical analyses were supplied by Laudan for other aspects of scientific change.

Clearly, the historical record, far from justifying the view that a change in methodology necessarily results from a change in paradigm, suggests, on the contrary, that methodological change can occur independently of any other sort of scientific change. Thus, when qualitative researchers suggest that their methodological approach necessarily stems from a different set of ontological assumptions, they do so not only in the absence of any historical support whatsoever but in the face of contrary historical evidence. It should be emphasized that qualitative researchers, like Kuhn, have offered no evidence for their view that methodological change necessarily occurs as a result of a wholesale change in paradigm. Given these circumstances, the view embraced by qualitative researchers that an emphasis on qualitative methods necessarily involves a break from quantitative science is totally without evidentiary foundation and can only be considered an unjustified opinion. As Weinberg (2002), a qualitative researcher himself, has noted, qualitative researchers have the duty and obligation to justify their methodological predilections by meeting the legitimate objections raised by the quantitative methodologists. Because the argument that the qualitative approach involves a paradigm change is contradicted by the historical record, some other justification must necessarily be supplied. So far, no evidence along this line has been provided by the qualitative researchers.

Misunderstanding of Positivism

Many qualitative researchers indicate that quantitative researchers are dominated by adherence to positivism. They are mistaken in this, as they are about their understanding of the positions that positivists are supposed to embrace. In identifying contemporary psychology with positivism, qualitative researchers are probably referring to logical positivism, which, as described in Chapter 2, was influential in psychology in the middle part of the 20th century. However, they are not specific on this point, often using only the term "positivism," which *Webster's New World Dictionary of the American Language* (1980) defines as follows:

> A system of philosophy basing knowledge solely on data of sense experience; esp., a system of philosophy, originated by Auguste Comte, based solely on observable, scientific facts and their relations to each other: it rejects speculation about or search for ultimate origins. (p. 1112)

Most quantitative psychologists are not positivists in the sense of this definition or in the sense of logical positivism. Notice that this definition suggests that the proper subject matter of psychology is observed experience and observed experience alone. However, most quantitative psychologists postulate unobservable entities such as attention, habits, desires, working memory, and so on. Postulation of such entities is definitely not a characteristic of positivism.

Another mistaken idea of qualitative researchers is that positivists favor quantitative methods to the exclusion of qualitative methods. No positivist would reject any method that produced "data of sense experience," as indicated in the above definition. Qualitative researchers suggest that positivists are interested in cause and effect relations. This, too, is a mistake because the categories of cause and effect are not themselves observable entities and, therefore, do not occupy the attention of positivists. Another example of their mistaken ideas about positivism is their characterization of it as embracing realism. One meaning of realism is that the entities postulated to explain sense data, such as memory, really exist. Because a positivist would not posit memory as an explanatory category in the first place, it is clear that he or she could not believe in it as "a real thing" in the second place.

It is ironic that qualitative researchers characterize quantitative researchers as positivists, when the positions of qualitative researchers are closer in many respects to those of positivism than are the positions of current-day quantitative researchers. For example, qualitative researchers place a much heavier emphasis on direct experience than do quantitative researchers. As another example, qualitative researchers place more emphasis on induction than do quantitative researchers, induction being the favored logical procedure of positivists (see Chapters 2 and 3). In our opinion, qualitative researchers are really not objecting to positivism when they reject quantitative methods. What they really object to, in our view, is experimentation, which they mistakenly identify as a methodological position that flows from positivism and positivism alone. It is true, of course, that positivists accept experimentation, but so too do a variety of other scientists who either have no particular philosophy of science or, if they have one, embrace some variety of postpositivist position.

Note that there is at least one advocate of qualitative methods, Michell (2003), who would agree with the major outlines of the criticisms expressed above. Michell asks, "So why are qualitative researchers so hostile towards positivism" (p. 6)? Answering his own question, he says, "The answer is complex, but the puzzle is partly resolved by noting the tendency of qualitative researchers to systematically misunderstand positivism" (p. 6).

Specific Positions of Qualitative Researchers

As indicated in earlier chapters, qualitative researchers often adopt various positions associated with **postmodernism**. Among other things, this means that they adhere to the view that there are many realities and that none of these is worthy of more intellectual respect than any other. This leads many qualitative researchers to adopt the position of **relativism** (see, e.g., Camic et al.'s, 2003a, statement in this regard in the previous chapter). Often these ideas are represented as being new to scientific methodology when in reality they are old ideas repackaged under new names. Let us deal with these various postmodernist positions one at a time.

Relativism

The adherence of qualitative researchers to relativism seems to stem from their desire to differentiate themselves from their non-relativistic counterparts in academic psychology. First of all, we can note that there is nothing new in the relativistic position. It was already an old position when it was adopted by various Greek philosophers (Zeller, 1955). Secondly, there is no necessary relationship between qualitative methods and relativism. Non-relativists are as fully capable of adopting and using qualitative methods as are relativists. What seems to be the case is that their relativism stems not so much from the use of qualitative methods as from a desire to avoid quantitative methods.

Experimentation is seen by relativists as having many undesirable characteristics, some of which we will discuss in due course. These would include linear causality, limiting findings to the specific context in which data were obtained, and the treatment of participants as subjects or objects to be manipulated. None of these, as will become clear, are necessary characteristics of quantitative methods. If we are correct in this, the reliance on relativism represents an effort to distinguish qualitative researchers from quantitative researchers and to suggest that qualitative research is as good as, or better than, quantitative research. Qualitative researchers seem to chafe under the idea that quantitative researchers consider qualitative methods to be a valuable, but necessarily limited, approach to science. Of course, as indicated, most quantitative researchers do not consider quantitative methods to be of universal applicability.

Causal analysis

Although some qualitative researchers strive for **causal analysis**, most do not and instead seek understanding, as illustrated by the quotes cited in the previous chapter. They describe qualitative research as providing descriptions and interpretations, rather than causal relations. The tendency to seek understanding, rather than causation, seems to be another factor fostering the embrace of qualitative methods. As with relativism, there seems to be no necessary relationship between the desire for description and understanding and embracing qualitative methods. This is recognized by some qualitative researchers, who suggest that qualitative methods can be used in the quest for causal analysis.

Restriction to sane, intelligent adult humans

Qualitative methods in principle can be applied to a variety of participants, ranging from infants to the elderly, from the mentally stable to psychotics, from the simplest animals to humans, and from neurophysiological measures to verbal behavior. Despite this, qualitative researchers in general tend to restrict the object of investigation to fully mentally functioning adult human beings who are mentally healthy. The reason for this restriction is that qualitative researchers appear to be primarily interested in the inner experience of the individuals they study. Qualitative researchers seldom, if ever, comment on how the narrowness restricts the data they collect and the types of problems they investigate. Consider some of the fertile areas of investigation that are beyond the scope of this narrow approach. In animals, for example, many important processes have been investigated, ranging from emotions to learning and complex cognitive processes. Much of this work that stems from animals is foundational in various branches of psychology, ranging from cognitive neuroscience to clinical application. Too, a variety of participants who lack any semblance of coherent verbal ability, either because they are too young to have yet developed language or because they are psychologically impaired, as in severe autism, cannot be studied. That is, verbal communication with either infants or autistics is severely limited or impossible.

Given these limitations, it is clear that qualitative methods as they are used by qualitative researchers deal with only a highly restricted portion of psychology, primarily the inner experience of mentally capable adult humans. It is ironic that qualitative researchers, who tend to see themselves as more broadminded than quantitative researchers, restrict the information they gather to a highly limited set of conditions. Even under the most optimistic set of assumptions, the approach of the qualitative researchers could be considered to be extremely impoverished. Under a less optimistic set of assumptions, it may be considered to be impoverished to the point of irrelevance. For example, there are many who believe that conscious processing of information, even for functioning human adults, plays only a small role in causing human behavior (see, e.g., the recent volume, *The New Unconscious*, edited by Hassin, Uleman, & Bargh, 2004, for which the front piece states that "a new picture of the cognitive unconscious has emerged from a variety of disciplines," and "According to this picture, unconscious processes seem to be capable of doing many things that were thought to require intention, deliberation, and conscious awareness"). Consider the views of some prominent researchers and theorists in various areas of psychology:

- Daly and Wilson (1988) noted, "We have known at least since Freud that people may have little insight into their own motives" (p. 50).
- The prominent theorist Endel Tulving (2002) stated with reference to human memory that studies conducted since his 1983 book, *Elements of Episodic Memory*, indicate that "there is no necessary correlation between behavior and conscious experience" (p. 4).
- The prominent attention researcher, Steven Yantis (2001), notes that it is generally accepted with respect to vision that "there are aspects of visual functioning . . . to which we do not have conscious access" (2001, p. 376).

- Regarding selection of strategies that people may employ to perform tasks, Cary and Reder (2002) conclude that strategy selection "can occur without (a) conscious consideration of different strategies or (b) conscious awareness of factors influencing one's strategy use" (p. 63).
- Lakin, Jefferis, Cheng, and Chartrand (2003) indicate that much mimicking of the behavior of others "occurs outside of conscious awareness, and without any intent to mimic or imitate" (p. 145).

The question arises as to why it has only recently occurred that qualitative methods have been strongly recommended as the primary methodology in psychology (Camic et al., 2003b). Although opinion on this matter can only be speculative, it seems worthwhile to consider one major possibility. It is to be noted that qualitative methods were accepted in fields such as anthropology and sociology long before they were recommended in psychology. A characteristic of these areas is that they tend to deal primarily with human beings in cultural settings. Qualitative methods such as narrative, participatory action, and so on, are certainly useful in these areas, particularly when dealing with cultural factors. But, although some investigators are interested in the psychological effects of culture, this is an important part, but only a part, of the vast field of psychology. One whose primary interest is culture is much less likely to use a variety of methods that are commonly employed in other areas of psychology, as for example classical conditioning of infants and animals, psychophysical methods to measure basic perceptual processes such as dark adaptation in adults, or reaction time and event-related potentials to stimuli of various intensities and qualities. It is possibly because psychologists know of the worth of all of these other various methods and procedures for many of the problems of concern in psychology that they were not inclined as much as individuals in other areas of investigation to see all of psychology as dependent upon qualitative methods. To put it differently, psychologists are aware that much useful information can be produced employing methods other than quantitative ones in relation to certain kinds of participants and problems. However, they are also aware of the limitations of these methods, even in the cases for which they seem appropriate.

Looking forward to the past

Qualitative researchers see themselves as adopting a new paradigm that is both different from and superior to that employed by quantitative researchers. The paradigm they adopt has many features in common with that embraced by various relativists and postmodernists. It may be doubted that the paradigm explicitly acknowledged by qualitative researchers is either new or novel. Indeed, in our view it represents a return to older pre-scientific thinking.

First of all, the view that there is not a single objective reality but rather multiple realities that are a product of human construction is not a new view, but one embraced in ancient philosophy. As one example, consider the Greek **Sophists**, whose views were popular in the 5th century BCE. Their views sound very much like those adopted by current postmodernists. The Sophists believed that all knowledge, laws, and morality were created by individuals, and thus the Sophists can be regarded as the forerunners of current social constructionists. Zeller (1955) says of Protagoras, the leading Sophist, "There can be . . . little doubt that Protagoras regarded all morals and laws as only relatively valid, that is binding only on the human community which formulated them and only so long as that community holds them to be good" (p. 99). A contemporary postmodernist could not have expressed it better! The Sophists eschewed truth and any form of absolute knowledge, seeking instead to provide insights into the ambiguities of life. Zeller says of the Sophists, "Sophism had by its philosophic skepticism not merely thrown doubts on the possibility of science but by its relativistic theories and thorough-going individualism of some of its members had shaken the existing authority of religion, state and the family to their foundations" (p. 111).

The Sophists placed emphasis on personal experience and rejected any claim of abstract knowledge. According to De Romilly (1992), "In the Sophists' intellectual world, where nothing was accepted a priori any more, the only sure criterion was immediate, concrete human experience . . . Our own judgements, our own feelings, and interests now constituted the sole criteria. 'Man is the measure of all things,' Protagoras used to say" (p. 9). Moreover, De Romilly (1992) suggests that by the 5th century BCE, due to the Sophists, "Philosophy shifted its attention to man himself, and from cosmogony to morality and politics" (p. 11). Note that this emphasis on human experience and politics corresponds closely with major objectives of qualitative researchers who have increasingly turned to a concern with practical matters and activism of various sorts (see Gaventa, 1993).

The Sophist Protagoras restricted reality only to that which could be observed. Sextus Empiricus, another Sophist, quoted by Kerferd (1981, p. 108), says of Protagoras's view, "Thus, according to him, Man becomes the criterion of things that are; for all things that appear to men also are, and things that appear to no man, also are without being." Kerferd notes that Protagoras's "doctrine that there are not entities other than phenomenal entities involves the denial that there are any non-phenomenal objects for the understanding" (p. 109). In other words, Protagoras and other Sophists were radical empiricists who rejected any and all attempts to form inferences about underlying reality. This emphasis on personal experience is central to the approach of most qualitative researchers.

The views described above, rather than representing new ideas that antedate science, are old ideas that pre-date science. Science in its modern form was not developed until some 2000 years following the Sophists. What the qualitative researchers are embracing are not ideas born of a failed quantitative approach to science, but old ideas that were rejected by the likes of **Galileo**, **Newton**, and a host of other more modern thinkers. We find it ironic that qualitative researchers regard their ideas as new ones that displace a quantitative approach. It should be understood that we are not denigrating qualitative research methods, nor are we denigrating the paradigm adopted by qualitative researchers, even though we reject it. What we are objecting to is the belief of qualitative researchers in particular, and of postmodernists in general, that they are offering new ideas utterly unknown before the **Enlightenment** and the birth of scientific thought. In actuality, the ideas they are embracing were old when the Enlightenment and science were born.

Another indication that qualitative researchers are embracing pre-scientific ideas is the rejection of hypothesis testing by many of them. As we have mentioned earlier in this chapter, the hypothesis testing method so popular in science today was not seriously considered as a major methodological approach until about the middle of the 19th century. Thus, in rejecting hypothesis testing in favor of either induction or descriptive science, qualitative researchers, far from suggesting a new approach to psychology, are taking us back to a form of science practiced roughly from 1600 to 1850.

Linear causality

Qualitative researchers suggest that they are concerned with recip-rocal interaction, meaning cause-to-effect and effect-to-cause relations, whereas quantitative researchers are concerned with causality in one direction only, from cause to effect. This is one of the more serious of various misunderstandings of experimentation and quantitative research (see Capaldi & Proctor, 1999). The misunderstanding arises from a failure to differentiate tactical and strategic considerations employed in experimentation. The tactical consideration is that for purely pragmatic reasons it makes sense to look for cause–effect relationships under particular sets of conditions. This in no way means that quantitative researchers are unaware that causality goes in another direction. But, investigation of this matter occurs in separate experiments. So, strategically, the experimentalist approach may be represented as *examine the effects of a on b* and subsequently *examine the effects of b on a*. A good example of reciprocal causality may be found in physics. When motion from object *a* is imparted to object *b*, the physicist is well aware that *b* is also affecting *a*. But these things are measured in separate experiments. In psychology, when two individuals interact, each influences the other in reciprocal fashion.

Experiments are not descriptive, according to qualitative researchers

Qualitative researchers suggest that whereas they are interested in description, rather than causation, quantitative researchers are interested in only cause–effect relations. It may be true that qualitative researchers are more concerned with description than with causation. But it is a serious misunderstanding of quantitative research to suggest that it is not concerned with description, as well as causation. In truth, descriptive statements abound in experimental psychology and in experimental science generally. One of the more famous lines in all of science is the statement by Isaac Newton, "Hypotheses non fingo" (loosely translated, "I don't entertain hypotheses"), which expressed Newton's idea that he was merely describing how gravity worked, not supplying a causal mechanism for gravity. For example, in learning and skill acquisition, it is commonplace to note that, generally speaking, performance increases as number of training trials increases. As another example, in both skill acquisition and forgetting, serious attempts are made to determine the precise nature of the relationship between the independent and dependent variables (e.g., does skill acquisition follow a power function or an exponential function?). It is true that individuals may attempt to supply causal analyses of the qualitative relationships, but that in no way invalidates the idea that the nature of the relationship is sought, and necessarily so, before serious attempts to interpret it occur. It is commonplace in experimental science to inductively seek out descriptive relationships among phenomena before serious attempts to interpret them occur (see, e.g., Hull, 1943).

Chapter Summary

According to most qualitative theorists, their methods that rely heavily on the lived experience of persons stem from a unique ontology. This position seems to arise from Thomas Kuhn, who suggested that a paradigm determines the methods and problems of an approach. We agree with Larry Laudan that historical analysis shows that this is not the case, and methodology can change independently of one's ontology, or paradigm, and vice versa. Moreover, according to the naturalistic approach, decisions about what constitutes proper methodology are to be decided on empirical grounds, not on general philosophical or logical grounds. We characterize the ontology of qualitative theorists as being relativistic. We show that their approach, contrary to what qualitative theorists suggest, is not new and has much in common with various pre-scientific points of view that go back as far as ancient Greece. We also show that the reliance on human experience as the primary source of data unnecessarily restricts the study of psychology. For example, it does not allow the study of infants, autistics, and other individuals who have impaired linguistic abilities. Too, it does not allow studies of animals and many phenomena in neuroscience that occur independently of conscious experience. We demonstrate that qualitative theorists, in suggesting that qualitative methodology stems from a misplaced emphasis on positivism, are incorrect and, ironically, positivism is more characteristic of the qualitative approach than of the quantitative one. Though qualitative methods can be useful under a wide variety of circumstances, like any other methodology, including experimentation, there are many circumstances in which other methods may be more useful. Rather than making general methodological claims, the more fruitful approach to devising useful methodologies is to determine the specific circumstance under which a given methodology is most informative about the questions of interest.

INTERNAL AND EXTERNAL VALIDITY

Introduction

The reach of science, of course, extends beyond its own boundaries into society at large. Clearly, scientific theorizing has a profound effect on society, both in terms of the technology it produces and the increased understanding it provides of the world around us. The technology that issues from science is sometimes truly astounding, as in the case of NASA's Cassini mission to Saturn, some 930 million miles from earth. It is also often beneficial, as in the invention and widespread use of microcomputers over the past 25 years. However, it sometimes happens that the technology that science produces may have negative consequences. For example, because of the destructive capacity of the nuclear weapons bequeathed to us by physics, arguably the world would be better off without them. Science also influences our conception of ourselves and of our place in the universe. Modern astronomy has this effect by indicating that the earth is merely one planet among billions in our galaxy, and our galaxy is itself one among billions. These facts remove the earth, and hence its habitants, from being the center of the universe.

Although few would deny the proposition that science in general deeply affects our lives in many ways, this is often doubted when it comes to scientific psychology in particular. This is a position held, for example, by social constructionists, postmodernists, and relativists of various sorts who do not think that psychological science is very applicable to everyday life and experience. Within psychology, there are also those who are not relativists but think that laboratory experiments provide little that is useful in the way of data (see Berkowitz & Donnerstein, 1982, and Mook, 1983, for criticisms of this view). For example, Ulrich Neisser (1982), hardly a relativist, suggests that laboratory studies of memory tell us little beyond what is revealed by common sense. Regarding empirical generalizations found in laboratory research on memory, Neisser says,

> Every one of the generalizations I have mentioned is familiar to the average middle-class third-grader in America from his own experience! Indeed, most of them are known to kindergartners. If the psychology of memory must rest its case on accomplishments like these, it has little to boast of. (p. 6)

According to Neisser, memory has to be studied in real-world settings to be of much relevance. This view has been criticized and rejected by some memory researchers (see, e.g., Banaji & Crowder, 1989).

One way to frame this issue of relevance of laboratory findings to real-world situations is in terms of **internal validity** and **external validity**, a distinction first made by the social psychologist **Donald Campbell** (1957). Much of this chapter will be devoted to examining the concepts of internal and external validity both at a logical level and at an empirical level. The purpose of this analysis is twofold: to better understand the concepts of internal and external validity, and to demonstrate that scientific findings obtained in the laboratory often have implications that generalize to real-world settings.

Internal validity concerns the correct isolation of causal relations among variables. It is defined by Anderson and Bushman (1997) as follows: "If the design and structure of a study are such that one can confidently conclude that the independent variable caused systematic changes in the dependent variable, then the study is said to have *high internal validity*" (p. 20). Conversely, a study that fails to establish causal relations between independent and dependent variables is said to have low internal validity. On the other hand, external validity concerns generalizability to other settings. Anderson and Bushman define external validity as typically referring "to the generalizability of the results of a study to other (usually real world) settings or populations" (p. 21). Sometimes the term **ecological validity** is used instead when the concern is specifically with generalizability to real-world settings. Whereas internal validity is usually associated with laboratory studies, external validity is usually associated with real-world studies. However, this is an oversimplification. A laboratory study may have high external validity, and a real-world study may have high internal validity.

Other considerations are relevant to more fully understanding the distinction between internal and external validity. In many cases, research conducted in laboratory settings, in which high internal validity is typically sought, is not concerned with whether the specific procedures employed and results obtained generalize to the real world. Rather, the concern is primarily with establishing *principles and relationships* and secondarily with determining whether these have meaning in other contexts. For example, employing undergraduate students and word lists, psychologists found that our memory of earlier learned material may be reduced by learning subsequent similar material, a process called retroactive interference (see, e.g., Postman & Underwood, 1973, for a review). Interestingly, retroactive interference was also found to occur in cockroaches, where the original material learned was maze running and the subsequent interfering conditions were the activities involved in normal conditions of waking (Minami & Dallenbach, 1946). Notice that what generalized from one study to the next, in which different participants and procedures were used, was the principle of retroactive interference, namely that later learning can reduce memory of earlier learning.

Settings in which high external validity is sought often are concerned with whether specific procedures used in the study are similar enough to those in the real world to produce similar effects in both. For example, if a drug company is interested in whether a particular drug is useful for headaches, it may test the drug on both males and females to determine whether the beneficial effects extend to both sexes. This is because both males and females are potential consumers for the drug. Similarly, in evaluating a new interface for a word processor, participants will be required to perform tasks that are similar to those for which the word processor will typically be used. As Mook (1983) indicates, "External validity is not an automatic desideratum; it *asks a question....* To what populations, settings, and so on, do we *want* the effect to be generalized? Do we want to generalize it at all?" (p. 379).

As indicated, a common misconception is that laboratory experiments have low external validity, whereas studies conducted in real-world settings have high external validity. There is reason to question these common misconceptions. The real issue is to what extent findings obtained under one set of conditions generalize to other sets of conditions. There is only one way in which this can be known, and that is empirically. Could we reasonably guess that retroactive interference effects isolated in people would also be obtained in an organism as different from us as a cockroach? Again, the real issue is to learn what is and is not generalizable by empirical means. Unfortunately, often, many of the pronouncements about internal and external validity are made without reference to empirical information. Anderson and Bushman

(1987; Anderson, Lindsay, & Bushman, 1999), using a variety of empirical procedures, have determined that laboratory studies of aggression may have high external as well as high internal validity, and real-world studies of aggression may have high internal as well as high external validity. It is to be emphasized that they have come to this conclusion not on some a priori basis but by diligently consulting the aggression literature. They say,

> The external validities of studies done in laboratory versus field settings are entirely an empirical matter, and there appears to be no reason to assume that the latter type of study generalizes across settings or populations with greater relative frequency than does the former. (p. 21)

The lesson to be learned from Anderson and Bushman's analysis is that one cannot reach conclusions about generalizability on the basis of superficial appearance. Some findings generalize to situations that seem to be vastly different from those under which they were obtained. For example, **Gregor Mendel**'s findings concerning the mechanism of hereditability in garden peas turned out to apply not only to other sorts of vegetables but to animals as well, including humans. At the time Mendel conducted his study, there was no way to determine whether his findings were isolated to garden peas or generalized to many other species. There is only one way to judge whether findings and principles obtained under one set of circumstances generalize to another set of circumstances, and that is empirically.

Applications of Scientific Psychology

In this section, our objective is to provide several notable and outstanding examples of how findings obtained in the laboratory may be relevant to real-world settings. These examples illustrate that experiments that have high internal validity may also have high external validity, and thus that findings and principles obtained in experimental settings may generalize to problems of concern in the real world. Of course, the examples provided are but a small sample of the applications of scientific psychology to the real world.

False memories

It is natural to think of memory as providing a valid or correct representation of past events. However, it is not unusual for people to "remember" events that did not in fact occur. A laboratory demonstration of this propensity was provided by Deese (1959), an investigator in the verbal learning tradition, who presented human subjects with lists of words of greater or lesser similarity. Following presentation of a list, they were asked to recall the items in the list in any order. The interesting finding was that subjects were often sure that a word related to the items in the list occurred, even though it had not. For example, in a subsequent study by Watson, Balota, and Roediger (2003), when subjects heard the words *bed, rest, awake, tired, dream, wake, snooze, blanket, doze, slumber, snore, nap, peace, yawn, drowsy,* many recollected that the word *sleep* was in the list. This phenomenon is called **false memory**. It demonstrates, using an experimental procedure, that people are often reasonably sure that they remember events that never occurred. Many studies subsequent to Deese's, such as that by Watson et al. cited above, have examined in some detail many of the variables that influence the false memory effect and why they do. Interestingly, Deese's findings of false memory with word lists, which many people might dismiss as inconsequential, can be duplicated under more ecologically valid, real-life conditions and can be shown to have considerable implications for memories in everyday life.

This may be seen in the popular demonstrations of the false memory phenomenon in the extensive work of **Elizabeth Loftus**, summarized in her 2003 address for the award of Distinguished Scientific Applications of Psychology given by the American Psychological Association. In one interesting condition, people are shown a film involving a traffic accident. False memories of the accident may be implanted in several different ways, one of which is providing people with leading questions that distort their memory for events that did not occur in the film. For example, an observer might be asked, "Did you see the broken headlight?" Under these conditions, many more people reported a broken headlight than did control subjects provided a more neutral question. In other conditions, people are provided with misinformation, as, for example, the stop sign in the film was described as a yield sign. In that case, they often remember a yield sign rather than a stop sign as having been viewed. A really dramatic demonstration of the false memory phenomenon involves an individual accepting a whole series of events as having been experienced in the past, when in fact they did not occur. The famous example is of people believing that when they were 5 or 6 years of age, they were lost in a shopping mall, rescued by an elderly person, and subsequently reunited with their families. Many of the participants not only recall having been lost in the mall, as suggested by the experimenter, but they add additional embellishing details on their own.

It might be thought that false memories of this sort can be implanted only under laboratory conditions and would not occur in real life. This is not the case. An experiment by Ihlebaek, Love, Eilertsen, and Magnussen (2003) showed a "live" crime to some subjects and a videotape of the same crime to other subjects. They found that those who watched the video reported not only a greater number of details, but they reported them with greater accuracy than those who watched the real staged crime. Ihlebaek et al.'s results indicate that memory may actually be better for events when seen in a video than when actually witnessed.

These findings have very considerable generality and importance. First, and most obviously, they warn us that eyewitness testimony may be tainted in various ways. For example, if the police interrogate witnesses and ask them leading questions, the witnesses may remember events that did not occur. Loftus (2003) points out that false eyewitness testimony may be one reason why some criminal convictions are being overturned by new DNA evidence. As another example, therapists may, by asking their patients leading questions, implant false memories of parental abuse. In recent times, many treated these memories of abuse as true repressed memories that were released by the therapy itself. In many cases, the memories were actually implanted during the course of the therapy. What these findings demonstrate is that all sorts of recollections by people under everyday conditions should be treated with some degree of skepticism. This applies not only to patients in therapy but to any circumstance in which the recollection of others is communicated to us. This problem is of particular concern for the qualitative method approach described in the previous two chapters, which attempts to employ reports of people's experience as the primary source of data on which to base scientific inferences.

Behavior modification

Scientific study of the learning process in animals has led to a variety of very effective procedures for doing therapy in humans. Two of these procedures will be considered here, one based on Pavlovian conditioning and the other based on instrumental conditioning. Pavlovian conditioning is often referred to as classical conditioning. Referring to it in this fashion is a result of the early substantial influence that the learning procedures derived by Ivan P. Pavlov (1928) had in psychology. In Pavlovian conditioning, a neutral stimulus such as a tone may precede a biologically significant stimulus such as food, without reference to the behavior of the subject. That is, the two stimuli are presented in sequence regardless of whether the subject responds to them or not. As a specific example, in a fear conditioning experiment, shock may occur following the offset of a 10-s neutral stimulus such as a flower, and in consequence, the subject may come to fear the flower. In an instrumental conditioning experiment, a response in the presence of what is called a discriminative stimulus may result in reinforcement. For example, if a rat presses a bar when a light comes on, it may receive food.

Systematic desensitization (Wolpe, 1958) is based on laboratory studies of Pavlovian conditioning using animals. The first step in a laboratory experiment might be to get the animal to fear a tone by having the tone followed by shock. The animal's fear of the tone may be alleviated by employing a procedure known as counterconditioning. On the first counterconditioning trial, the tone might be presented at a very low intensity so as to prevent the fear reaction. On subsequent trials the intensity of the tone is increased by small amounts. On each of these counterconditioning trials the tone is followed by food, rather than shock. Employing this procedure, the subject comes not to show fear to the tone.

Systematic desensitization is employed in connection with people who have phobias such as fear of public speaking. The first step in the procedure is to get the subject to relax, employing specialized relaxation procedures. The behavior modifier makes up a number of scenes, say, 10 or so, that are increasingly threatening. For example, the first scene might portray the client as thinking about giving a talk, and the final, most threatening scene might involve the client giving a speech before a live audience. Each of these scenes is presented to the client while that person is in a relaxed state, less threatening ones prior to more threatening ones. The intention is to countercondition relaxation to each of the scenes. The behavior modifier presents a scene to the client and, if it fails to arouse fear, the next more threatening scene is shown. This procedure is very effective in curing phobias such as fear of public speaking, fear of flying, and so on.

Consider now a **behavior modification** procedure based on instrumental learning, that of aversive conditioning. In the laboratory version of the aversive conditioning task, a rat might be shocked for making some response. Of course, this procedure deters the rat from making the same response in the future. A similar procedure is employed in aversive conditioning. As one example, an alcoholic is made to take an alcoholic drink, and this is followed by a substance, called annabuse, which makes the client sick. In this way, the client's tendency to drink alcoholic beverages is reduced or eliminated.

Scientific Psychology Opposes Pseudoscience

Many claims are made about supernatural events such as communicating with dead people. Theory and findings obtained in scientific psychology have considerable implications for evaluating such beliefs. That is, scientific psychology can provide alternative, more plausible explanations for the supernatural phenomena in terms of natural psychological processes. A good example of this is provided by the link between thought and action, sometimes called **ideomotor action**.

Ideomotor action

There is considerable evidence that having an idea of performing an action can produce the action itself. People are often not aware of the link between ideas and actions. Consequently, when they engage in particular activities, they may attribute them not to the idea but incorrectly to various external sources. This lack of awareness may result in many superstitious beliefs being accepted.

Consider the practice of dowsing, or water witching (Vogt & Hyman, 1959). The dowser holds a stick in each hand, parallel to each other, in front of her or his body, and walks over terrain. The belief is that when the individual walks over an underground source of water, the two sticks will cross, indicating that this is a location at which a well can be dug. In a demonstration by Hyman (1999), he walked across a room and purposely allowed the sticks to cross at a particular location, while a group of students observed him. For a second group of students, Hyman had the sticks cross at another location in the room. Each student was allowed to walk about the room holding the dowsing rods. In the first group of students, the dowsing rods crossed at the first location but not elsewhere, whereas in the second group, the rods crossed at the second location and not elsewhere. Hyman has many other similar demonstrations, for example, with the Ouija board, making the following point: "Under a variety of circumstances, our muscles will behave unconsciously in accordance with an implanted expectation" (Hyman, 1999, p. 35).

Ideomotor activity has been uncovered by scientists in many areas who are interested in mental processes, including psychologists. These findings have important significance, practically as well as scientifically. Let us consider the practical first. One reason people believe that they can communicate with the dead is that in séances, events occur in ways that they are unable to explain in other than supernatural terms.

For example, the table at which they are seated at some point may appear to turn and possibly move about the room. People may have no awareness of doing anything to cause the table to move and thus attribute it to occult forces. However, controlled experiments have shown that the movements of the table are produced by the participants in the séance in the absence of conscious awareness, because of their expectation that it will move. Because of the lack of conscious awareness, participants in séances are very reluctant to believe that the table movements are caused by other than the spirits summoned by the spiritualist. Many experiments of this sort, dating back to the physicist **Michael Faraday** (1853), have shown that people themselves, in the absence of awareness, contribute to the movement.

More recently, autistic children, some of whom may have low IQs, have been said to be highly intelligent, to the understandable joy of their parents. The reason for this belief is the apparently effective communication of complex information by autistics by other than verbal means, in which they are deficient, when assisted by a facilitator (Biklen, 1990). The autistic child sits at a standard keyboard, and an adult facilitator steadies the hands of the child over the keyboard. Surprisingly, the autistic child types out many complex messages that otherwise seem to be beyond his or her intellectual capacity. When facilitated communication was initially reported, it was taken seriously by a great many people. Accepting the communication as valid could have considerable consequences, as in some cases the child's messages included tales of sexual abuse. It should be apparent from our discussion above that facilitated communication could result from ideomotor activity of the facilitator. Indeed, controlled experiments have shown this to be so (Jacobson, Mulick, & Schwartz, 1995). They have revealed that the facilitator unconsciously guides the hand of the child, much as the plangent of the Ouija board, to spell out the messages. This evidence comes from experiments in which the facilitator is unable to observe the child's movements, in which case no communication is forthcoming. Many individuals are quite prone to ascribing ideomotor action to outside causes such as the occult because the actions are occurring without conscious intent. Hyman has indicated that when some people are shown that the behavior is the result of ideomotor activity, rather than of some other cause, through the use of double-blind experiments, they will reject the experiment and still ascribe the behavior to the other cause or causes. Hyman (1999) states, "Many pseudo- and fringe-scientists often react to the failure of science to confirm their prized beliefs, not by gracefully accepting the possibility that they were wrong, but by arguing that science is defective" (p. 41).

Ideomotor activity has been of interest to scientists for a long time (Stock & Stock, 2004). The British branch of interest in ideomotor activity goes back to Laycock (1845) and Carpenter (1852). The German branch is even older, going back to Herbart (1816), Lotze (1852), and Harless (1861). It is well known that **William James** (1890), in his monumental *Principles of Psychology*, placed great emphasis on ideomotor activity. Although interest in ideomotor activity waned for a while, in the past decade there has been a resurgence of interest in it (see, e.g., Knuf, Achersleben, & Prinz, 2001). A common proposition, accepted by many, is that we associate the stimuli that accompany an action with the action itself. Consequently, when we later think of those stimuli, the action itself is initiated, often in the absence of conscious awareness.

Cold reading

Another way in which people may embrace false beliefs about occult powers or the psychic abilities of others is through supposedly psychic readings. The psychic provides to an unknown target individual, the mark, a reading that contains many items of correct information, which the mark recognizes as being applicable to him- or herself. It should be noted that there never has been a successful demonstration of such psychic powers under well-controlled laboratory conditions, despite a $1,000,000 prize offered by the James Randi Educational Foundation for the successful demonstration of such powers under proper, controlled observing conditions.

The reader may employ several different techniques, collectively known as **cold reading** (Hyman, 1977), to convince the mark of his or her psychic abilities. The term "cold" in cold reading refers to the fact that the person doing the psychic reading knows little or nothing about the mark and is doing it "cold." One technique is to provide the mark with certain generalities that are true of most people, as, for example, "You are proud of being an independent thinker, and you accept the opinions of others only when there is good reason to do so." One reason why this technique is successful is that people put the vague suggestion in a more specific context that applies to themselves. Such interpretation is normal in everyday life, where we use our background knowledge to interpret events.

Another cold reading technique is known as fishing for details. The psychic says something vague and suggestive, such as, "Does a name that begins with a *J* mean anything to you?" If the mark fails to warm to this suggestion, the reader moves on. However, in many cases, the mark will supply the reader with a positive indication and possibly a specific name and event, as for example, "Yes, I have an uncle named Joe who recently died." The reader will then follow up on the mark's comments by saying, for example, "You were close to Uncle Joe, weren't you?" Often times, the mark will later remember the psychic as the source of the information about Uncle Joe, rather than himself or herself. Selective memory of this sort often contributes to people's belief that some people possess psychic powers.

A third technique employed by readers is to carefully note the behavior of the mark. As Steiner (1989) has indicated:

> The reader begins with generalities which are applicable to large segments of the population. He or she pays careful attention to reactions: words, body language, skin color, breathing patterns, dilation or contraction of the pupils of the eye, and more. The subject of the reading will usually convey important information to the reader: sometimes in words, and sometimes in bodily reactions to the reading. (p. 21)

The mark typically fails to recognize that he or she is providing information to the reader by means of subtle facial and other muscular behaviors. Given our previous discussion of ideomotor activity, this should not be surprising.

It is not too surprising that humans are able to read the behavior of other humans since non-human animals are also able to read subtle human behaviors. One of the most well-known examples of this in psychology involves a horse known as Clever Hans. Hans was reputed to be able to add, subtract, multiply, and divide. He provided answers to these questions by tapping out the answer with his hoof. Many scientists were unable to determine how Clever Hans accomplished this, and Clever Hans's accomplishments were known throughout the world. However, **Oskar Pfungst** (1965), a psychologist, ultimately demonstrated that the horse was unable to perform mathematical calculations. Pfungst went about this in a systematic way. First, he established that Clever Hans was indeed clever, that is, Hans could answer the questions when in the presence either of his owner or other people. Pfungst then fit Hans with blinders so that he could not see the questioner. Under these conditions, Hans was not able to provide correct answers. Too, when the human questioners asked questions to which they did not know the answers, Hans again failed to provide correct solutions.

Pfungst ultimately established that Hans being correct depended on the horse's observation of subtle movements of the questioners. For example, when Hans was coming closer to the correct number of taps, questioners tended to straighten up, and that was a cue for Hans to stop tapping. Hans was also sensitive to other tiny bodily movements such as upward movements of the head. It is to be emphasized that people were unaware that they were cueing the horse. Rosenthal (1965) noted, "Most interesting was the finding that even after he had learned the cueing system very well Pfungst still cued Hans unintentionally, though he was consciously try to suppress sending the crucial visual messages" (p. xii).

Chapter and Book Summary

In this chapter, it was shown that the findings of science often have important applicability to real-world problems. Some have doubted this in connection with scientific psychology. However, in this chapter, we have provided a small number of the findings from scientific psychology that apply importantly in real-world settings. We began by discussing internal and external validity, emphasizing that external validity can only be evaluated empirically. Some of the basic principles and findings discovered in the laboratory and considered in this chapter that have applicability to the real world are as follows. It was found that it is relatively easy to implant false memories in people. These findings should be considered when evaluating the testimony of people in connection with crime or in therapy, where people may remember events that did not in fact happen, events that may have important consequences for themselves and others. The chapter considered how people may come to believe in supernatural phenomena because they are unaware that the thought of an action may unconsciously lead to the action itself. Another area of scientific psychology that has led to important practical application is learning. Two therapy techniques that come from the animal learning laboratory were discussed, systematic desensitization and aversion therapy. An observer keenly aware that the behavior of others may indicate their true thoughts and feelings can use this knowledge for various purposes. So-called mind readers may use the behaviors of a mark to perform a reading that seems to apply accurately to the mark. Non-human animals are also capable of reading the behavior of others. The chapter considered the case of a famous horse, Clever Hans, who by reading the behavior of people gave

---

the appearance of being able to solve complex numerical problems such as addition, subtraction, multiplication, and division.

The major objective of this book was to provide a clear understanding of theory and practice in modern science. It is our strong belief that a better understanding of modern science will allow the student to become a more knowledgeable consumer and practitioner of science in general and psychology in particular. The key to understanding modern science, as we have emphasized throughout the book, is to realize that scientific methods and procedures arise not only from logic but also empirically. This approach is known as **naturalism**. A proper science is a naturalized science, that is, one in which proper methodology is constructed by the same means used to construct proper empirical and theoretical propositions in any area of science. Naturalism is a relatively new movement in science studies that owes its modern origins to **Willard Quine** and **Thomas Kuhn**.

Initially, it was indicated that the origins of science extend back literally thousands of years with astronomy in the Middle East. A variety of developments in Greece, ranging from assuming that the nature of reality is best described mathematically to the view that all matter is composed of irreducible atoms, influenced the thinking of **Galileo**, who may be regarded as the first modern scientist, and many other early scientists such as Newton. In the Newtonian era, it was generally assumed that the proper method of science was **induction**. The view that induction was the main method of science was challenged by William Whewell in the mid 1800s. Whewell pointed out that **hypothesis testing** is an important component of the scientific method. Indeed, today, many scientists feel that hypothesis testing is *the* method of science.

The inductive method, so prized in the Newtonian era, was subsequently embraced by the logical positivists in the 20th century. Karl Popper pointed out the weaknesses of induction and suggested that the proper method of science involves the falsification of hypotheses. Popper's suggestion proved to be very popular among scientists. However, Popper's view was disputed by Thomas Kuhn, who approached science naturalistically, using historical analyses of scientific movements. Kuhn's (1962) book proved to be immensely influential in many quarters, among scientists, social scientists, and philosophers of science. Indeed, many post-Kuhnian conceptions of science have been developed either in agreement or disagreement with Kuhn. The naturalism that began with Kuhn is flourishing today and is in the process of producing an ever-increasing and better understanding of science.

Although induction and **deduction** are important methods of science, they are neither the only methods, nor in the opinion of many, the most important methods. That prize, in the opinion of many, goes to **abduction**. Surprisingly, although most scientists employ abduction in their scientific decision making, it is seldom recognized as a distinct and important methodological procedure. When employing abduction, a scientist looks over a variety of data and observes a pattern in it. The essential feature of abduction is that the pattern of data would make sense if a particular hypothesis were true. Note that reasoning of this type does not involve the simple enumeration of induction nor the testing of a deduction derived from a theory. Again, we emphasize that although induction and deduction are important in science, the most general theoretical statements of science are arrived at abductively.

Although Kuhn employed the historical method to arrive at his understanding of science, naturalism recommends that a variety of empirical procedures be employed to this end, many of which are the province of psychology. For example, the study of decision making, an area of concern to psychologists, is useful for understanding how decisions are arrived at in science. This would include employing analogy, various **heuristics**, or, following **Herbert Simon**, a procedure known as **satisficing**. With respect to science, satisficing, as discussed at some length in Chapters 3 and 6, may briefly be defined as selecting from available possibilities that outcome or model that best satisfies the scientist's aim. Other methods employed to understand science naturalistically include observing scientists working on tasks related to scientific discoveries, directly observing scientists in the laboratory environment, examining the notebooks and other work products of scientists, and developing computational models of scientific thought and discoveries. These newer methods for understanding science are, so to speak, in their infancy and offer many opportunities for new and informative research.

Another outgrowth of Kuhn's (1962) theorizing, ironically, is the development of various forms of **relativism**. These would include various forms of **postmodernism**, various forms of **social constructionism**, and various forms of **contextualism**. These approaches, which are basically antithetical to science, have many adherents in the social sciences, including psychology. For example, a popular relativist assumption is that there are many different realities, none of which has priority over the others. This implies that the scientific way of knowing is one among many and is no better or worse than any of the rest. One methodological outgrowth of the relativistic movement is an emphasis on **qualitative methods** and rejection of **quantitative methods** such as experimentation. As naturalists, we are prepared to regard any method, qualitative or quantitative, as useful, provided that it has been found to be adequate empirically. Qualitative methods, as recommended by many of their advocates, are justified not empirically, but on the basis of a priori ontological considerations.

Although relativists tend to denigrate the contributions of scientific psychology to the solution of real-world problems, we argue to the contrary in this final chapter. Using a few of many possible examples, the usefulness of scientific psychology in many areas was underlined. For example, knowledge of ideomotor activity allows psychology to provide a natural explanation of many so-called supernatural phenomena. Too, understanding how perception and memory are related provides a basis for understanding how people may come to believe that they experienced events that did not in fact occur. Psychology as a science has provided a deeper understanding of the phenomena mentioned in this chapter, such as false memory and false testimony, as well as many others. However, this capability will be enhanced by adopting a greater tendency to accept and employ a naturalistic approach to science. Not only will the field as a whole become more sophisticated methodologically speaking, but so too will each of the individual psychologists who employ naturalism in their daily professional lives. Naturalism, in our view, promises to make psychology and psychologists more effective producers of useful psychological information.

REFERENCES

Achinstein, P. (1994). Explanation v. prediction: Which carries more weight? In D. Hull, F. Forbes, & R. M. Burian (Eds.), *PSA 1994* (Vol. 2; pp. 156–164). East Lansing, MI: Philosophy of Science Association.

Andersen, H., Barker, P., & Chen, X. (1996). Kuhn's mature philosophy of science and cognitive psychology. *Philosophical Psychology, 9*, 347–363.

Anderson, C. A., & Bushman, B. J. (1997). External validity of "trivial" experiments: The case of laboratory aggression. *Review of General Psychology, 1*, 19–41.

Anderson, C. A., Lindsay, J. L., & Bushman, B. J. (1999). Research in the psychological laboratory: Truth or triviality? *Current Directions in Psychological Science, 8*, 3–9.

Anderson, J. R. (1990). *Cognitive psychology and its implications* (3rd ed.). New York: W. H. Freeman.

Anderson, J. R. (1996). ACT: A simple theory of complex cognition. *American Psychologist, 51*, 355–365.

Angell, J. R. (1908). The doctrine of formal discipline in the light of principles of general psychology. *Educational Review, 36*, 1–14.

Baigrie, B. (1992). The vortex theory of motion, 1687–1713: Empirical difficulties and guiding assumptions. In A. Donovan, L. Laudan, & R. Laudan (Eds.), *Scrutinizing science: Empirical studies of scientific change* (pp. 85–102). Baltimore: Johns Hopkins University Press.

Bamberg, M. (2003). Foreword. In P. M. Camic, J. E. Rhodes, & L. Yardley (Eds.), *Qualitative research in psychology: Expanding perspectives in methodology and design* (pp. ix–xi). Washington, DC: American Psychological Association.

Banaji, M. R., & Crowder, R. G. (1989). The bankruptcy of everyday memory. *American Psychologist, 44*, 1185–1193.

Barnes, B., & Bloor, D. (1982). Relativism, rationalism and the sociology of knowledge. In M. Hollis & S. Lukes (Eds.), *Rationality and relativism* (pp. 21–47). Canbridge, MA: MIT Press.

Bechtel, W. (1988). *Philosophy of science: An overview for cognitive science.* Hillsdale, NJ: Erlbaum.

195

Bechtel, W. (1992). Fermentation theory: Empirical difficulties and guiding assumptions. In A. Donovan, L. Laudan, & R. Laudan (Eds.), *Scrutinizing science: Empirical studies of scientific change* (pp. 163–180). Baltimore: Johns Hopkins University Press.

Bechtel, W., Mandik, P., Mundale, J., & Stufflebeam, R. S. (Eds.) (2001). *Philosophy and the neurosciences: A reader*. Oxford: Blackwell.

Bergmann, G., & Spence, K. W. (1941). Operationism and theory in psychology. *Psychological Review, 48*, 1–14.

Bergmann, G., & Spence, K. W. (1944). The logic of psychological measurement. *Psychological Review, 51*, 1–24.

Berkowitz, L., & Donnerstein, E. (1982). External validity is more than skin deep. *American Psychologist, 37*, 245–257.

Beyer, H., & Holtzblatt, K. (1998). *Contextual design*. San Francisco: Morgan Kaufmann.

Biklen, D. (1990). Communication unbound: Autism and praxis. *Harvard Educational Review, 60*, 291–314.

Blank, T. O. (1986). Contextual and relational perspectives on adult psychology. In R. L. Rosnow & M. Georgoudi (Eds.), *Contextualism and understanding in behavioral science: Implications for research and theory* (pp. 105–124). New York: Praeger.

Boring, E. G. (1950). *A history of experimental psychology* (2nd edn). New York: Appleton-Century-Crofts.

Bridgeman, P. W. (1927). *The logic of modern physics*. New York: Macmillan.

Broca, P. (1863). Localisations des fonctions cérébrales. – Siège du language articulé. *Bulletins de la Sociéte d'Anthropologie, 4*, 200–204.

Brush, S. G. (1989). Prediction and theory evaluation: The case of light bending. *Science, 246*, 1124–1129.

Callebaut, W. (1993). *Taking the naturalistic turn or how the real philosophy of science is done*. Chicago: University of Chicago Press.

Camic, P. M., Rhodes, J. E., & Yardley, L. (2003a). Naming the stars: Integrating qualitative methods into psychological research. In P. M. Camic, J. E. Rhodes, & L. Yardley (Eds.), *Qualitative research in psychology: Expanding perspectives in methodology and design* (pp. 3–15). Washington, DC: American Psychological Association.

Camic, P. M., Rhodes, J. E., & Yardley, L. (Eds.) (2003b). *Qualitative research in psychology: Expanding perspectives in methodology and design*. Washington, DC: American Psychological Association.

Campbell, D. T. (1957). Factors relevant to the validity of experiments in social settings. *Psychological Bulletin, 54*, 297–312.

Capaldi, E. J., & Proctor, R. W. (1994). Contextualism: Is the act in context the appropriate metaphor for psychology? *Psychonomic Bulletin & Review, 1*, 239–249.

Capaldi, E. J., & Proctor, R. W. (1999). *Contextualism in psychological research? A critical review*. Thousand Oaks, CA: Sage.

Capaldi, E. J., & Proctor, R. W. (2000). Laudan's normative naturalism: A useful philosophy of science for psychology. *American Journal of Psychology*, *133*, 430–454.

Carpenter, W. B. (1852). On the influence of suggestion in modifying and directing muscular movement, independently of volition. *Proceedings of the Royal Institution*, 147–154.

Cary, M., & Reder, L. M. (2002). Metacognition in strategy selection. In P. Chambres, M. Izaute, & P. Marescaux (Eds.). *Metacognition: Process, function and use* (pp. 63–77). Dordrecht, Netherlands: Kluwer Academic Publishers.

Chalmers, A. F. (1999). *What is this thing called science?* (2nd edn). Indianapolis, IN: Hackett.

Chen, X., Andersen, H., & Barker, P. (1998). Kuhn's theory of scientific revolutions and cognitive psychology. *Philosophical Psychology*, *11*, 5–28.

Christensen, L. B. (2001). *Experimental methodology* (8th edn). Boston: Allyn & Bacon.

Coleman, S. R., & Salamon, R. (1988). Kuhn's *Structure of Scientific Revolutions* in the psychological journal literature, 1969–1983: A descriptive study. *Journal of Mind and Behavior*, *9*, 415–446.

Collins, H. (1981). Stages in the empirical programme of relativism. *Social Studies of Science*, *11*, 3–10.

Curd, M., & Cover, J. A. (Eds.) (1998). *Philosophy of science: The central issues*. New York: Norton.

Daly, M., & Wilson, M. (1988). *Homicide*. Hawthorne, NT: Aldyne de Gruyter.

Dampier, W. C. (1952). *A history of science and its relation with philosophy and religion* (4th edn). Cambridge: Cambridge University Press.

Darwin, C. (1859). *On the origin of species*. London: Murray.

Davis, J. H. (2003). Balancing the whole: Portraiture as methodology. In P. M. Camic, J. E. Rhodes, & L. Yardley (Eds.), *Qualitative research in psychology: Expanding perspectives in methodology and design* (pp. 199–219). Washington, DC: American Psychological Association.

Dawson, M. R. W. (2003). *Minds and machines: Connectionism and psychological modeling*. Malden, MA: Blackwell.

Deese, J. (1959). On the prediction of occurrence of particular verbal intrusions in immediate recall. *Journal of Experimental Psychology*, *58*, 17–22.

De Romilly, J. (1992). *The great Sophists in Periclean Athens* (Janet Lloyd, translator). Oxford, UK: Oxford University Press.

Donovan, A., Laudan, L., & Laudan, R. (Eds.) (1992). *Scrutinizing science: Empirical studies of scientific change*. Baltimore: Johns Hopkins University Press.

Dougher, M. J. (1993). Interpretive and hermeneutic research methods in the contextualist analysis of verbal behavior. In S. C. Hayes, L. J. Hayes, H. W. Reese, & T. R. Sarbin (Eds.), *Varieties of scientific contextualism* (pp. 211–221). Reno, NV: Context Press.

Dunbar, K. (1997). How scientists think: On-line creativity and conceptual change in science. In T. Ward, S. Smith, & S. Vaid (Eds.), *Conceptual structures and processes: Emergence, discovery, and change* (pp. 461–492). Washington, DC: American Psychological Association.

Dunbar, K., & Fugelsang, J. A. (2005). Causal thinking in science: How scientists and students interpret the unexpected. In M. E. Gorman, R. D. Tweney, D. C. Gooding, & A. P. Kincannon (Eds.), *Scientific and technological thinking* (pp. 57–79). Mahwah, NJ: Erlbaum.

Ebbinghaus, H. (1964). *Memory: A contribution to experimental psychology* (H. A. Ruger & C. L. Bussenius, Translators). New York: Dover Publications. (originally published in 1885, *Über das Gedächtnis*. Leipzig: Duncker and Humblot)

Eisner, E. (2003). On the art and science of qualitative research in psychology. In P. M. Camic, J. E. Rhodes, & L. Yardley (Eds.), *Qualitative research in psychology: Expanding perspectives in methodology and design* (pp. 17–29). Washington, DC: American Psychological Association.

Encyclopaedia Britannica. (1771). Edinburgh, Scotland: C. Macfarquhar.

Ericsson, A., Charness, N., Feltovich, P., & Hoffman, R. (Eds.) (in press). *Cambridge handbook of expertise and expert performance.* London: Cambridge University Press.

Faraday, M. (1853). Experimental investigation of table-moving. *The Atheneum,* July 2, 801–802.

Feist, G. F., & Gorman, M. E. (1998). The psychology of science: Review and integration of a nascent discipline. *Review of General Psychology, 2,* 3–47.

Festinger, L. (1957). *A theory of cognitive dissonance.* Evanston, IL: Row, Peterson.

Feyerabend, P. (1970). Consolations for the specialist. In I. Lakatos & A. Musgrave (Eds.), *Criticism and the growth of knowledge* (pp. 197–230). New York: Cambridge University Press.

Fine, M., Torre, M. E., Boudin, K., Bowen, I., Clark, J., Hylton, D., Martinez, M., Missy, Roberts, R. A., Smart, P., & Upegui, D. (2003). Participatory action research: From within and beyond prison bars. In P. M. Camic, J. E. Rhodes, & L. Yardley (Eds.), *Qualitative research in psychology: Expanding perspectives in methodology and design* (pp. 173–198). Washington, DC: American Psychological Association.

Finocchiaro, M. A. (1992). Galileo's Copernicanism and the acceptability of guiding assumptions. In A. Donovan, L. Laudan, & R. Laudan (Eds.), *Scrutinizing science: Empirical studies of scientific change* (pp. 49–67). Baltimore: Johns Hopkins University Press.

Follette, W. C., & Hayes, S. C. (2000). Contemporary behavior therapy. C. R. Snyder, & R. E. Ingram (Eds.), *Handbook of psychological change: Psychotherapy processes & practices for the 21st century* (pp. 381–408). New York: John Wiley.

Ford, D. H., & Lerner, R. M. (1992). *Developmental systems theory: An integrative approach.* Newbury Park, CA: Sage.

Francis, G. (2003). Developing a new quantitative account of backward masking. *Cognitive Psychology, 46,* 198–226.

Fritsch, G., & Hitzig, E. (1960). On the electrical excitability of the cerebrum. In G. von Bonin (Trans.), Some papers on the cerebral cortex (pp. 73–96). Springfield, IL: Charles C. Thomas. (original work published 1870)

Gardner, H. (1983). *Frames of mind: The theory of multiple intelligences*. New York: Basic Books.

Gaventa, J. (1993). The powerful, the powerless, and the experts: Knowledge struggles in an information age. In P. Park, M. Brydon-Miller, B. Hall, & T. Jackson (Eds.), *Voices of change: Participatory action research in the US and Canada* (pp. 21–40). Westport, CT: Bergin and Garvey.

Gazzaniga, M. S., Ivry, R. B., & Mangun, G. R. (1998). *Cognitive neuroscience: The biology of the mind*. New York: Norton.

Gentner, D., & Jeziorski, M. (1989). Historical shifts in the use of analogy in science. In B. Gholson, W. R. Shadish, Jr., R. A. Neimeyer, & A. C. Houts (Eds.), *Psychology of science* (pp. 296–325). New York: Cambridge University Press.

Gergen, K. J. (1985). The social constructionist movement in modern psychology. *American Psychologist, 40*, 266–275.

Gergen, K. J. (1988). If persons are texts. In S. Messer, L. Sass, & R. Woolfolk (Eds.), *Hermeneutics and psychological theory: Interpretive perspectives on personality, psychotherapy, and psychopathology* (pp. 28–51). New Brunswick, NJ: Rutgers University Press.

Gergen, K. J. (1992). Toward a postmodern psychology. In S. Kvale (Ed.), *Psychology and postmodernism* (pp. 17–30). Thousand Oaks, CA: Sage.

Gergen, K. J. (2001). Psychological science in a postmodern context. *American Psychologist, 56*, 803–813.

Gergen, K. J. (2002). Beyond the empiricist/constructionist divide in social psychology. *Personality & Social Psychology Review, 6*, 188–191.

Gholson, B., & Barker, P. (1985). Kuhn, Lakatos, and Laudan: Applications in the history of physics and psychology. *American Psychologist, 40*, 755–769.

Giere, R. N. (1985). Philosophy of science naturalized. *Philosophy of Science, 52*, 331–356.

Giere, R. N. (1988). *Explaining science: A cognitive approach*. Chicago, IL: University of Chicago Press.

Giere, R. N. (2001). Critical hypothetical evolutionary naturalism. In C. Heyes & D. L. Hull (Eds.), *Selection theory and social construction: The evolutionary naturalistic epistemology of Donald T. Campbell* (pp. 53–70). Albany, NY: State University of New York Press.

Giere, R. N. (2003). Computation and agency in scientific cognition. *Proceedings of the 25th Annual Conference of the Cognitive Science Society*. Mahwah, NJ: Erlbaum. (Downloaded 9-14-04 from http://www.tc.umn.edu/~giere/R&Fpubs.html)

Gilligan, C., Spencer, R., Weinberg, K. M., & Bertsch, T. (2003). On the *Listening Guide*: A voice-centered relational model. In P. M. Camic, J. E. Rhodes, & L. Yardley (Eds.), *Qualitative research in psychology: Expanding perspectives in methodology and design* (pp. 157–172). Washington, DC: American Psychological Association.

Glaser, B. (1992). *Emergence versus forcing: Basics of grounded theory analysis*. Mill Valley, CA: Sociology Press.

Glaser, B., & Strauss, A. (1967). *The discovery of grounded theory*. New York: Aldine.

Gorman, M. E., Tweney, R. D., Gooding, D. C., & Kincannon, A. P. (Eds.) (2005). *Scientific and technological thinking*. Mahwah, NJ: Erlbaum.

Gould, S. J., & Lewontin, R. C. (1979). The spandrels of San Marco and the Panglossian paradigm: A critique of the adaptationist program. *Proceedings of the Royal Society of London B, 205*, 581–598.

Green, C. D. (1992). Of immortal mythological beasts: Operationism in psychology. *Theory & Psychology, 2*, 291–320.

Greene, B. (1999). *The elegant universe*. New York: Norton.

Greenwald, A. G., Pratkanis, A. R., Leippe, M. R., & Baumgardner, M. H. (1986). Under what conditions does theory obstruct research progress? *Psychological Review, 93*, 216–229.

Guba, E. G. (1990). The alternative paradigm dialogue. In E. G. Guba (Ed.), *The paradigm dialogue* (pp. 17–27). Thousand Oaks, CA: Sage.

Guttman, B. S. (2004). The real method of scientific discovery. *Skeptical Inquirer, 28 (No. 1)*, 45–47.

Hall, B. (1993). Introduction. In P. Park, M. Brydon-Miller, B. Hall, & T. Jackson (Eds.), *Voices of change: Participatory action research in the US and Canada* (pp. xiii–xxi). Westport, CT: Bergin and Garvey.

Hanson, N. R. (1958). *Patterns of discovery: An inquiry into the conceptual foundations of science*. Cambridge, UK: Cambridge University Press.

Harless, E. (1861). Der Apparat des Willens. In I. H. Fichte, H. Ulrici, & I. U. Wirth (Eds.), *Zeitschrift für Philosophie und philosophische Kritic: Vol. 38* (pp. 50–73). Halle, Germany: Pfeffer.

Harman, G. (1965). The inference to the best explanation. *Philosophical Review, 74*, 88–95.

Hassin, R. R., Uleman, J. S., & Bargh, J. A. (Eds.) (2004). *The new unconscious*. New York: Oxford University Press.

Hayes, S. C., & Hayes, L. J. (1989). Is behavior analysis contextualistic? *Theoretical & Philosophical Psychology, 9*, 37–40.

Hayes, S. C., Hayes, L. J., Reese, H. W., & Sarbin, T. R. (Eds.) (1993). *Varieties of scientific contextualism*. Reno, NV: Context Press.

Hebb, D. O. (1949). *The organization of behavior: A neuropsychological theory*. New York: Wiley.

Heft, H. (2001). *Ecological psychology in context: James Gibson, Roger Barker, and the legacy of William James's radical empiricism*. Mahwah, NJ: Erlbaum.

Helmholtz, H. von (1852). On the theory of compound colours. *Philosophical Magazine, 4*, 519–534.

Hempel, C. G. (1966). *Philosophy of natural science*. Englewood Cliffs, NJ: Prentice-Hall.

Henwood, K., & Pidgeon, N. (2003). Grounded theory in psychological research. In P. M. Camic, J. E. Rhodes, & L. Yardley (Eds.), *Qualitative research in psychology: Expanding perspectives in methodology and design* (pp. 131–155). Washington, DC: American Psychological Association.

References

Herbart, J. F. (1816). *Lehrbuch zur Psychologie*. Königsberg, Germany: Unzer.

Hering, E. (1954). Outlines of a theory of the light sense (Trans., L. M. Hurvich). Cambridge, MA: Harvard University Press. (original published in 1920)

Hoffman, R. R., & Nead, J. M. (1983). General contextualism, ecological science, and cognitive research. *The Journal of Mind and Behavior, 4*, 507–560.

Hofmann, J. R. (1992). Ampère's electrodynamics and the acceptability of guiding assumptions. In A. Donovan, L. Laudan, & R. Laudan (Eds.), *Scrutinizing science: Empirical studies of scientific change* (pp. 201–217). Baltimore: Johns Hopkins University Press.

Holcomb, H. R., III. (1998). Testing evolutionary hypotheses. In C. Crawford & D. L. Krebs (Eds.), *Handbook of Evolutionary Psychology: Ideas, issues, and applications* (pp. 303–334). Mahwah, NJ: Erlbaum.

Holland, J. H., Holyoak, K. J., Nisbett, R. E., & Thagard, P. R. (1986). *Induction*. Cambridge, MA: MIT Press.

Holzman, L. (1999). Introduction. In L. Hozman (Ed.), *Performing psychology: A postmodern culture of the mind*. New York: Routledge.

Howson, C. (2000). *Hume's problem: Induction and the justification of belief*. Oxford: Oxford University Press.

Hull, C. L. (1943). *Principles of behavior*. New York: Appleton-Century-Crofts.

Hull, C. L. (1952). *A behavior system: An introduction to behavior theory concerning the individual organism*. New Haven, CT: Yale University Press.

Hume, D. (1748). *An enquiry concerning human understanding*. (Republished in 2000 by Oxford University Press)

Hurvich, L. M. (1981). *Color vision*. Sunderland, MA: Sinauer.

Hyman, R. (1977). "Cold reading": How to convince strangers that you know all about them. *The Zetetic*, Spring/Summer 1977, 18–37.

Hyman, R. (1999). The mischief-making of ideomotor action. *The Scientific Review of Alternative Medicine, 3*, 34–43.

Ihlebaek, C., Love, T., Eilertsen, D. E., & Magnussen, S. (2003). Memory for a staged criminal event witnessed live and on video. *Memory, 11*, 319–327.

Jacobson, J. W., Mulick, J. A., & Schwartz, A. A. (1995). A history of facilitated communication: Science, pseudoscience, and antiscience. *American Psychologist, 50*, 750–765.

Jaeger, M. E., & Rosnow, R. L. (1988). Contextualism and its implications for psychological inquiry. *British Journal of Psychology, 79*, 63–75.

James, W. (1890). *Principles of psychology*. New York: Holt.

James, W. (1976). *Essays in radical empiricism*. Cambridge, MA: Harvard University Press. (original work published 1912)

Johnson, A., & Proctor, R. W. (2004). *Attention: Theory and practice*. Thousand Oaks, CA: Sage.

Jost, J. T., & Kruglanski, A. W. (2002). The estrangement of social constructionism and experimental social psychology: History of the rift and prospects for reconciliation. *Personality & Social Psychology Review, 6*, 168–187.

Kagitçibasi, Ç. (2000). Cultural contextualism without complete relativism in the study of human development. In A. Comunian & U. P. Gielen (Eds.),

International perspectives on human development (pp. 97–115). Lengerich, Germany: Pabst Science Publishers.

Kanwisher, N., & Duncan, J. (Eds.) (2004). *Functional neuroimaging of visual cognition: Attention and performance XX.* New York: Oxford University Press.

Kerferd, G. B. (1981). *The Sophistic movement.* Cambridge, UK: Cambridge University Press.

Ketelaar, T., & Ellis, B. J. (2000). Are evolutionary explanations unfalsifiable? Evolutionary psychology and the Lakatosian philosophy of science. *Psychological Inquiry, 11,* 1–21.

Kidder, L., & Fine, M. (1987). Qualitative and quantitative methods: When stories converge. In M. M. Mark & R. L. Shotland (Eds.), *Multiple methods in program evaluation* (pp. 57–75). San Francisco, California: Jossey-Bass.

Kitao, N. (2002). A review of research on the spacing effect in memory. *Japanese Psychological Review, 45,* 164–179.

Kitcher, P. (1993). *The advancement of science: Science without legend, objectivity without illusion.* New York: Oxford University Press.

Klahr, D., & Dunbar, K. (1988). Dual space search during scientific reasoning. *Cognitive Science, 12,* 1–48.

Klahr, D., & Simon, H. A. (1999). Studies of scientific discovery: Complementary approaches and convergent findings. *Psychological Bulletin, 125,* 524–543.

Klahr, D., & Simon, H. A. (2001). What have psychologists (and others) discovered about the process of scientific discovery? *Current Directions in Psychological Science, 10,* 75–79.

Kopala, M., & Suzuki, L. A. (Eds.) (1999). *Using qualitative methods in psychology.* Thousand Oaks, CA: Sage.

Kosslyn, S. M., & Andersen, R. A. (1992). General introduction. In S. M. Kosslyn & R. A. Andersen (Eds.), *Frontiers in cognitive neuroscience* (pp. xv–xxix). Cambridge, MA: MIT Press.

Knuf, L., Aschersleben, G., & Prinz, W. (2001). Analysis of ideomotor action. *Journal of Experimental Psychology, 130,* 779–798.

Krueger, J. (2001). Null hypothesis significance testing: On the survival of a flawed method. *American Psychologist, 56,* 16–26.

Kuhn, D. (1989). Children and adults as intuitive scientists. *Psychological Review, 96,* 674–689.

Kuhn, T. S. (1962). *The structure of scientific revolutions.* Chicago: University of Chicago Press. (revised edition published in 1970 and 3rd edition in 1996)

Kuhn, T. S. (1970a). Logic of discovery or psychology of research? In I. Lakatos & A. Musgrave (Eds.), *Criticism and the growth of knowledge* (pp. 1–23). New York: Cambridge University Press.

Kuhn, T. S. (1970b). Reflections on my critics. In I. Lakatos & A. Musgrave (Eds.), *Criticism and the growth of knowledge* (pp. 231–278). New York: Cambridge University Press.

Kuhn, T. S. (1977). *The essential tension: Selected studies in scientific tradition and change.* Chicago: University of Chicago Press.

Kulkarni, D., & Simon, H. A. (1988). The processes of scientific discover strategy of experimentation. *Cognitive Science, 12*, 139–175.

Kvale, S. (2003). The psychoanalytical interview as inspiration for qualitative research. In P. M. Camic, J. E. Rhodes, & L. Yardley (Eds.), *Qualitative research in psychology: Expanding perspectives in methodology and design* (pp. 275–297). Washington, DC: American Psychological Association.

Lachman, R., Lachman, J. L., & Butterfield, E. C. (1979). *Cognitive psychology and information processing: An introduction.* Hillsdale, NJ: Erlbaum.

Lakatos, I. (1970). Falsification and the methodology of scientific research programmes. In. I. Lakatos & A. Musgrave (Eds.), *Criticism and the growth of knowledge* (pp. 91–196). New York: Cambridge University Press.

Lakin, J. L., Jefferis, V. E., Cheng, C. M., & Chartrand, T. L. (2003). The chameleon effect as social glue: Evidence for the evolutionary significance of nonconscious mimicry. *Journal of Nonverbal Behavior, 27*, 145–162.

Lamarck, J. B. (1809). *Zoological philosophy.* New York: Macmillan and Company. (English translation in 1914)

Lashley, K. S. (1929). *Brain mechanisms and intelligence.* Chicago: University of Chicago Press.

Lashley, K. S. (1951). The problem of serial order behavior. In L. A. Jeffress (Ed.), *Cerebral mechanisms in behavior* (pp. 112–131). New York: Wiley.

Laudan, L. (1977). *Progress and its problems: Toward a theory of scientific growth.* Berkeley, CA: University of California Press.

Laudan, L. (1984). *Science and values: The aims of science and their role in scientific debate.* Berkeley, CA: University of California Press.

Laudan, L. (1990). *Science and relativism: Some key controversies in the philosophy of science.* Chicago: University of Chicago Press.

Laudan, L. (1996). *Beyond positivism and relativism: Theory, method, and evidence.* Boulder, CO: Westview Press.

Laudan, L. (1997). How about bust? Factoring explanatory power back into theory evaluation. *Philosophy of Science, 64*, 306–316.

Laycock, T. (1845). On the reflex functions of the brain. Reprinted from N. XXXVII of the *British and Foreign Medical Review* (pp. 1–16). Bartolomew Close, UK: Adlard.

Leondes, C. T. (Ed.) (2002). *Expert systems: The technology of knowledge management and decision making for the 21st century.* San Diego, CA: Academic Press.

Lewis, M. (1997). *Altering fate.* New York: Guilford Press.

Litton, I., & Potter, J. (1985). Social representations in the ordinary explanation of a "riot." *European Journal of Social Psychology, 15*, 371–388.

Loftus, E. F. (2003). Make-believe memories. *American Psychologist, 58*, 867–873.

Logan, G. D. (2002). An instance theory of attention and memory. *Psychological Review, 109*, 376–400.

Losee, J. (2001). *A historical introduction to the philosophy of science.* Oxford, UK: Oxford University Press.

Lotze, R. H. (1852). *Medizinische Psychologie oder Physiologie der Seele* (pp. 287–325). Leipzig, Germany: Weidmann'sche Buchandlung.

Lutgens, F. K., & Tarbuck, E. J. (1998). *Essentials of geology*. Upper Saddle River, NJ: Prentice Hall.

Maguire, P. (2001). The congruency thing: Transforming psychological research and pedagogy. In D. L. Tolman & M. Brydon-Miller (Eds.), *From subjects to subjectivities: A handbook of interpretive and participatory methods* (pp. 276–289). New York: New York University Press.

Malinowski, B. (1922). *Argonauts of the Western Pacific*. New York: Dutton.

Marecek, J. (2003). Dancing through minefields: Toward a qualitative stance in psychology. In P. M. Camic, J. E. Rhodes, & L. Yardley (Eds.), *Qualitative research in psychology: Expanding perspectives in methodology and design* (pp. 49–69). Washington, DC: American Psychological Association.

Mauskopf, S. H. (1992). Molecular geometry in 19th-century France: Shifts in guiding assumptions. In A. Donovan, L. Laudan, & R. Laudan (Eds.), *Scrutinizing science: Empirical studies of scientific change* (pp. 125–144). Baltimore: Johns Hopkins University Press.

McGrath, J. E., & Johnson, B. A. (2003). Methodology makes meaning: How both qualitative and quantitative paradigms shape evidence and its interpretations. In P. M. Camic, J. E. Rhodes, & L. Yardley (Eds.), *Qualitative research in psychology: Expanding perspectives in methodology and design* (pp. 31–47). Washington, DC: American Psychological Association.

McGuigan, F. J. (1960). *Experimental psychology: A methodological approach*. Englewood Cliffs, NJ: Prentice-Hall.

Michell, J. (2003). The quantitative imperative: Positivism, naïve realism and the place of qualitative methods in psychology. *Theory & Psychology, 13*, 5–31.

Miller, N. E. (1959). Liberalization of basic S-R concepts: Extensions to conflict behavior, motivation, and social learning. In S. Koch (Ed.), *Psychology: A study of science (Vol. 2: General systematic formulations, learning, and special processes)* (pp. 196–292). New York: McGraw-Hill.

Miller, P. J., Hengst, J. A., & Wang, S.-H. (2003). Ethnographic methods: Applications from developmental cultural psychology. In P. M. Camic, J. E. Rhodes, & L. Yardley (Eds.), *Qualitative research in psychology: Expanding perspectives in methodology and design* (pp. 219–242). Washington, DC: American Psychological Association.

Minami, H., & Dallenbach, K. M. (1946). The effect of activity upon learning and retention in the cockroach. *American Journal of Psychology, 59*, 1–58.

Minsky, M., & Papert, S. (1969). *Perceptrons*. Cambridge, MA: MIT Press.

Mook, D. G. (1983). In defense of external invalidity. *American Psychologist, 38*, 379–387.

Moser, K., Gadenne, V., & Schröder, J. (1988). Under what conditions does confirmation seeking obstruct scientific progress? *Psychological Review, 95*, 572–574.

Murray, M. (2003). Narrative psychology and narrative analysis. In P. M. Camic, J. E. Rhodes, & L. Yardley (Eds.), *Qualitative research in psychology: Expanding perspectives in methodology and design* (pp. 95–112). Washington, DC: American Psychological Association.

Neath, I., & Surprenant, A. (2003). *Human memory: An introduction to research, data, and theory* (2nd edn). Pacific Grove, CA: Wadsworth.

Neisser, U. (1982). Memory: What are the important questions? In U. Neisser (Ed.), *Memory observed: Remembering in natural contexts* (pp. 3–19). San Francisco: W. H. Freeman.

Newell, A., & Simon, H. A. (1967). An example of human chess play in the light of chess-playing programs. In N. Weiner & J. P. Schade (Eds.), *Progress in cybernetics* (Vol. 2, pp. 19–75). Amsterdam: Elsevier.

Nicholas, J. M. (1992). Planck's quantum crisis and shifts in guiding assumptions. In A. Donovan, L. Laudan, & R. Laudan (Eds.), *Scrutinizing science: Empirical studies of scientific change* (pp. 317–335). Baltimore: Johns Hopkins University Press.

O'Donohue, W. (1993). The spell of Kuhn on psychology: An exegetical elixir. *Philosophical Psychology, 6,* 267–286.

Oreskes, N. (1999). *Rejection of continental drift.* New York: Oxford University Press.

Park, P. (1993). What is participatory research? A theoretical and methodological perspective. In P. Park, M. Brydon-Miller, B. Hall, & T. Jackson (Eds.), *Voices of change: Participatory action research in the US and Canada* (pp. 1–19). Westport, CT: Bergin and Garvey.

Pashler, H. (1998). *Attention.* Cambridge, MA: MIT Press.

Pavlov, I. P. (1928). *Lectures on conditioned reflexes* (W. H. Grantz, Trans.). New York: International Publishers.

Peirce, C. S. (1940). Abduction and induction. In J. Buchler (Ed.), *The philosophy of Peirce: Selected writings* (pp. 150–156). London: Routledge and Kegan Paul.

Pepper, S. C. (1942). *World hypotheses.* Berkeley, CA: University of California Press.

Perrin, C. E. (1992). The chemical revolution: Shifts in guiding assumptions. In A. Donovan, L. Laudan, & R. Laudan (Eds.), *Scrutinizing science: Empirical studies of scientific change* (pp. 105–124). Baltimore: Johns Hopkins University Press.

Pfungst, O. (1911/1965). *Clever Hans: The horse of Mr. Von Osten* (Carl L. Rahn, Trans.). New York: Holt, Rinehart, and Winston.

Piaget, J. (1975). *The child's conception of the world.* Totowa, NJ: Littlefield, Adams. (originally published in 1929)

Pigliucci, M. (2003). 'Elementary, Dear Watson'. *Skeptical Inquirer, 27 (No. 3),* 18–19.

Piran, N. (2001). Re-inhabiting the body from the inside out: Girls transform their school environment. In D. L. Tolman & M. Brydon-Miller (Eds.), *From subjects to subjectivities: A handbook of interpretive and participatory methods* (pp. 218–238). New York: New York University Press.

Platt, J. R. (1964). Strong inference. *Science, 146,* 347–353. Reprinted in J. R. Platt (1966), *The step to man.* New York: Wiley.

Ponterotto, J. G., & Grieger, I. (1999). Merging qualitative and quantitative perspectives in a research identity. In M. Kopala & L. A. Suzuki (Eds.), *Using qualitative methods in psychology* (pp. 49–62). Thousand Oaks, CA: Sage.

Popper, K. R. (1959). *The logic of scientific discovery*. New York: Basic Books.

Popper, K. R. (1963). *Conjectures and refutations*. London: Routledge and Kegan Paul.

Popper, K. R. (1970). Normal science and its dangers. In I. Lakatos & A. Musgrave (Eds.), *Criticism and the growth of knowledge* (pp. 51–58). New York: Cambridge University Press.

Posner, M. I., Snyder, C. R. R., & Davidson, B. J. (1980). Attention and the detection of signals. *Journal of Experimental Psychology: General, 109*, 160–174.

Postman, L., & Underwood, B. J. (1973). Critical issues in interference theory. *Memory & Cognition, 1*, 19–40.

Potter, J. (2002). Experimenting with reconciliation: A comment on Jost and Kruglanski. *Personality & Social Psychology Review, 6*, 192–193.

Potter, J. (2003). Discourse analysis and discursive psychology. In P. M. Camic, J. E. Rhodes, & L. Yardley (Eds.), *Qualitative research in psychology: Expanding perspectives in methodology and design* (pp. 73–94). Washington, DC: American Psychological Association.

Pratto, F. (2002). Integrating experimental and social constructivist social psychology: Some of us are already doing it. *Personality & Social Psychology Review, 6*, 194–198.

Quine, W. V. (1953). Two dogmas of empiricism. In W. V. Quine, *From a logical point of view*. Cambridge, MA: Harvard University Press.

Quine, W. V. (1970). On the reasons for indeterminacy of translation. *The Journal of Philosophy, 67*, 179–183.

Rachlin, H. (2002). Altruism and selfishness. *Behavioral & Brain Sciences, 25*, 239–296.

Ramón y Cajal, S. (1999). *Advice for a young investigator* (N. S. Swanson & L. W. Swanson, Trans.). Cmabridge, MA: MIT Press. (original work published 1897)

Reichenbach, H. (1947). *Elements of symbolic logic*. New York: Macmillan.

Ricoeur, P. (1991). Life: A story in search of a narrator. In M. J. Valdes (Ed.), *A Ricoeur reader: Reflection and imagination* (pp. 137–155). Toronto: University of Toronto Press.

Rocke, A. J. (1992). Kekulé's benzene theory and the appraisal of scientific theories. In A. Donovan, L. Laudan, & R. Laudan (Eds.), *Scrutinizing science: Empirical studies of scientific change* (pp. 145–162). Baltimore: Johns Hopkins University Press.

Roediger, H. L., III (1980). Memory metaphors in cognitive psychology. *Memory & Cognition, 8*, 231–246.

Rorty, R. (1989). *Contingency, irony, and solidarity*. New York: Cambridge University Press.

Rosenberg, A. (1995). *Philosophy of social science* (2nd edn). Boulder, CO: Westview Press.

Rosenblatt, E. (1962). *Principles of neurodynamics*. Washington, DC: Spartan Books.

Rosenthal, R. (1965). Introduction. In O. Pfungst, *Clever Hans: The horse of Mr. Von Osten* (Carl L. Rahn, Trans.). New York: Holt, Rinehart, and Winston.

Rosnow, R. L., & Georgoudi, M. (1986). The spirit of contextualism. In R. L. Rosnow & M. Georgoudi (Ed.), *Contextualism and understanding in behavioral science: Implications for research and theory* (pp. 3–22). New York: Praeger.

Ruse, M. (2001). On being a philosophical naturalist: A tribute to Donald Campbell. In C. Heyes & D. L. Hull (Eds.), *Selection theory and social construction: The evolutionary naturalistic epistemology of Donald T. Campbell* (pp. 71–100). Albany, NY: State University of New York Press.

Rychlak, J. F. (2003). *The human image in postmodern America*. Washington, DC: American Psychological Association.

Salmon, W. C. (1988). Rational prediction. In A. Grünbaum & W. C. Salmon (Eds.), *The limitations of deductivism* (pp. 47–60). Berkeley, CA: University of California Press.

Sarbin, T. R. (1977). Contextualism: A world view for modern psychology. In A. Landfield (Ed.), *Nebraska symposium on motivation, 1976: Personal construct psychology* (pp. 1–41). Lincoln: University of Nebraska Press.

Schaller, M. (2002). Any theory can be useful theory, even it if gets on our nerves. *Personality & Social Psychology Review, 6,* 199–203

Schunn, C. D., & Anderson, J. R. (1999). The generality/specificity of expertise in scientific reasoning. *Cognitive Science, 23,* 337–370.

Shraagen, J. M. (1993). How experts solve a novel problem in experimental design. *Cognitive Science, 17,* 285–309.

Shweder, R. A. (1996). *Quanta* and *qualia*: What is the "object" of ethnographic method? In R. Jessor, A. Colby, & R. A. Shweder (Eds.), *Ethnography and human development: Contextual meaning in social inquiry* (pp. 175–182). Chicago: University of Chicago Press.

Simon, H. A. (1983). *Models of bounded rationality.* 2 vols. Cambridge, MA: MIT Press.

Simonton, D. K. (1992). Leaders in American psychology, 1879–1967: Career development, creative output, and professional achievement. *Journal of Personality and Social Psychology, 63,* 5–17.

Singley, K., & Anderson, J. R. (1989). *The transfer of cognitive skill.* Cambridge, MA: Harvard University Press.

Slife, B. D., & Williams, R. N. (1995). *What's behind the research? Discovering hidden assumptions in the behavioral sciences.* Thousand Oaks, CA: Sage.

Smith, J. A. (Ed.) (2003). *Qualitative psychology: A practical guide to research methods.* Thousand Oaks, CA: Sage.

Snyder, L. J. (1994). Is evidence historical? In P. Achinstein & L. J. Snyder (Eds.), *Scientific methods: Conceptual and historical problems* (pp. 95–117). Malabar, FL: Krieger.

Sober, E. (2000). *Philosophy of biology* (2nd edn). Boulder, CO: Westview Press.

Steiner, R. A. (1989). *Don't get taken! – Bunco and bunkum exposed – How to protect yourself.* El Cerrito, CA: Wide-Awake Books.

Stock, A., & Stock, C. (2004). A short history of ideo-motor action. *Psychological Research, 68,* 176–188.

Strauss, A., & Corbin, J. (1998). *Basics of qualitative research* (2nd edn). London: Sage.

Thagard, P. (1988). *Computational philosophy of science.* Cambridge, MA: MIT Press.

Thagard, P. (2005). How to be a successful scientist. In M. E. Gorman, R. D. Tweney, D. C. Gooding, & A. P. Kincannon (Eds.), *Scientific and technological thinking* (pp. 159–171). Mahwah, NJ: Erlbaum.

Tolman, D. L., & Brydon-Miller, M. (2001). Interpretive and participatory research methods: Moving toward subjectivities. In D. L. Tolman & M. Brydon-Miller (Eds.), *From subjects to subjectivities: A handbook of interpretive and participatory methods* (pp. 3–11). New York: New York University Press.

Tooby, J., & Cosmides, L. (1992). The psychological foundations of culture. In J. H. Barkow, L. Cosmides, & J. Tooby (Eds.), *The psychological foundations of culture* (pp. 19–136). New York: Oxford University Press.

Tulving, E. (2002). Episodic memory: From mind to brain. In *Annual Review of Psychology* (Vol. 53, pp. 1–25). Palo Alto, CA: Annual Reviews.

Tversky, A., & Kahneman, D. (1974). Judgment under uncertainty: Heuristics and biases. *Science, 185,* 1124–1131.

Tweney, R. D. (1989). A framework for cognitive psychology of science. In B. Gholson, W. R. Shadish, Jr., R. A. Neimeyer, & A. C. Houts (Eds.), *Psychology of science* (pp. 342–366). New York: Cambridge University Press.

Tweney, R. (1991). Faraday's notebooks: The active organization of creative science. *Physics Education, 26,* 301–306.

Uttal, W. R. (2001). *The new phrenology: The limits of localizing cognitive processes in the brain.* Cambridge, MA: MIT Press.

Vogt, E. Z., & Hyman, R. (1959). *Water witching, USA.* Chicago: University of Chicago Press.

Wason, P. C. (1960). On the failure to eliminate hypotheses in a conceptual task. *Quarterly Journal of Experimental Psychology, 12,* 129–140.

Watson, J. D. (2000). *A passion for DNA: Genes, genomes, and society.* Cold Spring Harbor, NY: Cold Spring Harbor Laboratory.

Watson, J., Balota, D. A., & Roediger III, H. L. (2003). Creating false memories with hybrid lists of semantic and phonological associates: Over-additive false memories produced by converging associative networks. *Journal of Memory & Language, 49,* 95–118.

Webster's New World Dictionary of the American Language (2nd college edn). (1980). Cleveland: OH: Collins.

Weinberg, D. (2002). Qualitative research methods: An overview. In D. Weinberg (Ed.), *Qualitative research methods* (pp. 1–22). Malden, MA: Blackwell Publishers.

Weismann, A. (1893). The germ plasm: A theory of heredity. Translated by W. N. Parker & H. Ronfeldt. New York: Charles Scribner's Sons.

Wernicke, C. (1874). *Der aphasische symtomenkomplex.* Breslau: Cohn & Weigert.

Whewell, W. (1840). *The philosophy of the inductive sciences, founded upon their history.* London: J. W. Parker.

Whewell, W. (1984). *Selected writings on the history of science.* Chicago: University of Chicago Press.

Williams, L. P. (1970). Normal science, scientific revolutions and the history of science. In I. Lakatos & A. Musgrave (Eds.), *Criticism and the growth of knowledge* (pp. 49–50). New York: Cambridge University Press.

Willig, C. (2001). *Qualitative research in psychology: A practical guide to theory and method.* Oxford: Oxford University Press.

Wilson, E. O. (1987). Kin recognition: An introductory synopsis. In D. J. C. Fletcher & C. D. Michener (Eds.), *Kin recognition in animals* (pp. 7–18). Hove, UK: Wiley.

Wilson, E. O. (1998). *Consilience: The unity of knowledge.* New York: Vintage.

Wolpe, J. (1958). *Psychotherapy by reciprocal inhibition.* Stanford, CA: Stanford University Press.

Yantis, S. (Ed.) (2001). *Visual perception: Essential readings.* Philadelphia, PA: Psychology Press.

Young, T. (1802). On the theory of light and colours. *Philosophical Transactions of the Royal Society of London, 92,* 12–48.

Zandvoort, H. (1992). Nuclear magnetic resonance and the acceptability of guiding assumptions. In A. Donovan, L. Laudan, & R. Laudan (Eds.), *Scrutinizing science: Empirical studies of scientific change* (pp. 337–358). Baltimore: Johns Hopkins University Press.

Zeller, E. (1955). *Outlines of the history of Greek philosophy* (13th edn). New York: Meridian.

Zuckerman, H. (1977). *Scientific elite.* New York: Free Press.

GLOSSARY OF TERMS

Abduction – A procedure, initially made popular by the philosopher C. S. Peirce in the late 1800s, that has been used in three different senses: explaining patterns of data, entertaining multiple hypotheses, and arguing to the best explanation. As a means of evaluating theory, it is superior to either induction or deduction.

Affirming the consequent – A reasoning fallacy of accepting an empirical observation consistent with a deduction from an hypothesis as confirming that hypothesis. Such an observation does not necessarily imply that that hypothesis is true because there may be many other hypotheses consistent with the observation.

Analytic statements – A term used by logical positivists to designate statements that are true by definition but lack empirical content. An example is "All bachelors are unmarried." See also synthetic statements.

Behavior modification – A variety of techniques for changing the behavior of humans derived from the scientific study of the learning process in animals.

Causal analysis – To say that an effect has a cause is to suggest that the cause provides a necessary and sufficient condition for the effect to occur.

Cold reading – Techniques employed to provide personalized details about some aspect of an individual's life by a reader who knows little or nothing about the person being described.

Confirmation bias – A tendency for researchers to persevere by revising experimental procedures until they obtain a result consistent with their favored theory.

Consilience – A term used to describe situations in which particular propositions are supported by evidence from a variety of different sources.

Context of discovery – Refers to the processes involved in the formulation of an idea, concept, or hypothesis. See also Context of justification.

Context of justification – Refers to the various methodological procedures that scientists might use to confirm or justify their hypotheses and theories.

Contextualism – A variety of relativism that rejects the idea that general laws can be discovered, accepts the fact that novel events can appear at any time, rejects conventional science, accepts radical empiricism, and tends to see experimentation as merely one context among many.

Deduction – The procedure of deriving specific predictions from general premises.

Discourse analysis – The study of how talk and texts are used to perform actions.

Discursive psychology – Application of discourse analysis to issues in psychology, with the intent of providing a perspective of meta-theoretical, theoretical, and analytical principles closely related to those of social constructionism.

Duhem–Quine thesis – Concerns the logical difficulties of being unable to reject a hypothesis when obtaining a result that is not consistent with it. The basic idea is that there may be a variety of reasons why an inconsistent result was obtained.

Ecological validity – Concerns whether findings generalize to relevant real-world settings.

Empiricism – The view that knowledge should be generated by observation through the senses.

Enlightenment – The Enlightenment is an intellectual movement beginning in the 17th century and associated most notably with the 18th century in which reliance on the writings of the ancients as a basis for knowledge was rejected in favor of observation and reasoning.

Epistemology – The philosophical analysis of the principles and procedures of inquiry used to acquire knowledge.

Ethnographic methods – Methods, originally employed by anthropologists and sociologists, and more recently adopted in psychology, that are concerned with meaning that is structured by particular cultures.

Explanatory theory – A theory that is devised primarily to explain known facts.

External validity – Concerns the generalizability of results. Results are considered to have high external validity if they generalize broadly to a variety of novel settings.

False memories – The phenomenon of "remembering" events that did not in fact occur.

Falsificationism – The view, suggested by Karl Popper, that the proper approach in science is to do one's best to falsify hypotheses.

Foundationism – The procedure of justifying core methodological beliefs and practices using intuition and logic.

Grounded theory – An approach developed by sociologists that employs semi-structured interviews, case-study notes, and field observations. The basic idea is that the researcher begins with minimal preconceptions, collects observations, revises his/her interpretation of the observations, and repeats this process until a satisfactory theoretical explanation is achieved.

Heuristics – Rules of thumb used to provide a solution to a complicated problem by conceptualizing as a simpler one. The solution is often, but not always, satisfactory. See Satisficing.

Hypothesis testing – Deriving predictions from an hypothesis or theory and evaluating them employing experimentation or some other research method. According to some individuals, hypothesis testing is identified as the scientific method.

Ideomotor action – Action produced automatically, and often unconsciously, simply by having an idea about the action. It is thought to be the explanation for many so-called paranormal phenomena involving movement, such as table turning in a séance and movement of a Ouija board plangent.

Incommensurability – The opinion that the basic assumptions of individuals who adhere to different paradigms are so different that the individuals cannot understand or communicate with each other.

Induction – A reasoning process that moves from the observation of a variety of specific instances to a general characterization of the observations.

Inference to the best explanation – Attempting to come to a conclusion as to which among several alternative theories best satisfies the available evidence. A given theory is to be accepted only if it is superior to its rivals.

Internal validity – The extent to which results obtained in a given study are valid for that situation. Internal validity is said to be high when the design of a study is sufficiently controlled that one can confidently conclude that the independent variable caused observed changes in the dependent variable.

Listening guide method – A qualitative method intended to provide insight into the human psyche by listening to the distinctive voices possessed by individual human beings.

Localization of function – The view that distinct regions of the brain control specific perceptual, cognitive, and motor functions.

Logical positivism – A European movement in the first half of the 20th century that saw induction from observations as the central method of science, distinguished between analytic and synthetic statements, emphasized the context of justification, and used a verifiability criterion of meaning.

Metaphysical – A term used to refer to propositions that cannot be verified empirically. The goal of logical positivism and operationism was to rid science of metaphysical concepts.

Modernism – The view, stemming from the Enlightenment, that lawful relations can be discovered and that sound methodology will ultimately be able to isolate the truth, or at least approximations to it.

Narrative – An approach concerned with the structure, content, and function of the tales that we tell ourselves and others. Individuals who use the narrative approach believe that it is through people's narratives that we come to understand them.

Naturalism – A movement in philosophy based on the view that nature is the totality of reality and that it can be understood only through scientific methods. Naturalism is incompatible with metaphysics.

Natural selection – The central idea in Darwin's theory of evolution. It requires variability, selection, and heredity.

Normal science – In Kuhn's view of science, this applies to the period in which a paradigm is accepted and determines the problems and issues that are researched.

Normative naturalism – The view that a naturalistic approach to scientific methodology can be not only descriptive but also provide norms concerning how science should best be practiced.

Ontology – Refers to the sort of fundamental entities that a particular theory posits. An ontology is sometimes called a worldview.

Operational definition – Defining concepts in terms of the operations, or methods, used to measure them.

Operationism – The approach, first advocated by Bridgeman, that scientific concepts are synonymous with the operations used to measure them.

Paradigm – The term used by Kuhn to specify the ontological and methodological commitments accepted in a particular area of science at a given time.

Participatory action research – A qualitative method that involves participants as equal partners in the research process, often with the intent of accomplishing some particular action to improve the lives of the people in the community of interest.

Portraiture – A qualitative method in which the researcher attempts to produce an authentic, coherent portrait of the individual or individuals of interest.

Positivism – An approach emphasizing the central role of experience in science.

Postmodernism – A reaction to modernism that rejects its core conceptions of truth, reality, and objectivity.

Postpositivism – A term used to refer to the varieties of philosophy of science that have been developed since the influence of logical positivism and falsificationism waned in the latter part of the 20th century.

Predictive theory – A theory from which predictions can be derived deductively and tested.

Psychoanalytic interview – The dialogue between a psychoanalyst and patient. It has been suggested that the psychoanalytic interview can serve as a qualitative research method.

Pythagoreanism – Followers of Pythagorus who accepted the view that anything that was real should and could be described in mathematical terms.

Qualitative inquiry – An approach to psychological research that uses methods that focus on the reported experiences of individuals.

Qualitative methods – As employed by qualitative theorists, the term refers to methods intended to provide a detailed description of individual experience. More generally, qualitative methods refer to a variety of procedures that are not specifically quantitative, as, for example, employing naturalistic observation.

Quantitative methods – The term used by qualitative researchers to refer to experimentation and other methods that emphasize control and quantified measures of performance.

Radical empiricism – A view that science should be concerned only with observable sense data.

Relativism – Denial that there is any privileged methodological basis for creating theory. It suggests instead that truth is created rather than found or discovered.

Research program – Lakatos's term for the general theoretical and methodological commitments accepted by scientists that are more fundamental than the specific theories to which they give rise.

Research traditions – Laudan's term for the idea that there are overarching ideas that relate a particular group of theories, similar to Kuhn's concept of paradigm.

Revolutionary science – Kuhn's term for science as practiced when a crisis arises for the currently accepted paradigm.

Satisficing – The name given by Simon to the procedure of searching in difficult cases for a satisfactory solution to a problem or choice rather than for a completely adequate one.

Social constructionism – A relativistic approach that views knowledge about the world as an artifact of the social interchange among individuals.

Sophists – Ancient Greek philosophers who believed that all knowledge, laws, and morality were created by individuals.

Synthetic statements – A term used by logical positivists to designate propositions that have empirical content, for example, "grass is green." See also Analytic statements.

Systematic desensitization – A procedure, based on Pavlovian conditioning, used in connection with people who have phobias. The intent of the procedure is to countercondition relaxation to increasingly threatening scenes. This procedure is effective in curing phobias such as fear of public speaking.

Underdetermination – The view that a given body of evidence does not uniquely determine any particular theoretical position.

GLOSSARY OF NAMES

Aristotle (384–322 BCE) – Outstanding Greek philosopher who was noted for contributions in a variety of knowledge areas, including the philosophy of science and logic.

Bacon, Sir Francis (1561–1626) – An English noble who proposed a new system of knowledge based on empirical and inductive principles with the ultimate goal of producing knowledge for both theoretical and practical purposes.

Campbell, Donald T. (1916–1996) – A social psychologist who founded evolutionary epistemology. He was concerned with methodological issues such as internal and external validity.

Darwin, Charles (1809–1882) – British naturalist who developed the idea that evolution occurred by means of natural selection, an influential view that is accepted as the primary engine of evolution to this day. After developing his evolutionary ideas in 1859, Darwin invested a great deal of theorizing in psychology. Two well-known examples are his theory of sexual selection and his idea that emotion is similar between humans and animals, and that all humans share similar emotions.

Duhem, Pierre (1861–1916) – French philosopher of science who proposed that the role of scientific theory is to systematize relationships. He is known for advocating the view that any evidence counter to a theory is unable to specify which of several interrelated elements of the theory is at fault.

Faraday, Michael (1791–1867) – Pioneering physicist and chemist who is noted for his work in electricity and magnetism.

Galilei, Galileo (1564–1642) – He defended the heliocentric theory the solar system. His research overturned the Aristotelian approach to motion, establishing the modern conception. Dampier, in his history of science, said that Galileo was the first modern scientist.

Gergen, Kenneth – Relativist and social constructionist who believes that reality is socially constructed. According to Gergen, even emotions are social constructions.

Giere, Ronald – A philosopher of science whose naturalistic approach is informed by his interest in cognitive psychology and cognitive science.

Hanson, Norwood R. (1924–1967) – A philosopher of science who emphasized that our empirical judgments and perceptions are influenced by the conceptual framework in which they are embedded.

Hempel, Carl (1905–1997) – A logical positivist who was most concerned with identifying the conditions under which scientific ideas can be explained.

Hume, David (1711–1776) – A Scottish philosopher who suggested that induction does not establish cause and effect relationships.

James, William (1842–1910) – Philosopher and psychologist who had an enormous impact on both fields. In philosophy, he emphasized pragmatism and radical empiricism. In psychology, his best known work is the *Principles of Psychology*, in which many of his original ideas were expressed.

Kuhn, Thomas S. (1922–1996) – An internationally known historian and philosopher of science who suggested that science could be studied empirically, and thus may be regarded as one of the primary founders of the naturalistic approach to science.

Lakatos, Imre (1922–1974) – A philosopher of science and follower of Karl Popper whose major concern was with developing a view of falsification that he called sophisticated falsification.

Lamarck, Jean Baptiste (1744–1829) – A French naturalist who suggested that evolution occurs through the inheritance of acquired characteristics. His early views of evolution, considered at one time to be opposed to those of Darwin, have been discredited.

Laudan, Larry – Philosopher of science known for his view called normative naturalism. Laudan believes that naturalism can be prescriptive as well as descriptive.

Locke, John (1632–1704) – English empiricist who believed that all knowledge originated in the senses. His views were very popular in Europe because they suggested that knowledge could be derived from other than reading the texts of Greek philosophers.

Loftus, Elizabeth – A psychologist who has investigated a variety of conditions under which false memories can be implanted in people. She is known particularly for her work on the unreliability of eyewitness testimony.

Mendel, Gregor (1822–1884) – Austrian monk whose groundbreaking work on the inheritance of phenotypes in garden peas laid the groundwork for the modern theory of genetics.

Mill, John Stuart (1806–1873) – English philosopher who described the logic behind a variety of experimental procedures. He was of the opinion that explanatory theories were as valuable, scientifically speaking, as predictive theories.

Newton, Isaac (1642–1727) – A physicist and mathematician. Included among his many accomplishments were the invention of Calculus and his description of the variables involved in gravitational attraction. One of the foremost intellects of all time.

Peirce, Charles S. (1839–1914) – One of the foremost American philosophers. In addition to being the father of pragmatism, he contributed original ideas in many areas, including logic and semiotics.

Pepper, Stephen C. (1891–1972) – American philosopher who described major movements in philosophy, including mechanism, formism, contextualism, and organicism. In psychology, he influenced a variety of individuals who would be classified as contextualists.

Pfungst, Oskar – A German psychologist who demonstrated that the horse Clever Hans, said to be able to count by tapping his hoof, actually was sensitive to small movements on the part of his trainer and others as the correct answer to a particular problem arose.

Popper, Sir Karl (1902–1994) – A prominent philosopher of science who suggested that the proper approach to testing scientific ideas was to do our best to falsify them. Popper's views were widely accepted when first proposed and continue to be popular to this day.

Rorty, Richard – An American philosopher who said that truth is invented and not found. His brand of relativism is widely accepted and influential.

Ruse, Michael – A philosopher of biology whose philosophic views have been shaped by the theory of evolution. He has been an outspoken critic of scientific creationism.

Quine, Willard Van Orman (1908–2000) – A philosopher who suggested that all propositions could be rescued from falsification by a suitable combination of assumptions. This thesis was advanced strongly in his famous paper, *Two Dogmas of Empiricism*. Quine was a naturalist who suggested that philosophy could be understood through psychology.

Simon, Herbert (1916–2001) – A cognitive psychologist who was also a computer scientist and economist. Among his many accomplishments was his work in artificial intelligence and simulation of human thought processes. He suggested that people, when faced with complex problems that were too difficult to solve easily, would seek a satisfactory outcome, which he called satisficing.

Wegener, Alfred (1880–1930) – A geologist who advanced a novel theory of plate tectonics, the view that the continents float on giant plates. The original formulation of his view was based entirely on already known information and thus was not popular among those who favor hypothesis testing theories.

Whewell, William (1794–1866) – An English philosopher and scientist who introduced hypothesis testing and the concept of consilience into science.

Wilson, Edward O. – A biologist whose expertise is in ants. In 1975 he wrote a book called *Sociobiology* that was very controversial. More recently, he wrote a book called *Consilience*, which promotes the unity of all sciences.

AUTHOR INDEX

SUBJECT INDEX

Subject Index

strong inference 75
synthetic statements 21–24, 27, 215
systematic desensitization 186, 191, 216

underdetermination 52, 54, 122–127, 141, 216

verification 13, 22, 32

229